project phoenix   the birth of the

project phoenix the birth of the

 **M**  **G** **F**

ian adcock

B L O O M S B U R Y

First published in Great Britain in 1996
Bloomsbury Publishing Plc, 38 Soho Square, London
W1V 5DF

Copyright © 1996 Ian Adcock

The moral right of the author has been asserted

A CIP catalogue record for this book is available from
the British Library

ISBN 0 7475 2695 8

10 9 8 7 6 5 4 3 2 1

Designed by Bradbury and Williams
Printed in Italy

FOREWORD BY JOHN TOWERS, CHIEF EXECUTIVE, ROVER GROUP

Rover's product line-up made spectacular progress during the late 1980s and the early 1990s, with new model ranges being developed and introduced at an unprecedented rate. But there were many people – including some within the company itself –who felt that Rover's regeneration would not be complete without a new MG sports car.

The emergence of the legendary MG marque into the contemporary world brought with it enormous responsibilities. We knew there would be no compromise: the new MG had to represent a technically sophisticated, genuine two-seater sports car which would sustain the MG traditions of affordability and a distinctive British identity.

Our concept was to design and develop a product which would demonstrate that we were proud of our past – proud to acknowledge the unique heritage of MG – but that we were equally committed to the future by creating an advanced, highly developed car which would meet the most demanding expectations of the modern sports car driver.

We undertook comprehensive research into the proposition of the new MG, asking potential customers around the world what they liked and disliked about contemporary sports cars and what developments they hoped to see in the future. That research clearly showed that the classic heritage and emotional appeal of the MG name would once more give us an opportunity to lead the sports car sector. But, it was equally clear that to do so we had to create a product which provided class-leading design, technology and value for money.

The MGF is neither a nostalgic trip nor simply a competent open-top sports car. It represents a series of values which have been diligently developed and followed through during the evolution of the car – the values of Britishness, desire, distinctiveness and, perhaps most important of all, exhilaration.

Ian Adcock's book comprehensively describes the challenges we faced. I am delighted to welcome it as an impressive addition to the library of MG literature. It is a book which combines superbly the factual story of the development of the MGF with the very human story of sheer dedication, enthusiasm and personal emotion that helped to recreate a legend.

THE EARLY YEARS

It is impossible for those born into the age of the motor car to imagine life without cheap personal transport. It is equally impossible to imagine the pioneering spirit which drove early founders of the young motor industry; men like Herbert Austin, William Morris and Henry Ford, who built great industrial empires and brought mobility to the middle and working classes. Or engineers, like Henry Royce and Ettore Bugatti, who combined sophisticated technology with elegance and style to elevate the car from being merely a convenient method of getting from A to B and back to A to a contemporary art form as a breathing, moving sculpture.

In the post-war years it has become virtually impossible for imaginative opportunists to establish their own car companies; Ferrari managed it and so did Colin Chapman with Lotus, but both marques have survived only through the generous patronage of others.

Perhaps the nearest we get today to bright young engineers bringing about fundamental changes in the way society behaves and thinks is with people like Bill Gates. Computer geniuses are the contemporary equivalent of the founding fathers of the motor industry.

Cecil Kimber's birth, on 12 April 1888, came six years before that of the British car industry and although they grew up alongside each other it was some years before their paths crossed. Kimber's father, Henry Francis, ran a successful business manufacturing printing machinery, but in 1896 he uprooted his family from their home in Dulwich, South London, and moved north to Stockport, Lancashire, where he set up a printing-ink business with one of his brothers. He had to leave behind £10,000 in the family business, which eventually failed, while his new venture didn't do much better.

The Kimbers' uncertain financial status seemed to have ruled out a university education for Cecil and he was eventually - and reluctantly by all accounts - drafted into the family business on the sales side.

Although he had no formal mechanical or engineering training Kimber, like many of his peers, quickly showed his aptitude when he bought his first motorbike, a second-hand 1906 33/8th hp Rex. Within weeks the belt-driven machine had been stripped down and rebuilt, and over the ensuing years Kimber bought, sold and modified numerous motorcycles until in 1910 one nearly cost him his life.

Riding another Rex, Kimber was involved in an accident with a car sustaining serious leg injuries, with a smashed kneecap and broken right thigh bone; for the next two years he was a regular patient at Manchester's Royal Infirmary as surgeons tried first to plate the thigh bone and then to wire it together. It was only the chance inspection of an X-ray which showed the bone starting to knit that dissuaded the surgeons from amputating Kimber's right leg. Had that operation gone ahead, this story might never have been told.

The accident left Kimber with a pronounced limp as his leg was two inches shorter than it had been originally, but the local stockbroker who had caused the accident - and admitted liability - paid the young Kimber enough to purchase his first car, a 1912 Singer 10. The car, the first of its type to be seen in Manchester, was delivered to Kimber in February of the following year.

It must have been a melancholy period in Kimber's life as the Great War loomed; his mother had died of cancer in 1911 and his father's business was crumbling. In fact matters got so bad that Kimber Senior asked Cecil to put the

remainder of his settlement into the business to help shore it up. Kimber refused and after a bitter row his father never spoke to him again, even on his death-bed.

A year after war started, in 1915, Kimber married Irene Hunt and crossed the Pennines to start a new life with Sheffield-Simplex, who at that time rivalled Rolls-Royce with their luxury cars, distinguished by round radiators and a single-speed transmission.

An indicator of things to come was a paper Kimber published on works organisation: and it was, perhaps, his impatience with Sheffield-

MG's founder, Cecil Kimber, at his office in Abingdon.

Simplex management that drove him to join AC Cars in 1916 as their buyer.

Three years later the Kimbers were again on the move, this time to Birmingham, where Kimber worked for E. G. Wrigley Ltd either as a works organiser or as a draughtsman. Wrigley were one of the infant motor industry's suppliers, providing the likes of Morris with major components such as transmissions and steering racks.

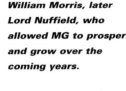

William Morris, later Lord Nuffield, who allowed MG to prosper and grow over the coming years.

Kimber's relationship with Wrigley could easily have led to financial ruin, as it is thought that he put the rest of his accident compensation into a new car company that eventually went broke. The Angus-Sanderson project concentrated on one model produced from a number of bought-in components - transmission and steering from Wrigley, Woodhead springs, Goodyear wheels and tyres, etc; Kimber was responsible for the radiator.

In 1921 Kimber quit to become manager for Morris Garages in Oxford, just a couple of years before Wrigleys collapsed.

William Morris, later Lord Nuffield, became one of the cornerstones of the British motor industry not so much through his engineering flair, but because of his purchasing and marketing strategy. Morris had drifted into selling cars after establishing a bicycle-repair business in his mother's front room. In 1910 he opened the Morris Garage in Oxford and three years later assembled his own car, the 'Bullnose' Morris, in nearby Cowley. These cars distinguished themselves from their rivals by being a jigsaw of bought-in components: engines from White and Poppe, wheels by Sankey, bodies by Raworth and rear axles from Wrigley -which is probably how Kimber and Morris first met. At only £175, the little 'Bullnose' was an instant hit and Morris quickly laid plans to build a bigger, 1.5-litre Cowley in 1915. When British producers failed to meet his requirements, Morris crossed the Atlantic and imported engines and gearboxes from the Continental Motors Corporation of Detroit.

When Kimber arrived as sales manager, he found himself promoted within months to general manager when Armstead resigned in March 1922 and then committed suicide.

After years of restless wanderings round the motor industry, Kimber at thirty-four seemed to have landed on his feet and was determined to make the most it, if Morris would let him. At the best of times Morris was an autocrat who ruled employees with a rod of iron, rarely letting them stray beyond their briefs. But there must have been something about Kimber which persuaded Morris to turn a blind eye to the goings-on in his Oxford showrooms.

Kimber's policy was to rebody and modify the chassis of the original, and rather dull-looking, 11.9hp Hotchkiss-powered Cowleys with the 1920s equivalent of a 2+2 body, called in those days a 'Chummy'. A pure two-seater version was introduced in 1923, probably inspired by Kimber's success in the March 1923 London-to-Land's End Trial in which he won a gold medal driving one of his own modified Chummies. There is some debate as to whether these two-seaters can be considered the first proper MGs, but Wilson McComb's authoritative book on MG certainly seems to confirm that they were.

Throughout 1923-24 a number of Morris Garages specials appeared, based on Cowley and Oxford chassis, but often with chassis and engine modifications as well as new bodywork. Although the cars sold in limited numbers they were hardly a runaway success, as the base Morris products were substantially cheaper and not that much different from the Specials.

Still, Kimber persevered and in March 1924 an advertisement appeared in The Morris Owner for the 'M. G. Saloon', the first time the initials had been used; two months later an advertisement for the 'MG Super Sports Morris' included the famous Octagon for the first time.   Since then everyone has accepted that MG stands for Morris Garages, especially as it was confirmed in a 1929 statement that 'we named our production the MG Sports, the letters being the initials of his [William Morris's] original business undertaking, "The Morris Garages", from which has sprung. . .the MG Car Co.'

Kimber's MGs were little more than modified versions of Morris's standard products: chassis, suspension and steering were optimised, a little more power coaxed from the engines, more tasteful bodywork designed, but in essence these MGs were nothing more than the GT, hot-hatch or coupé equivalents of today's cars. It wasn't until 27 March 1925 that the first true embodiment of what was to become the MG creed appeared.

'Old Number One' started life as a standard Morris Cowley chassis in spring 1924. Over the next twelve months, and under Kimber's instructions, it was heavily modified with the rear sawn off and replaced by a pair of hand-forged side members; it also boasted a specially prepared 11.9hp overhead valve Hotchkiss engine. Somewhere along the way it got the latest, and bigger, Oxford brakes and in March 1925, Carbodies of Coventry were asked to build a slim two-seater body for the car. Kimber and Wilfrid Mathews, an Oxford insurance broker, took 'FC 7900' on that year's Land's End Trial, where it easily qualified for a gold medal.

MG sales prospered during the Roaring Twenties that it quickly became evident that the Alfred Lane works - where Morris Garages had moved in 1923 after outgrowing their original Longwall Street site - had, likewise, become too small. Kimber asked W. R. Morris if a bay at the under-utilised Bainton Road radiator factory could be made available to MG. So in September 1925 a partition was erected within the factory and MG's fifty employees and all their equipment transferred.

Little could Kimber and Morris have foreseen the success that MG continued to enjoy - despite the General Strike of 1926 - with more than 400 Bullnose MGs being built between 1923 and 1926. This number was equalled in 1927 by the Bullnose's inferior successor - 'inferior' because in 1926 Morris had brought out a new chassis which was wider, had a shorter wheelbase and was heavier, which meant the little MG had to be restyled to accommodate its new underpinnings. Despite this discouraging start the 14/28 Mark lll and 14/40 Mark lV MGs

were steadily improved and enjoyed growing sales success. Production eventually reached the heady rate of ten cars a week.

Such was the pressure on Bainton Road's capacity that Kimber proposed to Morris that £10,000 be invested in a new factory at Cowley, solely for MG production. Kimber's powers of persuasion must have been considerable, for Morris agreed. In the end the factory ran £6000 over budget - how do you explain that to your boss? - but took only six months to build. In September 1927 MG took another momentous step forward when they started production at their Edmund Road factory.

During the same period the famous enamelled Octagon MG badge appeared for the first time on a production car and MG won their first international motor race - somewhat bizarrely in Argentina. Although MGs had won gold medals in various trials and Brooklands speed events, the marque's first genuine race victory came in a one-hour event held at the San Martin track near Buenos Aires. The winning car, a 14/40 four-seater, averaged 62mph in the hands of Alberto Sanchiz Cires.

Now that MG had their own dedicated factory with more space, even more care and attention were lavished on the standard rolling chassis delivered from Morris: engines were stripped ports and cylinder-heads polished, clearances optimised and stronger valve springs fitted. The reassembled chassis and engine were tested on a series of crude rolling roads called comparators, which allowed engineers to test the power train up to maximum engine speeds in each gear. Using special carburettors so that the engines could run on coal gas, they covered the equivalent of 750 road miles before the head was decoked, the valves ground in and the proper carburettor fitted.

The chassis underwent detailed tuning to the brakes, springs and shock-absorbers and were then driven up to Carbodies in Coventry - who have consistently played a major role in MG's history, as we will learn - for the coachwork to be fitted.

Determined to emphasise that his cars were more than just revamped Morrises, Kimber showered these MGs with Octagon motifs: oval instruments gave way to octagonal ones, octagons were cast into the aluminium toe-board and the accelerator, MG hubcaps replaced the standard Morris ones and even the tool-box carried the MG symbol.

Until this time MGs had still been heavily modified Morrises, even if their components were being delivered individually rather than assembled. But Kimber had a wider vision in which MG would become a manufacturer in its own right. However, he must have appreciated that MG would never be able to finance the cost of design and development of unique engines, transmissions - that would have pushed development and manufacturing costs up, resulting in excessively high sales prices. What he, and MG, needed to do was follow the example they had set themselves with 'Old Number One' - pick 'n' choose the best components from within the Morris empire and develop them to MG's precise

Kimber at the wheel of 'Old Number One'.

Old Number One is fully restored and in running order, kept at the British Motor Industry Heritage Trust.

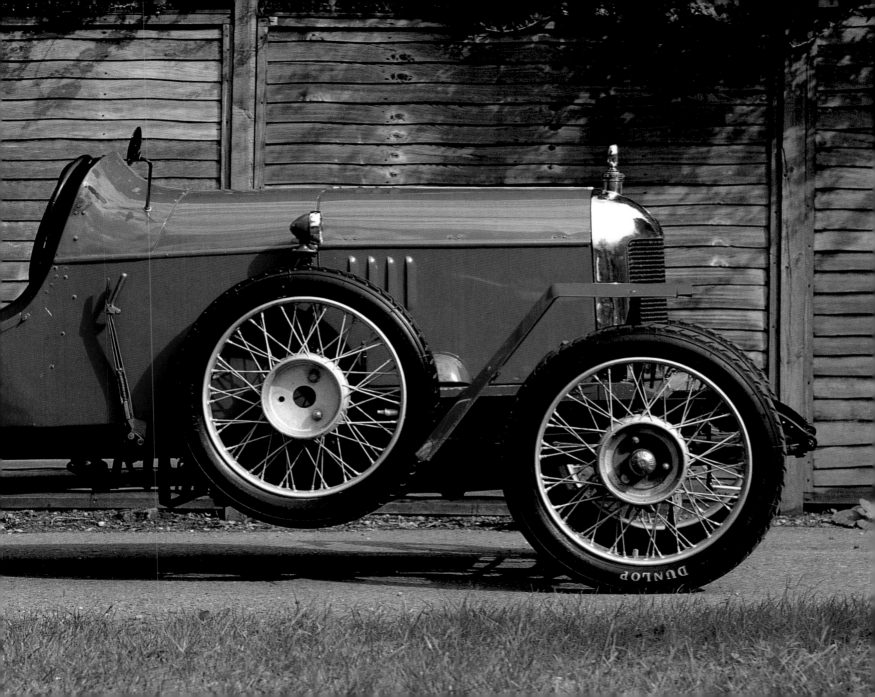

requirements.

The first of these components was a new 2468cc overhead-cam straight-six that Kimber got Morris Engines to design and build, before seeking approval from W. R. Morris himself. Such a venture was risky, but no doubt Kimber's bravado was spurred on by Frank Woollard, who headed Morris Engines and knew him from their time together at E. G. Wrigley.

It wasn't until MG got hold of one of these engines in late 1927, modified it to take twin carburettors and installed it in a chassis of their own design that its potential started to be realised. The finishing touch was a new radiator design penned by Kimber which formed the basis for all MG radiators for the next twenty-six years. Launched at the 1928 Olympia Motor Show in London, the 18/80 MG Six was an immediate hit and, with its top speed of 80mph, outperformed rivals like the 3-litre Lagonda and Alvis Silver Eagle.

With prices ranging from £420 for a bare chassis to £555 for the four-door saloon, the MG Six was out of the reach of most people's pockets. However, it shared the stand at Olympia with a car that would change the marque's future for ever and secure for it a niche in the marketplace that MG would dominate, at home and abroad, for more than half a century.

W. R. Morris unwittingly sowed the seeds for this success when he bought the bankrupt Wolseley Motors in February 1927. For some years Morris had been suffering a decline in sales as his products went upmarket with bigger engines, while arch-rival Herbert Austin had been enjoying continued success with the baby Austin Seven. Part of this success was due to the antiquated tax system which favoured cars of 10hp or less - never mind petrol tax, which was imposed for the first time in 1928. Morris desperately needed a rival engine and, fortunately, Wolseley had one.

During the First World War Wolseley built the Type W4A Hispano-Suiza aero engine under licence and had used lessons learned from that to develop a 847cc 8hp engine, It was just what Morris needed, but when installed in a prototype chassis it was deemed too fast for the average motorist and production versions were subsequently detuned.

Kimber somehow got hold of one of these prototype Minors, as the car was called, stripped off its bodywork and got Carbodies to replace it with a little two-door convertible complete with spindly cycle wings. Everything was kept as simple - and cheap - as possible; the radiator was a smaller version of the MG Sixes and the standard wire wheels were retained but sported MG badging. The chassis itself remained virtually untouched, apart from lowered suspension and a few other modifications. Weighing in at just 1100lb, the tiny 20hp two-seater offered performance on a par with the bigger 14/40 model, but at a price of just £175 - only £50 more than the standard Minor. Such was MG's confidence in this little car that 498 bodies were ordered from Carbodies and a separate assembly line at Edmund Road built in readiness for production to start in March 1929.

The Autocar of the time predicted that the MG Midget would 'make sports car history'. Little did they know what an understatement that would turn out to be.

As the 1920s drew to a close, MG's production rose rapidly, so that by the time of the 1929 Motor Show production had trebled and must have been approaching a thousand a year. It was plain that Edmund Road had served its purpose and that MG needed to move once again.

The next move was to be MG's last. Kimber suggested to Morris that £100,000 be invested in a disused extension of Pavlova Leather Company, which had made saddles and leather coats during the war but was now empty. By the standards of the time this was a big investment, even more so when you consider that it was for a fledgling sports-car producer, but Sir William Morris (as he then was), was obviously convinced that Kimber and his MG team were worth the money and would deliver the goods.

So, in September 1929, the MG Car Company transferred to the site that would be their home for the next fifty years - Abingdon.

It was the little MG Midget that really set the marque on the road to fame and fortune.

ABINGDON'S LEGACY

2

MG's move to Abingdon meant more than just an increase in production capacity, it established the marque as a manufacturer in its own right. It also allowed Kimber to surround himself with the management team who would forge MG's destiny, H. N. Charles, who headed design and development, general manager George Propert and George Tuck, in charge of publicity. One newcomer to the fold was a former Morris Garages apprentice, Syd Enever, who in years to come was to have a profound influence on the marque's development.

The inaugural luncheon for MG staff was held on 20 January 1930, but the MG Car Company Ltd didn't officially come into being until it was registered on 21 July of that year with Sir William Morris as its governing director and Kimber as managing director.

The company's first official race car was based on 18/80 Mark ll running gear, but with a highly modified engine that incorporated twin spark plugs per cylinder. Designated as the 18/80 Mark III, it was Bentley-like in its proportions and weight, but with only 83bhp on call the 3000lb car was more of a tourer than a racer; not only that, but it suffered humiliation in its first race at Brooklands when it ran its bearings during the 1930 Double Twelve Hour race and was comprehensively beaten by a modified M-type Midget.

Half a dozen specially prepared Midgets with 27bhp engines were privately entered in this twenty-four-hour race (it was split into two twelve-hour stints on consecutive days), and although one failed, the leading car finished at an average speed of 60.23mph. Backed up by the remaining four Midgets, the MGs captured the team prize from a works-entered trio of Austin Sevens. It was the start of an illustrious competition history for the Midget.

Amid all this activity MG adopted its famous 'Safety Fast!' slogan, which virtually became the company's motto in years to come; a group of keen owners also formed the MG Car Club. Its first honorary secretary was a young accountant called John Thornley, who joined MG in 1931, becoming general manager twenty-one years later.

During the 1930s, record-breaking became a national obsession. The newsreels and newspapers of the time were full of the titanic battles for the ultimate land-speed record between Sir Malcolm Campbell and George Eyston, each grabbing the headlines - and records - from the other as they pushed past the 200, 250, 300mph barriers. As the battle for the title of 'the fastest man on earth' raged manufacturers locked horns to prove that they could build cars capable of reaching, for those days, outrageous speeds. So, for instance, Malcolm Campbell was striving to build the first 750cc car capable of 100mph, powered by a highly tuned Austin engine.

At around this time, H. N. Charles was busily redesigning the Midget's chassis. Fabricated from mild steel tubing, EX.120's chassis went under rather than over the rear axle, thus allowing lower bodywork. It was simple and effective - so effective that it remained in use on Midgets for the next twenty years.

George Eyston learned that MG was planning an attack on the 750cc hour record and got in contact with Kimber. Immediately realising the publicity value of a man like Eyston, Kimber made the EX.120 chassis available to him and ordered a special Midget engine.

On 30 December 1930 Eyston drove MG's first record-breaking car at Montlhéry, near Paris, covering 100km (62½ miles) at an average speed of 87.3mph before a valve broke. The magic 100 miles in an hour had eluded them.

Spurred on by the news that Campbell and Austin were determined to break through that barrier before MG, Kimber's team worked frantically over the next few weeks fitting a supercharger to the engine and further streamlining the bodywork. It all came together late on 16 February when Eyston, despite battling with a fearsome cross-wind, established four new records at speeds up to 103.13mph.

Two weeks after breaking the record, Kimber announced that 750cc racing replicas, the Montlhéry Midget, would go on sale. The timing of such an announcement was odd, as the Depression was strangling the global economy; MG's labour force was slashed by a third and the remaining employees had their salaries cut by 10 per cent. Yet amid this, Kimber persuaded Morris that MG should build a squad of cars for that year's Double Twelve race at Brooklands.

MG built fourteen new Midgets in fourteen days. Not only that, but H. N. Charles designed and had built a new 746cc engine. Not bad, considering it was all done by paper, pencil and hand-machining - computer-aided design and machining were more than half a lifetime away.

Untested, the cars went to Brooklands, sup-

The C type (left) proved a popular car, especially amongst amateur racing drivers.

ported by 200 of the MG workforce. Their trip was worthwhile as the Midgets took the top five places and the team prize.

MG was still busy launching updated and new product: the Midget was now available in fabric- or metal-bodied versions; a two-door Salonette was available and the four-seater 'Magna' was launched. Despite having a six-cylinder 1271cc power unit - created by simply tacking two additional cylinders on to the Wolseley Hornet engine and then using sheet metal to try and disguise the fact - it was a fairly lethargic per-

former, although it proved quite popular, selling 1250 during 1931-32.

Eyston eventually cracked the magic 100mph in EX.120 at Montlhéry in the following September, covering 101.1 miles in the hour before the car burst into flames and was destroyed. Fortunately, MG already had EX.120's successor under way. Better known as the 'Magic Midget', EX.127 went on to dominate the 750cc world speed records up to late 1936. Over the years its performance improved consistently from 110.28mph (achieved first time out in

The J2, announced in 1931, set the MG style for the next fifty years and has been aped the world over as the quintessential British sporting two-seater.

1931 with Ernest Eldridge driving) to 140.6mph five years later when Bobbie Kohlrausch established a 750cc flying mile record that was to stand for the next decade.

Despite the race-track and record-breaking glory, MG sales were faltering, dipping to 1400 in 1931. This was partly due to the Depression, but must also be attributed in some measure to the products themselves: the 18/80 was outdated and the racing-bred C-type too costly, the D- and F-types underpowered and the M-type Midget just plain old-fashioned.

When the J.2 Midget appeared it set the style for open MGs for the next quarter of a century. It epitomised the British style of sports car - a long bonnet with the driver and passenger perched virtually over the rear axle. An exposed slab tank with the spare wheel bolted to it. and the deeply slashed doors which only went to emphasise the racing heritage. Early models had simple cycle-style wings, but within a couple of years these were melded into a continuous flowing sweep which incorporated a running board. This style evolved over the coming decades and its influence can still be seen in cars like the Morgan Plus 8. The chassis was a development of the original Montlhéry Midget and its 36hp engine an enlarged variation on the 750cc unit, increased to 847cc and fitted with a cross-flow

cylinder-head and twin SU carburettors.

The J.2 went into production in late 1931, selling for 10 shillings under £200, and was an instant success. The following year MG sales hit 2400, easily outstripping their 1930 record.

For 1932 MG announced their Magnette range, powered by a six-cylinder, 1087cc engine descended from the Magna's 1271cc with the idea of competing in 1100cc race class. At one stage the prospective Magnette owner had a choice of three chassis, four engines, three gearboxes and at least five body styles.

To confuse matters even further, the K.3 Magnette was then developed into arguably the most famous MG racer of all. The chassis came from the K.2- while its engine was a supercharged version of the 1087cc six and its body a modified C-type with characteristic cutaway doors.

Kimber was no longer satisfied with winning at home, he wanted to show what MG could do in the world's toughest road race - the Mille Miglia. MG drafted in some of the best known drivers of the time for the three-car squad: Earl Howe, 'Hammy' Hamilton, George Eyston, Count 'Johnny' Lurani and Sir Henry Birkin, one of the original 'Bentley Boys'. Birkin acted as the hare and disposed of the Maseratis, which were the MG's biggest threat, before his own car dropped a valve, but the strategy worked and the remaining MGs finished first and second in class, winning the team prize.

The most famous MG victory, however, belongs to the Michael Schumacher of his era, Tazio Nuvolari. On his way to winning the 1933 Ulster TT Nuvolari broke the class record seven times, leaving it at 78.65mph, where it remained for nearly two decades, until Stirling Moss won the 1951 TT in a Jaguar C-type.

Despite the fact that Abingdon was the only car plant in the world dedicated to sports cars and that MGs were amongst the most successful competition cars of their time, all was not well. Production started to waver in 1933 and continued its downward trend in '34 and '35, eventually bottoming out at about 1250. The problem was a tired model range that had become too expensive. Kimber was also coming under increasing pressure from Sir William Morris to limit the competition spend and improve profitability on production cars by purchasing more components from the Morris group. This led to a major saving late in 1933 when body production switched from Carbodies to the in-house Morris Bodies Branch.

MG needed to rationalise their model line-up. So in 1934 out went the numerous versions of the Magna and Magnette, to be replaced by the N-type Magnette; the successful J.4 Midget was superseded by the P-type Midget, a car that was to prove even more of a sales triumph.

The chassis of both cars had longer wheelbases for improved passenger comfort, while the P-type had a new three-bearing 847cc motor which ran more smoothly and was easier to tune. Meanwhile the N-type had new block and cylinder-head castings for its 1271cc power unit.

Visually the cars were a maturation of what had gone before, sweeping cycle wings joined in the centre section by a running board, a slab tank and an exposed spare wheel, the only real difference being that the N-type's fuel tank was enclosed within the rear bodywork section. While the Magnette might have looked a little tall and spindly, the Midget was blossoming into a truly handsome machine, having lost some of the crudity while retaining its youthful appeal. Perhaps one of the most attractive styling variations was the Airline Coupé, which can best be described as an early fastback.

MG's competition activities continued unabated, giving rise to the extraordinary Q-type with its 750cc engine and Zoller supercharger. Even with modest boost pressures the little engine would push out in excess of 100bhp, while the 1936 sprint version developed a shade over 146bhp at 7500rpm - the equivalent of 200bhp per litre. Put another way, that is almost double the 103bhp/litre produced by the 6.1-litre BMW V12 used to power the McLaren F1 in 1994. Not bad, considering that the MG's engine had started off producing just 20bhp from 847cc, i.e. 23.6 bhp/litre.

While MG concentrated its engineering efforts mainly on extracting more and more power from its little engines, European rivals had been racing ahead, developing more sophisticated independent suspension. Spurred on by these activities, Reg Jackson and Syd Enever cobbled together a crude independent set-up with wishbones and machined axle-shafts for torsion bars. Having approved the system, Kimber got Frank Stevens to fabricate a 'Y' chassis to take the Q engine and the new independent suspension, and so was born the R-type Midget racer.

The R type never fulfilled its true potential, partly because H. N. Charles had envisaged an advanced anti-roll system in which torsion bars were moved by a gyroscope operating via pressurised hydraulic cylinders, and partly due to a traumatic reorganisation within MG.

Since the late 1920s Lord Nuffield (he was made a baronet in 1934) had practically ceased attending Morris's weekly executive meetings He might have had a shrewd instinct for engineering, but he knew that he lacked basic skills in personal relationships, finding it difficult to communicate his ideas to others. Nuffield preferred one-to-one meetings with his senior managers and only grudgingly allowed his executives to make operational decisions in his absence. Moreover, his absences were becoming longer and longer: each year he would visit Australia for four months at a time - although this once stretched to seven - and would then fulminate about decisions taken while he was away. Here was a man who had built a great personal empire, acquiring companies like Wolseley, SU Carburettors and Riley along the way as they had gone bankrupt, but who couldn't work out how to deal with his growing family.

Typical of Nuffield was the unannounced appointment in 1933 of Leonard Lord, to reorganise Cowley. A dour, bitter man, Lord was just as irksome a character as his boss. His problem was that he knew he was good at his job and in a short space of time he had turned Cowley round and made it one of Europe's most efficient car-manufacturing facilities.

Leonard Lord, later Sir Leonard and finally Lord Lambury, first became involved with MG in 1933. Years later their paths would cross again.

This coincided with the transfer in 1935 of MG's ownership. From being part of Nuffield's personal fiefdom - which also included Wolseley - they now came under Morris Motors; this simultaneously relegated Kimber from managing director to a mere director and general manager answerable to Lord.

Leonard Lord was interested only in manufacturing efficiency and profitability, regarding such staff as accountants and salesman as extravagant overheads! If Morris 'makes proper bloody products. . . you don't need to sell 'em,' he maintained. The very thought of motor sport must have been anathema to him, so it is hardly surprising that on his first visit to Abingdon he took one look at the racing shop and said, 'Well, that bloody lot can go for a start.'

That might very well have been true, but Nuffield - who had never been keen on motor sport himself - was particularly annoyed by the death of a racing mechanic in May 1934; the driver lost control of his MG on the eve of a race, and the incident attracted bad publicity for MG. Such tragedies didn't go well with the company's motto. Furthermore, it is alleged that on one foreign trip Nuffield was angered by a business audience who failed to recognise 'the man who makes Morrises', but instantly showed their appreciation when it was explained that Nuffield also made MGs.

In Nuffield's biography the closure of MG's racing department is put down to something far less prosaic, money: 'Morris absolutely refused to allow the production model of the MG to be modified to suit these developments [in racing], nor did he wish the MG management to produce special racing models for official entries. He did not want people to be able to say, "Of course these are not cars they sell."'

Whatever the reasons, the repercussions for MG were deep. Apart from Syd Enever and Bill Renwick, the Abingdon design and engineering staff were either sacked or dispersed round the Morris empire. H. N. Charles was sent to Cowley. Furthermore, future MGs would contain a far higher percentage of Nuffield-sourced components.

Lord's tenure with Nuffield was successful but brief. By 1936 profits were up again and Morris Motors' share of the new car market had crept back to 33 per cent. Lord felt he deserved a share in these profits. Nuffield, not surprisingly, disagreed - and the two parted company. Although Lord instantly regretted the decision and returned to work for Nuffield as the manager of a fund to help areas of high unemployment, he left for good in 1938 to join Austin. But it wasn't the last that MG had seen of him.

3

The merger of MG's design and engineering staff was part of a larger vision to eliminate waste and reduce duplication between Morris, Wolseley and MG. Nuffield's senior management wanted to pare down overheads by centralising purchasing and making as many components as possible common to the three ranges, which would retain their own brand identity and, hopefully, customer loyalty.

For all the sporting enthusiasm which surrounded Abingdon's products, there was an equal amount of dissatisfaction which manifested itself in sales see-sawing throughout the 1930s. They reached their lowest ebb in 1935, when production shrank to fewer than 1300 cars. While this generation of MGs might have been loved by the gentleman racer, their single overhead-cam engines were temperamental and required expert fettling and tuning. Moreover, cars built with competition in mind invariably have firmer suspension to promote better handling and cornering, usually with a proportionate loss of ride quality. Neither trait endeared the cars to the expanding market of the 1930s. So a new product policy and line-up had to be developed.

The first project for the relocated MG design team was a new 2-litre six that would be shared with its sibling marques. However, when launched later that year, it bore no resemblance to any previous MG - it was a genuine four-door, four-seater saloon. Overhead valves had been replaced by pushrods, cable brakes by a hydraulic system and the gearbox eventually had syncromesh. To make matters even worse for the

for their new car and, one imagines, a fair number who wouldn't wait and took their money elsewhere. Neither did Roughly coinciding with the eventual availability of the Two-Litre was the new TA Midget. Again, purists were horrified by its push-rod ohv engine, syncro gearbox, hydraulic brakes and friendlier ride, but at £222 it was not only

Above and left: *MG tried to move up a class with its SA Tourer and four-door saloon, but was beaten to the market by SS Cars of Coventry, which later became Jaguar.*

aficionado, the engine came from Wolseley. But if there was to be 'commonisation' this car didn't achieve it, as the Morris and Wolseley variants were significantly different and even had their own unique chassis.

The one good point about the MG Two-Litre, was Kimber's handsome body style and low price tag - a mere £375, compared to the £399 asked for the KN Magnette.

Unfortunately, the Two-Litre also unmasked the inefficiencies of a large purchasing organisation like Nuffields. The problem was that it took the Nuffield Group over six months to get the new MG into production, by which time there were 500 seriously unhappy customers waiting

the same price as the car it succeeded, but roomier and smoother.

In 1936 MG launched their second saloon, a mid-size 1.5-litre badged as the VA. Like its bigger brother, which it closely resembled, it took months to get into production and went through as many technical alterations during its two-year production run from 1937.

Two years later, MG were pushed even further upmarket when the 2.6-litre WA saloon was announced. Based on a bigger version of the 2-litre Tourer's chassis its weight went up 300lb, which was hardly compensated for by the additional 20bhp the bigger engine produced. Fewer than 400 of these handsome machines were built and by all reports it was a roomy, comfortable tourer - although no real challenge to Jaguar's more powerful 2.5-litre saloon, which boasted an additional 10bhp over the MG's 95.

If motor sport was officially frowned on by the factory, that didn't stop a number of wealthy amateurs from competing in MGs. Privateers

From the mid-1930s the PB was a mainstay of MG's success as the countdown to the Second World War started.

such as Kohlrausch and Major 'Goldie' Gardner were upholding MG's record-breaking honour. Gardner had bought an offset single-seater K.3 back in 1936 and regularly campaigned it at Brooklands, taking the outer circuit 1100cc record to an unbeaten 124.40mph. But it was on the autobahn near Frankfurt, Germany, that Gardner and his MG really stole the limelight.

In 1937 Gardner had pushed the 1100cc class flying kilometre record to 148.8mph when

Eberan von Eberhorst, chief engineer of the all-conquering Auto Union team, suggested that even greater speeds would be achieved if a streamlined body were fitted to the K.3. At that time, the German motor industry were at the forefront of developing streamlined competition cars. This led Kimber to suggest cautiously to the ever-sceptical Nuffield that MG should build a record-breaker for Gardner to drive. Surprisingly Nuffield gave his consent and it was then decided to go one step further and buy Eyston's old record-breaking Magnette, EX.135, and rebody it.

Reid Railton, the man who penned John Cobb's sleek Railton-Mobil LSR car, was commissioned to draw up new bodywork. Reg Jackson and Syd Enever from MG worked on the engine with specialist tuner Robin Jackson and in November 1938 the first record attempt was made. Again the team went to the autobahn near Frankfurt where Gardner smashed the old record by 40mph, leaving it 187.62mph. Less than a year later the team returned to the same stretch of road where Gardner recorded an incredible 203.5 mph for the flying kilometre.

Die-hards might have grumbled about the

MGs were popular with the independent coachbuilders who thrived before 1939. This TA has bodywork by Tickford, a company which still lives on as a successful independent engineering consultancy.

effect the Cowley discipline had on MG products, but it's difficult to deny that as a sales philosophy it worked. Following 1935's disastrous slump, sales increased so that in 1937 nearly 2900 MGs were built.

From there on, though, it was downhill, caused more by the Munich Crisis and the gathering doom as war approached than by any deficiency in the products. Shortly before war was declared the TB Midget appeared with a modified short-stroke Morris M.10 engine. Like the little Wolseley engine that had gone before and soldiered on well beyond its sell-by date, this engine would still be in use in the early 1950s, powering another Gardner-MG to well over 200mph.

When war was declared in September 1939, Kimber stopped

production at Abingdon. Little did anyone suspect that when he watched 'his' 22,500th MG roll off the production line it would the last new MG he would see.

The sight of the Abingdon factory being cleared of all its MG tools and machinery must have been heartbreaking for men like Kimber and Enever, who had dedicated their lives to the marque. Their despondency must have worsened as the months went by and Abingdon stood empty and unused: Cowley seemed to pass on wartime contracts to everyone but MG.

Eventually Kimber and Propert resortd to traipsing from ministry to ministry, trying to get work to help the war effort. Gradually jobs trick-

The big 2.6-litre WA saloon was another attempt by MG to move into a bigger market dominated by makers such as Alvis.

led in: making shell racks, overhauling tanks, assembling trucks shipped from the States, repairing armoured cars and eventually assembling the frontal section of the Albemarle bomber.

However, the Albemarle also proved to be Kimber's downfall. In 1940, following the unexpected death of Oliver Boden - who had taken charge of Nuffield's following Leonard Lord's departure - Miles Thomas was appointed vice chairman and managing director and he planned to centralise the company's war effort. He was annoyed that Kimber had already secured the Albemarle deal for Abingdon, a move he described as a 'policy of non-conformity'. In November 1941 Thomas visited Abingdon to tell Kimber 'that he had better look out for another outlet for his energies, because he did not fit into the wartime pattern of the Nuffield Organisation'.

That was it. The summary dismissal of the man who had created an enduring legend.

For a short period in 1942 Kimber went to Charlesworth, the coachbuilders, and helped organise their production facilities to build aircraft. He then moved to Specialloid Pistons as works director to do the same job.

As war drew to a close Kimber started receiving approaches from men who were looking to a brighter, peaceful future. Tractor magnate Harry Ferguson talked to him and so did John Black, who had visions of Kimber doing for Triumph what he had done with MG. But Kimber was less optimistic. In a letter he sent to Harold Hastings, an old friend and founder member of the MG Car Club, he wrote prophetically, 'I feel somewhat pessimistic about the future of the real enthusiast's car. Sunbeam-Talbot, Riley and now MG have been or will be wrecked by the soul-deadening hand of the big business interests. . . .'

On Sunday 4 February 1945, five days after writing that letter, Kimber was travelling on the 6 p.m. train from Kings Cross to Peterborough on his way to visit Perkins, the diesel engine specialists, on behalf of Specialloid. Very shortly after leaving Kings Cross the track starts to climb through a series of tunnels. Kimber's train couldn't make the gradient, came to a halt and then started to slide slowly backwards. The signalman pulled the points to switch the train to another track, but it was too late - the rearmost carriage was over the points. The coach careered over against the signal bridge and was wrenched open by a steel stanchion.

Two passengers died that evening. One, just nine weeks short of his fifty-seventh birthday, was Cecil Kimber.

Abingdon was far from idle during the war, manufacturing tanks instead of cars.

July 1945. A new era dawns. Despite leading the nation through the horrors of the Second World War, Winston Churchill and his Conservatives are defeated by Clement Attlee's Labour Party and prophecies of a new promised land. The Bank of England, coal mines, civil aviation, cable and wireless services, steel, railways and road transport are nationalised. The National Health Service is launched and a new socialist order is developing in which the State will always provide.

However, the realities are different. The global economy is shattered by the conflict. Much of Europe, including substantial parts of the UK, is in ruins, and there seems to be little demand for any new cars, let alone sports cars.

MG's design and engineering teams went swiftly into action after the war ended and by the close of 1945 had produced a revamped version of the TB Midget, which had been launched shortly before hostilities began. It didn't matter much that its basic design was more than six years old, as what few rivals there were were also based on pre-war products. The outmoded sliding trunnion suspension was replaced by half-elliptical springs and lever arm dampers at the front and a live rear axle, but the original engine and transmission were retained. Although the car outwardly looked the same as its 1939 forebear the cockpit was a full 4in wider.

MG announced the TC in October 1945 - a matter of weeks after the war finally ended - and by the end of the year had built eighty-one. Cec Cousins - who had started with Kimber in Longwall Street - describing it as a 'lash-up'. But the following year 1500 customers - of whom a third were from overseas -decided it was anything but that and bought one.

Initially the overseas markets tended to be countries like Australia, New Zealand, Canada, South Africa and those Commonwealth nations who had fought with Britain. But gradually one export market emerged above all the others, a market that was to play a significant role, in more ways than one, in MG's future - the USA.

American servicemen, had come to know MG through being stationed in the UK during the war and wanted one when they went back home. Just as it did in the UK, the MG repre-

The archetypal post-war vision of Britain: a thatched cottage with an MG TC parked outside.

sented a break from conformity, a refreshing alternative to the bloated heavyweights being produced.

Despite the car's shortcomings - no left-hand drive, no heater, no bumpers, practically no service agents - overseas sales steadily increased, so that in 1948 it netted about a million pounds in foreign earnings, a fact which probably went a long way to assuring MG's future.

The man in charge of MG in the early years after the war was one H. A. Ryder, another who couldn't or wouldn't see the advantages of a competition or record-breaking programme, despite Lieutenant Colonel 'Goldie' Gardner's enthusiasm and determination to capture the 750cc record that had him eluded before the war.

Somewhat reluctantly, the factory agreed that Enever and Jackson could be seconded to the effort as long as the work was done off-site and the car prepared elsewhere. Following an unsuccessful attempt in Italy in the summer of 1946, the team headed for Jabbeke in Belgium This time Gardner succeeded and beat Kohlrausch's ten-year-old flying mile record with a speed of 159.15mph. Twelve months later Gardner captured the 500cc record at a speed of 118.06mph, using the same engine but with two cylinders blanked off.

MG's ambivalent attitude annoyed Gardner to such an extent that he stopped referring to the car as an MG and even went to so far as to use a prototype Jaguar XK120 engine for some attempts.

In February 1948 George Strauss, Labour's Minister of Supply, made a speech in Birmingham that was to have a profound effect on the UK's motor industry: 'Materials must go to firms who can export and do. And that means that those who do not, cannot have them. Needs must when the devil drives. And if that results in some firms having to close down, well, it is always regrettable when an organisation. . . has to disappear.' For Britain's car makers, that meant they had to export 75 per cent of their output, otherwise they wouldn't get their allocation of steel.

On the face of it these rules were draconian, but in the short term they had the desired effect; by 1950, Britain had overtaken the United States as the world's leading car exporter. Right at the forefront of the overseas sales drive was the MG TC. By the time it ceased production in 1949, 6592 had been sold overseas - out of a total production of 10,000 - of which 2001 found their way to the States.

The MG's racing potential was further enhanced by the availability of factory-designed, tested and produced tuning components which could increase the engine's output in varying degrees, from its standard 54.4bhp to a heady, supercharged 97.5. If that was to be welcomed, then the political battles raging within the British motor industry weren't and, though MG weren't directly involved, they did become a victim of the inevitable fall-out.

Leonard Lord got Austin off to a flying start as the war drew to a close, launching a six-cylinder, 16bhp car before VE Day. He also spent enormous sums on the Longbridge manufacturing site to put it on world terms with rival manufacturers as part of a million-pound investment programme agreed by Austin's board in April 1945.

Cowley, on the other hand, struggled to get going; by 1947 and '48 Morris's profits were once again slipping behind Austin's. Nuffield ousted Miles Thomas as chief executive and replaced him with Reginald Hanks, who ruthlessly set about reorganising the company, so that profitability steadily increased from £1.5 million in 1948 to £8 million two years later.

One positive outcome of Hanks's directorial reshuffle was the appointment of S. V. Smith at MG. Smith was no less a disciplinarian than his predecessor, but had a more relaxed attitude towards motor sport. He allowed Enever to modify further the six-cylinder Magnette engine Gardner had used in Jabbeke in 1946, so that

with only three of its six cylinders functioning it had a 497cc capacity. This allowed Gardner to recapture the 500cc record at 154.23mph. In July 1950 a fourth cylinder was disabled, taking the engine down to 350cc. With that Gardner set another class record of 121.09mph. This meant that the ageing Gardner-MG now held the outright record in half of the ten categories from 350 to 1500cc.

MG's new car sales were steadily improving throughout this period, in part due to the marque's first post-war saloon, the Y-type. Based on the Series E Morris 8, the Y-type was powered by a single-carburettor version of the TC's 1250cc engine and though it weighed 550lb more than the two-seater it was a reasonable cruiser. It proved relatively successful, selling over 8300 before being dropped in 1953, the least successful variant was the touring version.

In 1949 Abingdon underwent another change when production of Rileys was transferred there from Coventry and four years later a further 60,000sq. ft of work space was added to cope with increased demand for both marques.

With exports growing on a yearly basis it was inevitable that MG would have to start listening more to the demands of their new markets if they were to sustain the sales success. By 1949 the initial passion for the TC was beginning to wear a little thin; the export markets wanted something less crude, more comfortable and with left-hand drive. Recognising that the best people to design an MG were at Abingdon rather than Cowley or anywhere else, S. V. Smith set MG the task of coming up with a TC replacement.

Within a couple of weeks a prototype was being viewed by the Nuffield board. In their typically pragmatic manner, Syd Enever's Abingdon team had taken a Y-type chassis, complete with its independent front suspension and rack-and-pinion steering, chopped 5in out of the chassis and clothed it in a TC body. The project was approved and away it went to Cowley for the engineering drawings to be completed. By the

time the car went into production later that year it had put on 170lb in weight over the TC, but thanks to a lower axle ratio its performance was maintained.

As is the trend with MGs, existing TC owners thought the new TD soft and slow but, as usual, those that really mattered, potential TD owners, disagreed. By the time the TD ceased production in 1953, 29,664 had been sold.

Having patched up their differences, MG and Gardner set about attacking more world records, this time with a supercharged version of the TD's 1250cc engine. Enever's supercharging eventually resulted in a power unit pushing out 213bhp at 7000rpm, compared to the standard unit's 57bhp at 5500rpm. Several attempts were made at the Bonneville Salt Lake in Utah, but bad weather, problems with timing gear and a slight off which left Gardner concussed, conspired against the team. The hoped-for 210mph was not achieved - the best they could manage was a 202.14mph one-way run.

It was to prove the end of Gardner and MG's long-standing and very successful relationship, but not the end of MG speed

The Y-type, based on a pre-war design, was an early attempt by MG to cash in on the lucrative family motoring market, rather than confining their output to two-seaters.

attempts.

Meanwhile, it was still an uphill struggle for Hanks as Nuffield kept interfering and even delayed production of the Morris Minor, partly on the grounds that it looked like a 'poached egg' and partly because of a backlog of orders for the pre-war designs. Inevitably the relationship between Hanks and Nuffield deteriorated. Hanks recognised in Leonard Lord one of the ablest men in the post-war motor industry. Lord, meanwhile, had never forgotten - or forgiven? - the treatment meted out to him by Morris and Nuffield in 1935 and was still determined to fulfil his pre-war promise to take Cowley apart 'brick by bloody brick'.

Austin and Morris products were always priced within a few pounds of each other and both had tried unsuccessfully to sell cars in the USA. It was becoming obvious that a merger would strengthen them - Austin was strapped for cash, but had more modern facilities and products, while Morris was cash-rich, but lacked the products - but how to achieve it? Nuffield and Lord hadn't spoken for nearly fifteen years.

A private meeting was eventually arranged by Charles 'Carl' Kingerlee, a close friend of Lord, but also private secretary to Lord Nuffield. Lord phoned Nuffield on 10 October 1950 to

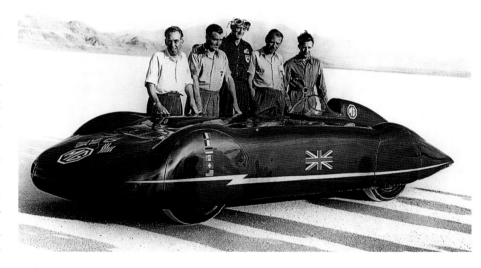

wish him a happy seventy-third birthday. Kingerlee followed up the call with a private visit to Lord and, with no prompting from anyone, suggested that a merger between Austin and Morris would benefit both organisations. Shortly afterwards Lord paid a visit to Nuffield and then

'Goldie' Gardner (centre) was still breaking records at Utah salt flats in 1952 with his pre-war EX.135.

met him at the factory, where they agreed that the merger should take place and a holding company be created. So much secrecy surrounded the visit that not even Hanks knew it was happening, but when Nuffield told him of the proposed alliance he opposed it vehemently. Reluctantly Nuffield backed down and called the agreement off.

Twelve months later the deal was on again, with Nuffield determined to sell his company whatever the other directors thought. Hanks eventually found out about the merger and confronted Nuffield with his objections in the nursing home where the old man was resting. Hanks's disapproval was ignored, the deal went ahead and Lord returned to Cowley as conqueror.

There was one final victory Lord wanted. He had already barred Lord Austin from Longbridge before his death in 1941 and now he wanted complete control of Morris without any interference from Nuffield. If he didn't get his way he threatened to quit and went so far as to send Nuffield a letter of resignation. Nuffield refused the letter and, instead, accepted the honorary post of president. He was a tired, beaten old man and never interfered with the way the company was run from that day until his death in 1963.

Leonard Lord had won.

The British Motor Corporation, as the new company was called, held 35 per cent of the UK market when it was formed in 1953 and was the fourth largest car producer in the world after Chrysler, Ford and General Motors. The year before BMC was created, John Thornley took over as MG's general manager. He had joined the company from the MG Owners' Club in the early days of Kimber and with boundless enthusiasm for the marque and its products. If there was one man who might be considered Kimber's heir apparent, it was Thornley. Just as Kimber before him had had to deal delicately with Nuffield, Thornley would have the same problems with Lord and they happened sooner rather than later.

Since 1949 a lightweight TC driven by George Phillips had competed in the Le Mans 24-hour race with reasonable distinction, finishing second in class in 1950. MG were so impressed with Phillips's efforts they agreed to produce a special body for him, based on a design Enever had penned for the next Gardner-MG project.

The low-slung car with its sleek bodywork and small frontal area was a radical departure from the TD, which still owed its design to the pre-war Midgets. Unfortunately, mechanical problems prevented UMG 400 from completing the 1952 Le Mans, but so taken with its looks were MG's management that they pressed ahead with a more refined prototype, EX.175. Enever designed a new chassis that allowed the driver and passenger to sit between the outer chassis rails, separated from one another by the transmission and prop-shaft. This allowed a much lower seating position than the original TD, which had the occupants perched on the chassis; bumpers, sidescreens, a windscreen, etc. were added to make the car look roadworthy.

Meanwhile, down the road at Warwick, a young man called Donald Healey was trying to make a go of his own embryonic sports-car company. At the 1952 London Motor Show Healey presented an aggressive looking two-seater prototype based on Austin A90 running gear and with a 2660cc engine. Lord was bowled over by the car and signed a deal with Healey for it to be built at Longbridge and wear the Austin-Healey badge.

But BMC already had a sports-car marque in MG. It is hardly likely that Lord had forgotten that, but by the time MG's management presented EX.175 to him the deal with Healey had been signed and sealed, and MG's proposal was turned down flat. After all, reasoned BMC's hierarchy, why did they need two modern sports cars in their line-up and anyway the TD was still selling well.

Instead of forging ahead with their new car,

MG were forced to soldier on with the rapidly ageing TD, updating it to the TF in time for the 1953 Motor Show. A new bonnet line, an imitation grille and headlamps faired into the wings were adopted; the TF was still powered by the

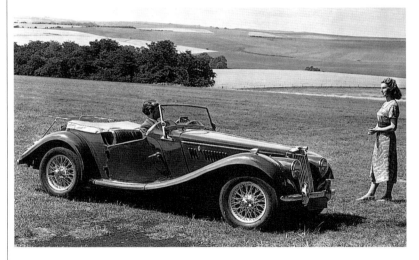

The TF model really marked the end of MG's traditional styling.

old 1250cc engine tuned to 57bhp, but the revamp did little or nothing to boost flagging sales.

To make matters worse, Triumph launched their 90bhp TR2 at the same Motor Show. Here was a car that could do a genuine 100mph and cost only five pounds more than the MG, which struggled to reach 80mph. The situation was further aggravated by the Healey's sales success; MG's overseas sales plummeted to half the previous year's and though a reduction in the UK's purchase tax provided a small sales boost, total MG production was down 40 per cent.

To add insult to injury, MG fans saw the Y-type replaced by a badge-engineered Wolseley 4/44 that had been launched twelve months earlier, but fitted with a mock MG radiator shell. The new ZA Magnette was powered by the first BMC engine, a 1489cc four developed by H. N. Charles, who had been with MG before the war. MG's star was waning and drastic action was called for if it wasn't to disappear altogether.

The Magnette ZA, so beloved of mid-1950s cops 'n' robbers films, was a true sign that badge engineering had arrived. It was little more than a Wolseley with a new grille.

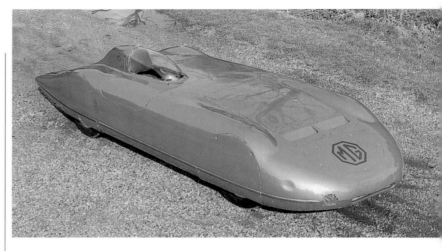

Given Lord's antipathy towards competition, Thornley and his team must have been pleasantly surprised when he gave the go-ahead for MG to build another record-breaker. Partially sponsored by Castrol, EX.179 was built up from a spare MGA chassis powered by a 1466cc development of the T-type's XPAG engine. During 1954 the car, driven by Eyston and American racer Ken Miles, set a number of records at Utah, including averaging more than 120mph for twelve hours.

While this record-breaking was going on, Leonard Lord seems to have had a change of heart about MG. He not only agreed that the nostalgic lines of the Midget were just too retro for the mid-1950s and that MG must have a new sports car, but he also decided that once again

Another record-breaker from MG, the EX.179, based around a spare MGA chassis.

The MGA proved a radical turnaround in MG's design and has acquired the status of a British design classic.

Abingdon should have its own design facility, headed by Syd Enever. After years of neglect, MG was returning to its spiritual home.

If competition does improve the breed, there can be no finer example of that than the MGA. BMC gave the go-ahead for this car in mid-1954 and Thornley, Enever and the Abingdon team had twelve months to bring the car into production. Fortunately for them many of the components already existed: there was the record-breaking EX.175 chassis which could be turned into the new car's underpinnings; Enever's body design for George Phillips' Le Mans racer was also pressed into service. The B series 1489cc BMC engine and new transmission had already proved their worth in the ZA Magnette and replaced the old TF engine, which immediately got rid of the bonnet hump.

A quartet of prototype MGAs powered by 82bhp Weslake tuned engines mated to a close ratio gearbox, débuted at the fated 1955 Le Mans 24-hour race as EX.182 prototypes. Early in the race Pierre Levagh's Mercedes-Benz careered off the track opposite the pits, killing the driver and eighty spectators. Overshadowed as it was by motor racing's worst ever accident, the fact that two of the MGs averaged 86.17 and 81.97mph to finish fifth and sixth in their class respectively had little meaning. And only a few weeks later a three-car team entered the Ulster TT, one powered by an experimental twin-cam engine. Only one of the cars survived to the chequered flag. Three drivers were killed during the race and Lord promptly withdrew MG from motor racing.

However, the tragedies did not seem to lessen the public's enthusiasm for the MGA when it was finally announced at the Frankfurt Motor Show. The new car was so obviously different from the Midget that it was decided to return to the first letter of the alphabet for its badging. With its sweeping lines, full-width windscreen and £844 price tag it was an instant success; in its first year of production, 1956, 13,000 MGAs were built. Add to that the revamped Magnette with its more powerful engine and higher final drive, and in 1956

One of motor sport's most famous poses. A young Stirling Moss takes a well-earned drink after shattering class land speed records in EX.181.

Abingdon produced over 20,000 cars, of which more than three-quarters were exported.

Those overseas sales were excellent news for MG, but on a wider front the British motor industry was beginning to lose out to continental rivals. Two years earlier, in 1954, British exports had plateaued while France and Germany's had increased so that by 1956 West Germany's production and export figures exceeded the UK's. In the long term, though, it was BMC's decision to sell technological know-how to Datsun (now Nissan) and the little heeded news that Toyota had built the first post-war Japanese-designed car that would have the most dire effects on BMC, MG and the British motor industry as a whole.

MG's obsession with speed records continued unabated. A twin-cam development of the B-type engine was installed in the EX.179 record car and taken to Utah, where it smashed sixteen international 1500cc class records, including ten miles at 170.15mph and averaging 141.71mph for twelve hours. But this was just an appetiser for what has become MG's most famous record-breaker.

EX.181 was a natural development of Enever's previous record cars, a slim teardrop standing just a fraction over 38in high and with 30 per cent less drag than EX.179. Its tubular

chassis had the driver pushed right to the front with the engine mounted immediately behind. MG was determined to beat the records that Gardner had set for them in 1939 and go one further. They wanted to hit the magic 250mph if possible and 240mph - four miles a minute - at the very least. To achieve this they needed at least 280bhp, so a super-charged version of the prototype 1.5-litre twin cam was developed and ended up producing 290bhp at 7300rpm.

On the evening of 23 August 1957 Stirling Moss set off across the salt flats in EX.181. By the time the runs were over he had broken five International Class F records with a top speed of 245.64mph.

This was an excellent platform for MG to launch a more powerful version of the standard 72bhp A. Using the record-breaker's twin-cam engine as a base, the new power unit had an alloy cross-flow cylinder-head and larger SU carburettors, while the bore was enlarged to 75.4mm, increasing capacity to 1588cc. This resulted in a

Based on EX.181's engine came the Twin-Cam MGA; though powerful, it proved fragile.

MGAs proved popular overseas as well. This is a left-hand-drive model destined for export.

hour race. However, while racing mechanics and drivers might be able to maintain the Twin Cam, ordinary buyers weren't having the same luck. For its time the Twin Cam had quite a high compression ratio -9.9:1 - and this meant running it on the rarer, and more costly, 100-octane fuel. It also meant the timing and the tuning of the carburettors had to be spot on. This wasn't happening and MG's reputation for reliability was beginning to suffer, especially in the vital American market. In April 1960, therefore, after 2111 Twin Cams had been built, the model was discontinued.

power increase to 108bhp at 6700rpm. Dunlop disc brakes were fitted all round with centre-lock disc wheels. The power improvement produced a welcome hike in performance: top speed was up to 115mph and 0-60mph time came down from fifteen seconds to 9.1. Not bad for a package costing only £1283.

Over the coming years the MGA Twin Cam had a reasonably successful competition life, including class records in the Sebring twelve-

Despite this set-back Abingdon had been going from strength to strength. By 1957 production was up to 28,500 cars a year, of which 20,000 were push-rod MGAs. But there were more revolutionary changes on the way. Also in 1957 BMC decided to transfer Austin-Healey production to Abingdon in place of Riley, which subsequently became nothing more than badge-engineered versions of existing Austin-Morris prod-

It might be wearing an MG badge, but this is little more than a Morris Oxford.

ucts. Within twelve months a brand-new Austin-Healey was announced, the 948cc BMC A series-engined Sprite. The little car turned out to be an unprecedented success and Abingdon's production rocketed to more than 41,000, of which 26,000 were MGs.

MG's hierarchy ought to have to taken note of what had happened to Wolseley and Riley in the past. Both marques had lost their identities and become little more than cloned versions of Austin-Morris mainstream products. The same thing was now happening with MG. Following their strategy of streamlining and badge engineering, BMC renamed versions of their Morris Oxford saloons as the MG Magnette Mark lll. It was the first time in thirty years that a car bearing the MG badge hadn't been built at Abingdon, and it created a trend which reached its nadir a quarter of a century later.

Taken as a whole 1959 was a pretty signifi-cant year for MG and the motor industry. Abingdon's production continued to rise, so they were building 52,785 cars a year (and exporting 47,000 of them) in a factory which hadn't had any major investment since its expansion in 1953. Product development also continued apace, with the MGA 1600 making an appearance in the same year. A push-rod cylinder-head was developed for the larger Twin-Cam block, improving power by 8bhp over the original 1500 to 80. It was upgraded further to 93bhp in 1961 when the 1600 Mark ll came out with a 1622cc engine. The Utah salt flats beckoned once more and the MG team set out with EX.181. This time engine capacity had been taken out to 1506cc so it could run in the two-litre category. Driving the car was Phil Hill, who would become the USA's first Formula One World Champion with Ferrari in 1961. The 254.91 mph he attained is the fastest an MG has achieved to date.

And as the glory of setting new records faded, an engineering revolution was

Unreliable the Twin-Cam might have been, but its block spawned a 1600 and then a 1622cc engine.

Launched in 1961, the MG Midget was yet another example of the growing trend of cloning marques from one to another.

taking place at BMC which would, ultimately, affect every major mass producer of cars in the world.

BMC had launched the Austin Seven or Morris Mini-Minor. With its tiny wheels and box-like shape it was quite unlike anything else seen on the roads up to that time. If that wasn't sufficient, then the engine sat across the front wheels and drove through them. It might not have been the world's first front-wheel-drive car, but Alec Issigonis' design was the most practical, reliable and easily manufactured. But could it form the basis of a small MG, a new Midget perhaps?

Well, a new Midget was on the stocks to join

the MGA, but not a Mini-derived front-wheel-drive model. Sales of the frog-eye Sprite were beginning to suffer, so Abingdon's design team developed a replacement complete with a conventional bonnet - rather than the original's one-piece bonnet-wing assembly - and boot. The 948cc engine was upgraded and now produced 46.4bhp and the competitions department had developed a close-ratio gearbox. A month after the Sprite was announced in May 1961, MG unveiled its Midget version of the same car. It wasn't a particularly quick little machine - it had a top speed of only 86mph and you'd be struggling to reach 60mph from standstill in under twenty seconds - but it evoked all the original thoughts that had led to the Midget being designed thirty years before, it was cheap 'n' cheerful sports-car motoring.

Unfortunately, time was beginning to catch up with the MGA. Sales had started to slide badly - from 1959's record of 23,000 they sank to a mere 6000 two years later. The search was on for an A replacement: the Italian styling house Frua produced a very attractive concept - EX.214 -on an A chassis, but while the design would have looked happy wearing a Lancia or Alfa Romeo badge, it definitely wasn't an MG. Chief body designer John O'Neill produced a fastback version of the car in two-tone colours, which betrayed very strong Aston Martin DB2/4 overtones in the sweep of its roofline from the cant rail, rearwards. It too was not an MG.

By 1962 the MGA had been in production seven years and during that 'never had it so good' era, design technology and manufacturing techniques had made huge strides forward. Unitary or monocoque construction was now a proven means of car design and production, while the MGA soldiered on with its separate chassis and labour-intensive body-assembly techniques. In spring of that year, the 100,000th MGA rolled off Abingdon's production lines and a few months later the 101,018th MGA marked the end of a remarkable career and the birth of a new one.

The MGA proved a bestseller for Abingdon both at home and abroad. A proud Syd Enever stands by the 100,000th example to be built.

5

The 'Swinging Sixties' had barely got into their stride when the MGB was launched at the London Motor Show on 20 September 1962. It was the perfect time to launch what eventually became one of the world's most enduring and best-loved sports cars, a 'classic' in the true sense of the word.

Over the years MG had developed to a fine pitch its philosophy of taking a mélange of mundane components and combining them to produce cars which were far better than the sum of their individual parts. The B turned out to be MG's finest example of that simple, cost-effective engineering policy for nearly three decades.

The MGB started life in 1958 as project ADO23, which itself had grown out of the earlier EX214 and EX205 styling exercises done by John O'Neill and his chief draughtsman, Don Hayter. While the decision had already been taken that unitary construction would be used,

there was a lot of serious debate about what should power the next generation MG.

Among the alternatives considered was a 60-degree V4/V6 with a single central cam operating the valves. Although a number of these were built the V4's inherent imbalance, as well as its cost, swiftly led to the V engines being dropped. Its legacy, however, lived on in the B's design and explains the car's wide engine-bay and bonnet.

Other options in the frame included a new small straight-six and a four-cylinder version of the three-litre C-series, while the Twin Cam's lack of reliability made that a non-starter.

Having ruled out these options, MG were forced to raid the corporate parts bin and came

In 1959 MG produced EX 205/1 as a replacement for the MGA. Note its obvious Aston Martin influences.

up with the smaller A-series 1588cc engine. Unfortunately as the B developed over the years it gained weight and ended up slower than the last 1622cc MGAs, so a late decision was taken to use the latest 1798cc version of the B-type engine that was being engineered. Its 95bhp wasn't much of an improvement over the last series A's, but the 107lb ft of torque was an 18 per cent increase.

The 'B' wouldn't be the first unitary-construction open-topped sports car, as both the Austin-Healey Sprite and Sunbeam Alpine used that build method. The result was a lighter and torsionally stiffer car than one with a separate chassis design. For the first time the MG was not to be wholly produced at Abingdon; the bodies were put together at Pressed Steel's new Swindon plant. MGBs would be assembled at Abingdon from components brought in from various corners of the BMC empire and independent suppliers. Although this broke with tradition, it meant that Abingdon's build capacity could be increased without too much expense being incurred in new buildings and facilities.

Pressed Steel didn't become part of the BMC empire until three years after the B was launched, but in the meantime Thornley was faced with the rising cost of developing the B. To disguise the increase in tooling expenditure, which was proving more costly than originally estimated, Pressed Steel agreed to Thornley's suggestion that it should accept a lower initial price and then make up the difference on the cost of each unit delivered. A nice example of financial two-stepping that ensured the MGB lived. However, the monetary constraints Thornley and his team were under meant that some of their more ambitious plans never materialised.

The biggest compromises were made over the B's suspension design. At the time independent rear suspension was just becoming a feature on more sophisticated British and European cars. Syd Enever, who was chief engineer for the MGB, and chassis designer Roy Brocklehurst wanted the B to have independent rear suspension to match the lever-arm system at the front.

Although both Watts linkage and De Dion rear suspensions were drawn up, they never got further than the concept stage. The development team then went down a blind alley designing a live rear axle using coil springs, trailing radius arms and a Watts linkage, which was later dropped in favour of a Panhard rod. Time was spent trying to tame the system's tendency towards rear-wheel steering and breaking mounting points, but to no real avail.

Late in the programme, the team resorted to

Thank God they don't build motor-show stands like this any more! Hidden beneath the travel rugs and mannequin is the new MGB.

the tried and tested leaf-spring set-up. This necessitated redesigning the rear of the car and lengthening it an inch to accommodate the longer cart springs demanded.

The knock-on benefit was a larger boot without any suspension turrets encroaching on luggage space and relocating the spare wheel flat on the boot floor rather than at an angle.

With its disc/drum brake set-up, rack-and-pinion steering, improved accommodation and a more forgiving ride than the MGA, but with equally good handling, the B was destined to appeal to a broad spectrum of buyers. Combine that with its 100+mph top speed and a £834 6s 0d price tag and it's not difficult to see why it became an instant success. For that price there was no heater or radio, while erecting the hood was like trying to fight a deck chair in a force 10 gale. Furthermore, BMC's chief engineer, Alec Issigonis, insisted that

first gear didn't need syncromesh.

Although the MGB had rivals like the Sunbeam Alpine and Triumph TR4, it appealed to a broader spectrum of buyers, from those who simply wanted reliable open-air motoring and weren't particularly interested in the finer points of ride, handling and performance, to those who revelled in the car's on-road abilities. Thornley's team had come up with a car that embodied the MG spirit of 'Safety Fast', so it is not surprising that by the end of 1962 more than 4500 MGBs

For a number of years the MGB altered little in its style or design, retaining its simple lines.

had been sold and twelve months later, at the end of the first full year of production, 23,308 had been built - just eleven short of the B's predecessor's best-ever year.

The MGB's début and its subsequent success completely overshadowed the appearance of what BMC's advertising somewhat fatuously called 'The Most Advanced MG of All Time', the MG 1100. In another instance of blatant badge-engineering, BMC tacked an MG-esque grille on the front of the Morris 1100 and added a few Octagon badges to exploit the marque's appeal. It was powered by the 1098cc A-series engine and was supposed to spearhead a sales initiative in the USA, where it proved a dismal failure.

The most intriguing aspect of the car was Alex Moulton's Hydrolastic suspension, which used rubber springs and liquid to absorb wheel movements and control pitch and roll, rather than conventional springing medium. Little did anyone realise at the time that MG would return to the same technology three decades later.

The Midget also came in for some minor improvements in 1962, with a 1098cc engine and front disc brakes. But it wasn't until the remodelled Mark lll version appeared in 1964 with a new windscreen and a few other cosmetic updates, as well as revised rear suspension and a 59bhp engine instead of 55, that Midget sales started to improve.

After an eight-year absence, MG returned to the race tracks with an Abingdon-built MGB entered in the 1963 Le Mans 24-hour race for Paddy Hopkirk and Alan Hutcheson. Even so, BMC insisted that the car was 'privately owned'. With its mildly tuned engine and taller gearing, the B reached 130mph on the long Mulsanne straight and, despite Hutcheson having to spend ninety minutes digging the car out of a sand trap after a minor off, won its class with an average speed of 92mph.

MG soldiered on with its singleton Le Mans entries until 1965 when it became obvious that the more specialised Porsches were making it difficult for the more standard MG to qualify. Even so in the 1964 race it averaged 99.9mph for the duration of the event, won the Motor trophy for the highest-placed British car, finished second in class and was eleventh overall. It went on almost to duplicate that feat the next year, with the exception that the Rover-BRM gas-turbine car took the Motor trophy.

A few updates had been made to the car since its 1962 launch, with much-needed over-

Unfortunately the B had to share its launch with another new 'MG', the 1100, which was nothing more than a badged Morris.

drive offered on US-bound cars in 1963 and a more user-friendly foldaway hood replacing the awkward demountable one as standard; an oil cooler became standard as well.

In 1965, though, MGB sales dipped to 24,703 from the previous year's record of 24,703. The majority was still going overseas, but the UK's growing financial crisis impacted on domestic sales as the credit squeeze and hire-purchase restrictions bit hard.

Furthermore the UK motor industry as a whole was beginning to tear itself apart. In 1965 six million days were lost due to strikes. The situation became so bad that Prime Minister Harold Wilson called the heads of the industry together and told them that if they didn't put their own houses in order, the government would step in and do so whether they liked it or not. It was the first sign of an interventionist policy that would have far-reaching repercussions for the UK's motor industry.

Despite all these problems, BMC's sales and profits were on the increase: between 1963 and 1966 they rose by 39 and 36 per cent respectively. The company's range of Issigonis-inspired front-wheel-drive cars - the Mini, 1100/1300 and later the 1800 - ruled the sales roost. However, even this masked the reality, for Alec Issigonis flatly refused to have any car styled or listen to

market research. 'Market research is absolute bunk,' he maintained. 'I design cars without any prompting from my employers to suit what they want from sales.... A stylist is employed to make things obsolescent.' Issigonis' arrogant stubbornness would cost BMC, and ultimately MG, dear in the long run.

Under the leadership of George Harriman, who took over from Leonard Lord in 1961, the company failed to address its manufacturing inefficiencies. The Mini, for instance, needed sixty different speedometers and the Minor was built in three different locations. From being a dominant world force in the mid-1950s the UK motor industry was fast deteriorating, until by the mid-1960s it was producing fewer cars per worker than Germany, France or Italy. Most ominously, the BMC factories were well behind either Vauxhall or Ford.

Nevertheless, in 1964 the MGB received the five-bearing engine that had been developed for the front-wheel-drive 1800 saloon. There weren't any power gains to be had with the new engine, it was just more refined, especially at lower engine speeds.

Ever since the start of the MGB programme, Thornley, Enever and Brocklehurst had wanted to produce a coupé version.

Thornley was a long-time admirer of Aston

John Thornley and his wife. Thornley effectively took over MG after the war.

Martins, as evidenced in the EX205/1 concept, and harboured ambitions for MG to build 'a poor man's Aston Martin'. Much of the design work was drawn by Don Hayter, an ex-Aston Martin man himself, so perhaps the styling overtones of these cars was only to be expected.

However, while Abingdon was still toying with the coupé concept a Belgian coachbuilder brought out his own Berlinetta. The Jacques Counes converted B, which first appeared at the Brussels Motor Show in early 1964, was no lash-up, but a neatly styled and well-finished conversion. Counes combined the B's rounded flanks with a Pininfarina-style roof line and fastback window that finished in an abrupt Kamm tail. The standard windscreen height was retained and a second side window cut into the C post; there was a conventional boot lid with access to the boot from inside the car as

Belgian coachbuilder Jacques Counes pre-empted the MGB GT with his own coupé in 1964

well. The headlights were cut well back into the wings and given Plexiglas covers, aping the style set by Jaguar's E-type in 1961 and, later, Ferrari's 275GTB.

The additional cost of £480 over the purchase price of an MGB made Counes's conversion expensive. Nevertheless, he built fifty-eight, and one even found its way to Abingdon. Walter Oldfield, manager of Nuffield Press, ordered one after meeting Counes at a motor show and had the finished car delivered in early 1964. Enever and his colleagues must have given the car a thor-

The MGB GT might not have been Pininfarina's most inspirational design, but it has weathered the test of time.

ough going-over, if only to see what the opposition was like.

Meanwhile the Abingdon design team were having problems mating their coupé's angular roofline to the bottom half of the B. Since the launch of the Austin A40 back in the 1950s, BMC had had a close relationship with Italy's premier design studio, Pininfarina, so it was to them that Enever and his team went to help sort the GT's styling problem. The Italians' breakthrough came when they altered the windscreen's angle and height as well as abandoning the alloy screen surround for a body-coloured one; the side windows were also changed and a full-size tailgate incorporated .

With its additional metalwork the MGB GT tipped the scales at some 250lb heavier than the convertible. No doubt much of this weight could have been pared off if BMC had been prepared to invest in redesigning the body shell, but they weren't. As a consequence the GT accelerated marginally more slowly to 60mph, but its cleaner aerody-

During its life the GT's interior remained largely unchanged. This is a 1972 version with vents and radio repositioned in the centre console.

namics meant its top speed - 107mph - was better.

When launched, the GT came with a front anti-roll bar and oil cooler as standard, but the heater was still an optional extra. Apart from that and slightly stiffer rear springs it was identical to the Roadster and in its most basic form sold for £998 8s 9d.

To describe the GT as a '2+2' would be an exaggeration, but at least the vestigial rear bench folded flat to extend the luggage area and it increased the car's appeal. In its first full year of production, 1966, 10,241 GTs were built, in addition to 22,675 Roadsters, underlining the fact that the new MG sales were incremental rather than substitutional.

Ominously, in 1966, the American safety movement was gathering pace, lead by a vociferous lawyer called Ralph Nader, who forced President Johnson to sign the Safety Act in September 1966. This legislation, together with the Clean Air Act that would follow two years later, would have far-reaching ramifications for the motor industry as a whole and MG in particular.

Closer to home, the structure of the British motor industry was undergoing radical changes. BMC had bought Jaguar, to form British Motor Holdings. BMH then went on to buy their body suppliers, Pressed Steel. A new overall managing director, Joe Edwards, was appointed. It was Edwards' second tour of duty at Longbridge - twelve years earlier he and Lord had had an acrimonious dispute which led to Edwards' resignation.

Unknown to everyone but the most senior levels of BMC/BMH's hierarchy, there had been secret discussions between BMC, Leyland (headed by Donald Stokes) and John Black of Standard about a grand alliance of the UK's motor industry to counter the growing threat from European rivals. That it fizzled out was, perhaps, to be expected, given the natures of the men involved, but what did emerge in the longer run were two automotive giants: BMH on one side with marques like Austin, Morris, Jaguar and MG, and the Leyland-Rover-Triumph axis on the other.

The immediate knock-on effect of the creation of BMH was the cancellation of a new, bigger-engined sports car powered by a 4-litre Rolls-Royce engine. One of the men involved in 'Project Fireball', which was targeted at Jaguar's E-type, was a young apprentice called Brian Griffin. Thirty years on the younger Griffin would play a pivotal role in MG's revival.

It was an unsettling period for Abingdon - now referred to as the MG Division. John

Thornley was slowly recovering from a major operation in September 1966 and Cec Cousins, had retired. Large amounts of time and money were being spent on ensuring that the Roadster and GT met with the impending American legislation. Abingdon's production slipped from the previous year's high of nearly 40,000 to below 35,000, with exports experiencing a similar decline.

In any car company, engineers love tinkering with 'what if' projects which combine unlikely power trains and body shells into improbable hybrids. So, during its time, development MGBs were powered by a Daimler V8, Jaguar's straight-six and, most improbable of all, a production version of a Coventry Climax V8

The unloved and short-lived MGC and MGC GT.

racing engine. One of the most attractive combinations was a BGT powered by the Australian-built 2433cc 'Blue Flash' six-cylinder engine. Effectively it was one and a half B-series engines fed by triple SU carburettors. That it was quick there is no doubt, as Brocklehurst was clocked at 127mph, but the drawback would have been shipping it back to Abingdon. Ultimately, in 1967, the B inherited the updated C-series straight-six that was destined for a new rear-drive saloon.

The new 3-litre was big, heavy and none too powerful. Even in its MG state of tune the engine produced only 145bhp and 170lb ft of torque, but what really threw the Abingdon team was its weight - 200 lb greater than the B-series engine.

This forced Roy Brocklehurst into some major design revisions at the front of the B, as the engine was both longer and taller than anticipated. Additionally the floor pan was beefed up, bigger brakes fitted, stiffer rear springs and a stronger Salisbury tubular axle introduced.

By the time all this was added up, the MGC, as the new car was christened, weighed 400lb more than the B. Not only that, but the weight distribution had altered, turning the car into a nose-heavy, ponderous understeerer which detracted from its 120mph top speed and ten seconds zero-to-60mph time.

When production of the unloved MGC ceased in 1969, 4550 roadsters and 4449 GTs had been built, the majority of which went across the Atlantic to the USA. Few mourned its passing.

The previous year the Abingdon works' competition team had won its last major track event, struggling to victory in the demanding 84-hour Nürburgring marathon, covering 5620 miles at an average speed of nearly 70mph. The victory marked the end of an illustrious forty-year competition history which had seen the marque tackle and win its class in the world's toughest motorsport events, from Brooklands to Le Mans, Targa Florio to Sebring, and not forgetting an enviable domination in land speed records.

Meanwhile, the Labour government was struggling to contain growing militancy among the trade unions and its fiscal policy was in ruins. The pound had been devalued in 1967 and HP restrictions were being tightened and loosened more often than a slimmer's belt.

During this period Abingdon was developing EX.234, a front-engined, rear-wheel-drive B replacement. The project started in 1967 under Roy Brocklehurst's direction, as a replacement not just for the B but also for the Midget, which would have used a smaller engine. MG again chose Hydrolastic suspension, but this time with

Pininfarina penned this suggested update for the 'B' – it's redolent of Alfa Romeo's Spyder.

wishbones at the front and trailing arms at the back. To minimise development and manufacturing costs a common 87in wheelbase was used for both the 1275cc Midget replacement and the larger, 1798cc-engined successor to the B.

Pininfarina built up a running prototype based on the Midget chassis in 1968. Visually it bears a close resemblance to the following year's Alfa Romeo Spider with EX.234 sharing the Alfa's short front overhang and longer rear one, but did without the Italian car's longitudinal side scallops.

At the time, though, BMH's management were immersed in a battle to save the entire group from going to the wall so, sadly, EX.234 was consigned to the 'what might have been' file.

With this as a backdrop, BMH was lurching from one problem to another. Quality was poor, production was constantly threatened by wild-cat strikes and the model line-up. Issigonis, for all his engineering and design genius, stubbornly refused to admit that products such as Ford Escorts and Cortinas or Hillman Avengers were successful rivals. BMH had too many sites, too many components and not enough reserves to save themselves. In short, while MG might have appeared safe, the parent company was in imminent danger of bankruptcy.

At the same time the smaller Leyland operation, headed by Donald Stokes, was making progress and profits, especially from overseas markets. Fearful of the consequences that a BMH collapse would precipitate, the Wilson government set about arranging a marriage between the two parties. The pressure that Stokes and Leyland, Harriman and BMH came under were immense, even to the extent of the Prime Minster inviting the two principals to dine and stay at Chequers to force the issue home. Also in attendance was Anthony Wedgwood-Benn, Minister of Technology, who had unsuccessfully tried to persuade Stokes and Leyland that they should buy Rootes and prevent it from falling into Chrysler's hands.

Inevitably, as with Nuffield and Lord, there were huge personality clashes between the Leyland and BMH directors over job titles and wording of press statements that constantly threatened the whole process. But eventually, on 17 January 1968, the two merged to create British Leyland Motor Corporation (later British Leyland Motor Holdings).

If ever there was a shot-gun marriage with a politician's finger on the trigger, this was it. The government couldn't afford to see BMH go under: its interventionist policy would probably-have been torn to shreds and if the arm-twisting Stokes and Harriman were put through hadn't succeeded Leyland and BMH would have been nationalised.

The new company, headed by Donald Stokes, was the second largest car manufacturer outside the United States (after Volkswagen) and the fifth largest non-nationalised company in the UK. It controlled 40 per cent of the domestic car market and 35 per cent of home truck sales. Its targets were Icarian to say the least: a billion pounds of annual sales, £50 million profit before tax, 45 and 40 per cent of the UK's car and truck sales respectively.

Stokes' appointment to the most senior post meant that MG was ultimately being run by the man who was also boss of MG's arch-rival, Triumph. It seemed as if history was repeating itself for MG - first Lord and Austin, now Stokes and Triumph.

6

That BMH was in a dire state was already a big enough problem for them to cope with, but additionally the 1970s proved to be the most depressing post-war decade yet for the motor industry. Whichever way they turned they were landed one knock-out punch after another: if it wasn't the unions calling wildcat strikes and demanding impossible pay increases, it was the American authorities imposing expensive safety and emission regulations, or global oil crises in the wake of the Yom Kippur War. If that wasn't enough to contend with, the Japanese exceeded the UK's vehicle production for the first time in 1968, import duties were slashed unleashing a flood of competitively priced foreign-built cars into the UK, and the government resorted to its old tactics of using the motor trade as the economy's throttle and brake.

It's inevitable given these circumstances that marques like MG should have been margin-alised. Having said that, some of the decisions taken in this era seem to have been triggered more by favouritism than sound business logic.

The new BLMH team set about the much-needed reorganisation and integration of the two giants with vigour, one of the first tasks being to amalgamate the various marques into their own business divisions. One, known as Specialist Car Division, included Standard-Triumph, Rover and Jaguar - but not MG. Much to their chagrin, the men from Abingdon found instead that they were part of the Austin-Morris Division.

The Leyland team had effectively taken over the running of the entire BLMH operation - apart from Jaguar, which remained steadfastly under the control of its founder, Sir William Lyons. A main objective of the new company was to rationalise production and delete competing marques. Riley and Wolseley were seen as superfluous rivals to both Rover and Triumph. A similar policy was adopted for sports cars: BLMH had two, the Triumph TR6 and the MGB. The question was, which marque should get the funds to develop a new sportster for the late 1970s and the 1980s - Triumph or MG? To settle the question, an internal 'competition' was staged between the rivals.

MG proposed a radical, wedge-shaped, mid-engined car on a chassis and power train developed by Don Hayter, with bodywork styled by Harris Mann. The power train was an Austin Maxi's 1750cc unit with the possibility that the Australian 2.2- or 2.6-litre E6 engine could have been adopted. Conventional MacPherson strut suspension was envisaged at the front, but there were two design proposals for the rear, both had coil spring/damper units and were based on De Dion set-ups.

The Triumph concept, code-named 'Bullet', was a more conventional front-engined, rear-wheel-drive project and eventually won out, although it was heavily restyled by Harris Mann before it was launched in 1974 as the TR7.

It would be too simplistic to say the dice were loaded against MG from the start. Developing a mid-engined car to meet the US impact regulations would have been tough and the tooling costs high, even if there was talk of badging the car both as an MG and Triumph. BLMH were struggling financially to get their mainstream programmes underway and MG was battling to meet the US emission laws. If, as Stokes and his team contended, the TR7 was going to be the group's main sports car, it makes you wonder why the MGB was allowed to stagger on for so many years, starved of development funds instead of being quickly put down.

This really was the start of a new régime. A year after the takeover, in July 1969, John Thornley retired at the age of sixty. Another link with Kimber had gone. Thornley's departure also coincided with Riley's disappearance; for many years the marque had been nothing more than badge-engineering standard Austin-Morris products. The cars possessed no real brand identity and its departure was of little loss to anyone.

Riley's death would be followed in 1976 by Wolseley's. The disappearance of these two badges should have set the alarm bells ringing in Abingdon.

In the meantime, though, MGs and especially the B Roadster and the GT were still sell-

Donald, later Lord Stokes, who championed Triumph and not MG.

ing strongly; there must have been quiet hope at Abingdon that an extensive face-lift for the B was on the cards. Instead, all that happened over the next couple of years was the odd cosmetic tweak, which included new wheels, seats, grille and hood; all welcome, even if the British Leyland badges which now adorned the cars were reviled. Most importantly, the Americans were still in love with MG and their purchase of 36,500 of them in 1970 helped MG production top 50,000 for the first time, of which 41,000 were exported.

If MG and Abingdon were holding their own, other parts of BLMH were tearing themselves apart. At Cowley, just a few miles down the road, there was an average of two and a half strikes a day - 600 a year - while Austin-Morris's £16 million loss that year seriously eroded the group's overall performance and must have led to the budgets of fringe operations being severely cut back. It was against this background that Abingdon had to develop increasingly old products to meet new safety and emission legislation.

The immediate effect of the American regulations was that over the next few years engine power was decreased, first by fitting an engine-driven air-pump, then by lowering the compression ratio to 8.0:1, which knocked its power down to a feeble 82bhp at 5400rpm. Matters were made even worse by the Californian legislature

in 1974. A catalytic converter had to be added, robbing the B of its 100mph top speed.

While BLMH were vacillating over MG's future development, an enterprising engineer had grasped the opportunity to show what could really be done with the BGT.

In 1965 Rover acquired the manufacturing rights to a 3.5-litre aluminium V8 that had been developed by GM's Buick division and then abandoned. Rover anglicised the engine with different inlet manifolds and SU carburettors, débuting it in the 1967 Rover 3.5-litre saloon.

Thanks to the BGT's wide engine bay, the lightweight V8 - without ancillaries it was 40lb lighter than the 1.8 could just about be shoe-horned in. The only problem came with the carburettors, which necessitated a bonnet power bulge; Costello even retained the MGB's standard gearbox and rear axle, although he did modify the steering and exhaust manifolds. With 144bhp at 5000rpm and 197lb ft of torque, the Costello V8 offered a genuine 115+mph top speed and 0-60mph in well under ten seconds.

There are two schools of thought as to what happened when Costello launched his car in 1970. One, that MG was already working on a V8 conversion, but that the inevitable delays which homologation, testing and engineering production cause led to the official BGT V8 not appear-

An early attempt at a safety car – a far cry from what we're used to in the mid-90s.

ing until 1973. The second, that when Stokes saw the Costello car he wanted to know why MG couldn't produce one and that within six weeks he was shown the first prototype.

Abingdon went further with its conversion than Costello: the B gearbox was swapped for the stronger C unit modified to take a bigger clutch and with higher intermediate gears to cope with the increased torque. A modified C rear axle with a lower ratio and stiffer springs was also developed and the tyres uprated to cope with the increased performance.

Unlike Costello, MG opted for the slightly less powerful Range-Rover specification V8, with 137bhp and 193lb ft of torque. The MGB GT V8's performance was impressive: 125mph top speed and 0-60mph in 8.5 seconds.

Despite everything going against it - legislation, lack of investment from BLMH - the 250,000th MGB, a left-hand-drive GT, rolled off the Abingdon production line in May 1971, just a few weeks after Syd Enever retired.

Before the V8 appeared, however, MG displayed an experimental version of the GT at a safety conference held in Washington DC in 1972. Safety Systems Vehicle One, as it was called, was intended to show that a small car could incorporate all the potential safety items that legislators wanted and that manufacturers were in the early stages of developing. Visually its most arresting features were a roof-mounted periscope-like rear-view mirror and low-mounted impact-absorbing bumpers. Foam-filled panels and reinforced doors intended to increase side-impact protection were included, as were door-mounted seat-belts designed to make it very difficult for the driver and passenger not to belt up. Air-bags were also included in the specification. Mechanically, the car's most intriguing developments were an electronically controlled anti-lock braking system and self-levelling suspension with parallel wishbones and telescopic shock-absorbers.

Meanwhile, that other stalwart from Abingdon, the Midget, soldiered on; following the demise of the Sprite in May 1971 it was rivalled only by the Triumph Spitfire. Like its bigger brother, the Midget's development languished under the BLMH flag, the yearly

ADO 34 – a Mini-based MG vetoed by Issigonis.

updates being nothing more than cosmetic tinkering: Rostyle wheels, different interior trims and developments to the engine that enabled it to perform within in the US emission regulations.

Aware that these regulations would only get tighter, MG started work in 1972 on developing a new 2-litre overhead cam engine - the O series - which was based round a modified B-series crankshaft, but with an aluminium cylinder-head; it was to be installed in the MGB.

If Abingdon's O-series project had gone ahead, the MGB's subsequent decline might

never have happened. But to say that is to reckon without what was happening in the world beyond Abingdon.

On the surface, 1972 was an excellent year for BLMC and the UK motor industry as a whole. Production, at 1,921,311 cars, was an all-time record, with exports accounting for over 32 per cent. New car sales in the UK, at 1,702,211, stood as a record for seven years, with eighteen British Leyland models taking a 33 per cent share and helping the company to a £21 million profit before tax.

Britain joined the Common Market, which led to the 25 per cent purchase tax being replaced by 10 per cent VAT and 10 per cent car tax, and BLMC dropped to seventh in the European car sales league with only 8.6 per cent of the market. Gloomy, but not disastrous.

What struck the almost fatal blow to BLMC was the after-shock of the 1973 Arab-Israeli war known as the Yom Kippur War. The OPEC nations united and in one year trebled the price of oil, bringing back the spectre of petrol rationing. Edward Heath's Conservative government was in tatters. Its anti-inflation strategy had collapsed, leading to the introduction of a three-day week; there were widespread power cuts and the miners won their battle for pay increases. Car sales tumbled from 1973's high to 1.26 million

two years later. As oil prices rocketed, rampant inflation then set in, rising from 9 per cent in 1973 to 24.2 per cent in 1975.

One of the tremors from the Yom Kippur War was a contributing factor in the demise of the MGB GT V8, even before it had got properly into its stride. Suddenly fuel economy was in vogue and a (comparatively) thirsty V8 sports car was unacceptable. Nor was the car sold in the States. Although eight were built to US specifications and shipped to America for assessment, they returned unwanted. At face value the GT V8 seemed an ideal car for the American market,

but it rivalled such in-house products as the 3-litre V8 Triumph Stag. At the same time its European sales were stifled through lack of engines. A mere 2591 were built in the car's four-year history, BL eventually blaming a shortage of engines for its termination in 1976.

American safety legislation demanded that as from late 1974 cars had to be fitted with bumpers that would absorb impacts up to 5mph. It was this regulation that gave rise to the heavy and ugly black rubber bumpers that blighted the B's looks in the final stages of its life. Not only did they add an extra 5in to the car's overall length,

In the name of US safety legislation the MGB was blighted with the ugliest set of bumpers ever contrived. What's worse is that BLMC's management insisted the rest of the world should suffer them as well.

V8 models suffered the same fate, even though they were never sold in the USA.

and 70lb to its weight, but the ride height was increased 1¹/₂ in so that the bumpers adhered to the new US standards.

The B's humiliation was complete. By complying with the US regulations, the Roadster and GT had been transformed from admittedly slightly dated-looking, benign-handling sportsters into a pair of disfigured wallowers. Jacking up the suspension had increased the ride height, increased roll-oversteer and created a rear end that would break into arm-twirling opposite lock if the driver so much as thought about cornering quickly.

It was bad enough that this abomination of an MG had to be inflicted upon the Americans, but it was then foisted on UK and European customers.

While the new-look MGs were being castigated by the press, BLMC were in severe financial difficulties. Years of mismanagement, underinvestment in manufacturing facilities and new product, and a growing militancy amongst the workforce finally forced Stokes to negotiate with the banks for increased loans just to keep BLMC's capital expenditure going. With the group heading for a £23.9 million loss, it became obvious the banks weren't going to risk their money.

Stokes had no alternative but to ask Whitehall for government backing. The recently elected Labour government eventually agreed to inject the massive sum of £1.4 billion into BLMC over the next eight years. But the company paid a high price for the rescue - 95 per cent of its shares were now held by the government. At last a Labour government had succeeded in getting what many of their politicians, supporters and union leaders wanted, a nationalised car manufacturer.

The National Enterprise Board, under the leadership of Sir Don Ryder, demanded and got radical changes. Stokes was given an honorary role and Alec Park made managing director, but he was virtually powerless unless his proposals were approved by Ryder and the NEB. Under his guidance the NEB produced the 'Ryder Report' on BLMC, which is now regarded as an ill-informed and misleading document on how to restructure the beleaguered company. In keeping with the left-wing sentiments of the time the unions became deeply involved in running the company, but their barons were more often than not more concerned with protecting their own fiefdoms and their members' interests than the company as a whole.

British Leyland Ltd, as it was renamed yet again, comprised four divisions: Leyland Cars (including MG), Leyland Truck and Bus, Leyland Special Products and Leyland International. Decades of motoring history were discarded as factories were given new Orwellian names - Jaguar's Browns Lane plant became 'Large/Specialist Vehicle Operations' and the Pavlova works were retitled 'Leyland Assembly Plant, Abingdon'.

Amidst all this furore MG persevered. To cope with US emissions regulations, the Midget's 1275cc Mini Cooper-type engine was replaced by the Triumph Spitfire's 1491cc unit. This went some way to retrieving the performance lost by the additional 170lb the Midget had put on due to impact-absorbing bumpers etc.

The MGB GT wasn't so lucky; due to its weight increase it went into a different category with more stringent emissions limits which the long-suffering 1.8 engine would probably have found it difficult to meet. As a result GT sales in the States were abandoned in 1975 -coincidentally just prior to the TR7's US launch.

The first nail had been hammered into MG's coffin and in the next five years the rest were driven home one by one. BGT exports ceased in 1976, the same year that the TR7 was launched on the Continent. Deprived of its profitable export markets and with the British buying public staying away in droves, production plummeted 37.5 per cent in three years to a low of 24,500 in 1975.

To add insult to injury British Leyland decid-

How much worse could things get than this so-called 'Golden Jubilee' model of the MGB GT?

ed to celebrate MG's golden jubilee in 1975 by building 750 gaudy British Racing Green and Gold GTs, ignoring the fact that MG production started in 1923/4. Despite its tinted glass, V8-style wheels and larger 175 tyres, the car was little more than a parody of its former self.

A slight recovery to 29,558 the following year helped, but the decline in sales had all the inevitability of an avalanche - nothing was going to stop it until disaster struck.

If life was gloomy at Abingdon, it must have been virtually suicidal within the parent group. In 1977 the toolmakers' strike cost 250,000 cars, a quarter of planned production, and the company was haemorrhaging cash at a frightening rate. It had too much production capacity and was overmanned. The policy outlined in the Ryder Report was still being stubbornly adhered to despite all the evidence that it was totally misguided.

Matters came to a head in October 1977 when Lord Ryder quit the NEB. Within weeks a fellow member of that board, Michael Edwardes, was in the hot seat at British Leyland. During his five years Edwardes did much to put Leyland

Michael Edwardes incurred the wrath of enthusiasts and MPs by closing down Abingdon.

back on its feet. He will, perhaps, be best remembered for three things: quelling the unions, extracting a further £1.4 billion from Margaret Thatcher's Conservative government, elected in 1979, and. . .

A second oil crisis in 1979 had precipitated another decline in the demand for new cars, but the UK's economy was aided by the discovery of vast oil reserves in the North Sea. This helped strengthen the pound against the US dollar, which partially disguised the £900 per car loss on each MG sold in the States. Just where that huge loss came from remains a mystery, for the development costs for the B Roadster and GT must have been amortised years before.

To celebrate MG's fifty-year association with Abingdon, a number of special events were held in the town, culminating on Sunday 9 September in a carnival parade through the streets with seventy different MGs present. The festive atmosphere was soured just twenty-four hours later with the news that Abingdon would close down and cease MG production in July 1980. Making such an announcement the day after the anniversary celebrations has got to be one of the clumsiest PR jobs of all time.

There was an immediate outcry, not just in Abingdon, but throughout the UK and from the States. The American dealers immediately offered to place $200 million worth of orders for MGBs, only to be assured by British Leyland that they could have TR7s instead. A mass demonstration led by Kimber's daughter, Jean Cook, marched on BL's Piccadilly headquarters in London and Robert Adley MP established an MG Emergency Committee which forced a debate on the closure in the House of Commons.

The most serious was a consortium led by Aston Martin-Lagonda's chairman, Alan Curtis, which proposed buying Abingdon and the right to build MGs. Even though an updated Roadster, designed by William Towns, with a GT windscreen and doors and neater bumpers was shown, the necessary financing just wasn't available and, perhaps inevitably, the negotiations collapsed in summer 1980.

With the Midget having been killed off by more emission regulations in 1979, Abingdon was reduced to producing a trickle of B Roadsters and GTs. Alongside the standard cars there were a 1000 Limited Edition models - 420 metallic bronze Roadsters and 580 metallic pewter GTs - built and a number of special Roadsters for the US market, which took ages to sell. On 22 and 23 October 1980 the last MGs built at Abingdon - a Roadster and a GT respectively - rolled out of the Pavlova works. After 521,111 cars the MGB was finished. Worse still, so was MG.

This was how MG enthusiasts were supposed to remember the marque, an emasculated, uglified parody of its former self.

THE DARK AGES

7

Michael Edwardes candidly admits in his book Back from the Brink that terminating MG was a mistake: '...you mess around with famous marque names that are loved and cherished by motoring enthusiasts at your peril!' But in truth he had no option and it would be some years before the Octagon badge reappeared.

BL's weakest models at the time were its small and mid-sized saloons, a market dominated in the UK by Ford's hyper-successful Escort and Cortina ranges. All BL could offer were cars like the Austin Allegro and Morris Marina; the Allegro had started life with a quirky Quartic steering wheel - imagine a box with rounded corners -and the Marina was dull and worthy. Neither appealed greatly to the buying public and their build quality was indifferent. Yet BL's priority at the time wasn't to replace these products with others that would challenge Ford in the

increasingly important fleet sector, but to build a new Mini.

ADO 88 had been approved by BL's board as the first in a trio of new cars that would set Austin and Morris back on the path to prosperity. It would be followed by LM10, the Maestro, in 1983 and LM 11, the Montego, a year later.

Some £300 million had been sunk into ADO 88's development and work was about to start on a £200 million refit at Longbridge, where the car was to be built. Yet there was growing disquiet within Leyland and the NEB that the car would not return its investment. Whereas the original Mini had started the trend for compact, front-wheel-drive runabouts, ADO 88 would be entering into a pitched battle against rivals like Ford's Fiesta, the Fiat 127, the Renault 5 and the VW Polo from Europe, never mind such Japanese contenders. In pre-launch customer clinics held in France, Germany and the Netherlands ADO88 fared very badly against this class of opposition.

The problem that Edwardes and his team faced was that nobody on BL's board had made a decision as to what should be done. In the end the new BL team decided to scrap ADO 88 as a Mini replacement and upgrade it one size while retaining all its best engineering and packaging elements. The BL board gave the go-ahead for

Aston Martin's proposed face lift for the MG.

was so severe that in spring 1981 TR7 production was suspended to try and get rid of unsold cars. A year after the Metro went on sale the TR7 ceased production. Since the Triumph Spitfire had been killed off the year before, BL no longer had an affordable sports car in its portfolio.

In one guise or another British Leyland had once dominated worldwide sales of affordable, mass-produced sports cars. Now they had fled the field and left the gate wide open for rivals to come in and eventually reap a ripe harvest.

Looking back, it is easy to cite a catalogue of poor management decisions which led to this inevitable decline, but that is also to ignore the climate of the late 1970s and early '80s, especially in the USA. Successful sports-car sales depended largely on a strong North American market and with the USA's obsession with safety, open-top cars of any description were at a severe disadvantage.

Additionally, there was a significant new trend in products that were taking over the traditional performance sector once dominated by two-seater sports cars'. The Golf GTi was launched at the Frankfurt Motor Show in 1976 and immediately started a trend which all other manufacturers would eventually follow. It was another nail in the MGB's coffin - here was a three-door hatchback which would seat four and

Leyland Cars 8, as the car was retagged, in July 1978, and on 8 October 1990 the Metro was launched at the Birmingham Motor Show.

While the car was welcomed with great critical approval at home and in Europe and sales took off, Edwardes was still faced with a multitude of problems - including the TR7. Despite all the claims that had been made for it and an international rally programme to boost its image, it had never been truly liked in the UK or overseas. What sales it did achieve were largely as a result of MGB's being withdrawn and discounts being offered by dealers.

In 1978 the strike-torn Triumph factory at Speke, near Liverpool, was closed down and TR7 production transferred to Coventry. But even this didn't help the car; the extent of the problem

MG reborn, once again as a badged variant, this time a Metro.

outperform a two-seater with its 108mph top speed and under 10 seconds 0-60mph time. Just to hammer home the message, in 1979 VW launched a convertible version made by the German coachbuilders Karmann. With its roll-over bar, which appeased the insurance companies and safety lobby, and its easily operated hood, a new generation of convertibles had effectively put an end to the open two-seater sports-car market.

Throughout this period Edwardes was aware that one solution to BL's lack of product would be to enter into a partnership with rival manufacturers to develop major components or, even, complete cars. Exploratory talks had been held with Renault and Volkswagen, but had never been satisfactorily concluded, often on the grounds that the companies product ranges clashed. Edwardes and his team started to look beyond Europe and negotiations with Honda started in 1978. Gradually the two sides moved closer together so that by 1980, with the approval of the Thatcher government, a

deal had been struck which would see the Honda Ballade built in the UK and sold as the Triumph Acclaim.

Amid all this MG's Octagon finally re-emerged on 5 May 1982, when the MG Metro 1300 was released.

It had taken BL's management eighteen months to appreciate the value of the MG badge. There are some claims that the decision to resurrect the Octagon was taken before the Metro was launched after market research showed that MG had more recognition that Triumph.

Much livelier than the 1300 Metro was this turbocharged version.

The original MG Metro wasn't a bad little car. Its 1275cc engine produced 72bhp and given a fair wind it would just about top 100mph. It offended MG die-hards as much as the TD and ZA Magnette had done in the past. In a blatant piece of opportunism, BL's marketing department distinguished the MG version of the Metro from its siblings with decals on the flanks and rear window, new alloy wheels and, inside, red seat-belts, carpeting and stitching. Apart from front and rear spoilers which cut the Cd down to 0.39 from 0.41, the car was mechanically identical to others in the Metro range. The MG Metro Turbo was a lively, 93bhp variant capable of 112mph and was claimed to dispose of the all-important 0-60mph in 10.9 seconds. The hatch inherited the same design of rear spoiler from the 1300 Metro, though there was a deeper front air dam which bled into front wheel arch spats that were mirrored at the rear. These weren't just for effect - they housed smart alloy wheels an inch larger than standard and wore lower profile tyres. To cope with the additional power and 85lb ft of torque at 2650rpm, the suspension geometry was altered, the springs and dampers stiffened all round, a rear anti-roll bar fitted and a larger front one added.

The turbocharger system comprised a single Garrett AiResearch T3 Turbocharger blowing through a single SU HIF 44 carburettor; excess boost was bled off through an electronically controlled waste-gate. Ensuring the extra power didn't blow the engine apart meant BL had to nitride the crankshaft and install stronger pistons and big ends. Both engine oiling and cooling rates were improved together with sodium-cooled exhaust valves and double valve-springs. Ventilated disc brakes at the front and different calipers ensured the car slowed down as effectively as it accelerated.

Like its less powerful sibling, the Metro Turbo suffered from a recurrence of Octagon-itis with an excess of MG and Octagon badges, while the styling department continued the red-with-everything theme established with the earlier MG Metro.

Apart from retaining the standard car's 6.6 gallon fuel tank, and the original four-speed gearbox, which made high-speed cruising noisy and tiresome, the Metro Turbo was well received. It had its drawbacks - the ride was harsh and uncompromising and the noise levels could get tiring. On the positive side the turbo installation provided a smooth, fairly constant stream of boost when the driver wanted it, unlike other cars in which waiting for the dreaded turbo lag to be overcome was a bit like waiting for Godot, only less exciting.

The early 1980s continued to be turbulent times for the BL Group. At one moment Edwardes would be cajoling the government into providing more financial backing, in the next he would be braving it out with the unions. His sacking of Longbridge's left-wing convenor, Derek 'Red Robbo' Robinson, was the most audacious piece of strong-arm management - some would say bullying - that British industry had seen in decades. And all the while, new faces were being drafted into BL to forge its long-term path: David Andrews, Ray Horrocks, John Baccus, Tony Gilroy, men not directly involved in MG's story, but who were striving for the good of the company as a whole. Others, like Mark Snowdon in sales and marketing, had a more direct influence, as did Harold Musgrove and Roy Axe.

Musgrove had taken over as Austin-Rover's (yet another name change instigated during the Edwardes régime) chairman and chief executive when Edwardes's contract expired in 1982. A blunt, no-nonsense man, he soon earned himself a reputation as a forthright talker who would browbeat journalists into submission if they had the temerity to suggest that Austin-Rover products weren't all he made them out to be.

It can hardly have been Musgrove's honeyed tones which persuaded Roy Axe to recross the Atlantic and join Austin-Rover, more his convic-tion that the company had turned the corner and was set well and truly on the path to success. Axe had been in the States since 1976, working his way through the Chrysler Corporation to become director of automotive design for America's third largest car manufacturer, when he was persuaded to return to the UK in 1982 and take over Austin-Rover's design. His American colleagues warned him he was making a mistake and even promised him a job if he should change his mind, which he almost did: 'I nearly died when I walked into this place in Longbridge which was like a railway shed with a few people working away, and then there was a little place at Canley. It was a total shambles, full of demoralised people. I am not a defeatist, but that was an appalling situation.'

Musgrove said he wanted to put design on the map and Axe admits that, to be fair, after a bit of niggling Musgrove backed a full reorganisation of styling within the Austin-Rover Group (ARG) and invested in a new design studio at Canley, near Coventry, which amalgamated the best of the design teams from Longbridge and Rover at Solihull.

There were a number of individuals already in place who would play pivotal roles in MG's future: Gordon Sked had been with Austin since 1970 and was appointed studio director, exterior design, and Gerry McGovern joined the styling team from Peugeot's UK office.

Roy, like so many other American-based observers, he had been astounded by BL's withdrawal from the sports car sector: '...the Americans in particular love them [sports cars] and they have the disposable income to afford a number of cars and those are the people that have them. So, to have walked away from that market by persuading yourself that you make too many of one thing, so you shouldn't make any at all...it was just mind-boggling that they should come to that conclusion.'

The most immediate product on the horizon was the Maestro, just four or five months away from launch. Horrified though he was by the car's design, Axe recalls that there was nothing to be done. Launched in March 1983, the Maestro was hardly a breakthrough in design or engineering. Austin-Rover had gone out of their way to be conventional: MacPherson struts at the front and trailing arms, torsion beam and coil springs at the back; a far cry from the innovative Hydragas suspension used on the Metro. Power came from the ubiquitous 1275cc A-series engine and the new 1598cc R series. The biggest change to both was the adoption of an end-on Volkswagen five-speed gearbox in place of Issigonis' more traditional under-engine design.

An MG model appeared at launch, thankfully without too many of the MG logos. However, apart from the 1600 engine getting revised timing and twin Weber 40DCNF carburettors, which pushed the power up 23bhp to 103, plus a close-ratio gearbox with a higher final drive, nothing mechanical was done to the car. A 111mph top speed was quoted, while standstill to 60mph took 9.6 seconds.

The decision to produce the Metro was probably the right one at the time, since this sector accounted for some 60 per cent of BL's car sales. However, the legacy of that decision was that the development of LM10 and LM11 - the Maestro and Montego - had slowed down and Axe found himself trying to inject new life into cars that were already past their sell-by date. To make matters worse, he adds, Austin-Rover's manufacturing facilities weren't up to scratch: 'There was nothing that could be done, just let it [the Maestro] go and swallow hard.'

The Montego was still a year away. When it was wheeled into a viewing room and Axe was asked what he thought of it, 'My immediate reaction was to ask if it could be stopped, only to be told my answer was "unacceptable" and that Austin-Rover were committed to the car. There was a fair bit of time spent trying to smooth it out. What came out, bad though it was and I am the first to admit it, was a damn sight better than when it started. But in hindsight I should have fought even harder and said there was nothing you can do with it, don't do it.'

If the car's styling was a worry, then Austin-Rover's build quality was of equal concern to Axe: 'The real horror story was that Harold [Musgrove] was wrong about manufacturing. Production wasn't capable of building the cars, or capable of doing anything as far as I was concerned without it falling apart.'

Cars like the Maestro and Montego, according to Axe, were badly engineered and poorly built. 'Those cars had been designed a long time ago and then put on hold while they did the Metro. They were three years old before they even got started on engineering them: I used to tell Harold that if a car has a six-year life and

An MG too far? That's what many felt about the slab-sided Montego version.

you've vacillated for three years, it doesn't still have a six-year life.

'The problem was, they had put the car on ice and tried to bring it back as it was, but the world had moved on substantially in that period of time. The cars were designed and constructed wrongly and could never, ever be made with reasonable quality.'

Launched in spring 1984, the Montego shared the Maestro's steering and suspension and some of the power plants; the major differences were ventilated front disc brakes and a Honda five-speed gearbox. The Maestro-derived floorpan had an extra 2in in the wheelbase and it was all clothed in a three-box saloon, with 60 per cent of the body panels Maestro sourced.

As a large, spacious, front-wheel-drive saloon the Montego was happier as a Vanden Plas than it ever was an MG. However, now that the Octagon had been revived Austin-Rover took every opportunity to exploit it to the maximum. Thankfully the

temptation to shower the Montego with Octagons and MG badges was resisted - there was a discreet red stripe in the rubbing strips and smart cast alloy spoked rims, though the front and rear spoilers might have been a little too aggressive. Inside, the grey and red theme which had become an MG signature since the Metro's introduction, continued with added veneer door cappings and the now usual MG Octagon moulded into the fascia's anti-slip mat.

Cutaway of the most outrageous MG yet – the rallying 6R4.

The most expensive MG to date at £8000 was powered by an updated version of the O-series engine that was once mooted as a possible replacement for the MGB's ageing B-series engine, but with a new alloy cylinder-head that had the inlet ports paired rather than alternating with the exhaust ports. A new Lucas electronic fuel-injection system was fitted which helped boost power to a useful 115bhp, giving the car a reasonable 8.9 seconds to 60mph before running out of steam at 115mph.

While the MG Montego might have been one Octagon too far, the marque's competition heritage was being fully exploited by Austin-Rover as it returned to racing and rallying. For the 1984 race season the Austin-Rover Group entered a pair of works-prepared MG Metro Turbos in the British Saloon Car Championship for drivers Patrick Watt and Robin Brundle (younger brother of F1 jockey Martin). Because of the regulations, the 1300cc Turbo was elevated to the 2.5-litre class, but with an estimated 190bhp available to them neither Brundle nor Watt disgraced themselves, winning their class in each of the four rounds entered.

As MG's return to racing was terminated through political wrangling and disputes, ARG's motor-sport division was busily developing one of the most bizarre-looking rally cars of its genera-tion. In the early 1980s motor sport's governing body changed the rules for international rallying; four-wheel drive was permitted and manufactur-ers had to build only 200 cars to achieve Group B homologation.

By 1981 ARG's motor-sport boss, John Davenport, had persuaded the powers that be to invest in an international Group B rally pro-gramme. Due to lack of engineering capacity Davenport approached Williams Grand Prix F1 designer, Patrick Head, to assist with the design. On the surface it might seem odd to approach a man steeped in Formula One racing to help develop a rally car, but at the time Leyland Vehicles were part-sponsors of the Williams team.

Head and his team spent much of 1982 eval-uating various concepts and eventually settled on a mid-engined, four-wheel-drive design pack-aged into a modified Metro body shell. Instead of going for the small capacity turbocharged engine for which arch-rivals Lancia and Peugeot had opted, ARG went for a bigger capacity, normally aspirated engine, reasoning that its more instant throttle response would be beneficial on stage events.

Until a pukka competition engine was devel-oped ARG's power train engineers hacked two cylinders off a 3.5-litre Rover V8 to create a 2.5-

The MG Montego Turbo, pictured here alongside Old Number One, was brutal in the dry and unforgiving in the wet.

litre V6 for the development programme. This ran throughout 1983 in great secrecy, ARG somehow managing not to get the car scooped by an intrepid photographer.

By the time the definitive car was launched to the media in May 1985 it was still a Metro, 'but not as we knew it'. During its gestation, long-travel front-suspension struts had been developed, resulting in blisters on top of the front wings, nearly 3in extra had been put in the front and rear tracks which necessitated box-like wheel-arch extensions and, at the rear, air intakes halfway along the doors; plus a pair of adjustable spoilers, one mounted on the roof and a second at the front which looked like a miniaturised snow plough.

Although the four-wheel-drive system remained, the engine was now an in-house 3-litre 90-degree V6 designed and developed by Dave Woods. With four valves per cylinder and multi-point fuel injection the international version was expected to produce 380-410bhp depending on its tune. A de-tuned 'Clubmans' variant destined for national rallies produced 250bhp.

The MG Metro 6R4 (six cylinders, rally car, four-wheel drive) spent the next six months being honed by the works' drivers, Tony Pond and the Belgian Marc Duez, before its international début in that year's RAC Rally. By then

Davenport had signed rising British rally star Malcolm Wilson to the team. It wasn't a dream début - despite all its testing the car proved fragile and at the end of the event Pond was the only finisher, in third place behind the two Lancias, although at one point he had been lying second.

In 1986. works-prepared 6R4s were entered into the Monte Carlo, Swedish, Portuguese and Corsican rallies, but none finished. They fared better in the UK, where national drivers won the Circuit of Ireland and Welsh rallies, but the car never realised its full international potential.

Pond repeated his third place in the 1986 RAC Rally, but it was effectively all over. Earlier that year the brilliant young rally driver Henri Toivonen and his co-driver had been killed in a high-speed crash on the Tour de Corse rally. effectively putting an end to Group B rallying and the MG Metro 6R4's works' participation.

Meanwhile, back in the real world, the MG Maestro had been turned into a more credible bearer of the MG motif when the 2.0i version débuted in October 1984. Essentially it was an engine transplant from the MG Montego plus ventilated front discs, uprated tyres and damper rates tuned in accordance with the thicker front and rear anti-roll bars. The additional power provided a useful hike in performance - 115mph maximum and 0-60mph in 8.5 seconds - which put it much nearer to rivals.

Visually the car had hardly changed, apart from body-coloured bumpers, grille, door mirrors and handles. As Gordon Sked recalls, there wasn't a lot of scope for radical thinking on a car like the Maestro: 'Basically the architecture of the product was there and there wasn't much we could do about it. OK, so we could put a spoiler under the front bumper, stuff one on the tail-gate and stick some nifty alloy wheels on, but there was a limit to how much you can con people into thinking this really meets the ethos of what MG is about.'

As both Axe and Sked recall, however, there was a genuine desire to keep MG alive. According to Sked, 'The rebadging of Metros, Maestros and Montegos was very much a stopgap. It came about at a period when the hot-hatch was beginning to take off. MG was a badge we had that represented sporting vehicles, but I don't think there was anyone in the company who had a huge amount of enthusiasm to see MG go to its grave in that particular way. There was a great desire to see MG seriously regenerated as a car that had sporting character, a car that actually evoked some of the driving aspirations of the MG marque.'

The problem was that ARG was far from out of trouble. This coincided with the news that ARG had struck a £15 million deal with Honda to build the five-speed gearbox - as used in the MGs -under licence rather than import them from Japan.

Even so, as Roy remembers, there was a strong desire, certainly within his styling area, to do more with MG than just plaster the badge on family saloons. A fringe product like a two-seater MG was always going to disappear to the bottom of the pile, but it was the likes of Axe and Sked and their team that kept pulling it back up to the top. In fact as early as 1983 they had mocked up a little MG just to prove that a real one wouldn't cost a corporate arm and a leg.

Once the Canley styling studio was nearing competition, Axe was keen to show it off to the media: 'People had forgotten we designed cars and I wanted to tell and show them we did.' The problem was what to show. The Metro, Maestro and Montego were well known, and the new Project XX/HX (Rover 800) saloon with Honda was too far down the line to be revealed.

'I felt it wasn't enough to walk the press through this room with a lot of current product in it. That wouldn't get anyone excited and the Rover 800 was a no-no. So I put forward the idea of doing a show vehicle.'

Meanwhile, down at ARG's recently opened technical centre at Gaydon, a team that included

Spen King was working on a lightweight experimental runabout called ECV3. Axe and his team styled a Metro-sized body for that car which eventually went on display when the press visited the Canley studio.

Axe takes up the story: 'After that I decided it would be interesting to take the top off it, do nothing more than that, and turn it into an MG. It looked rather square and parallel because it wasn't designed as a sports car, but as a saloon with the roof taken off.'

The object of the exercise was to show ARG's management that a new MG that could be spun off existing componentry, which would cut down on the number of tailor-made, unique parts required. 'It shared doors and various other parts such as the entire front end. I suppose what I was really trying to get across was that it's necessary to make MG separate from other cars, not just rebadge them.'

Looking at the Midget-sized car now, it's dated as kipper ties and flared trousers, but its stark straight razor-edge lines were all the rage at the time (think about the Mark I and II Golfs). It looks slightly odd proportionally because of the long deck aft of the front passengers which effectively covered the rear pair of seats, and its short nose with the steeply raked screen. 'Interestingly, it was, perhaps, a forerunner of what is now

called cab-forward design,' says Axe of a theme that would later re-emerge in a far more stylish project.

In the meantime ARG launched the fastest version of the Montego saloon yet seen, a 150bhp turbocharged bruiser that would eclipse 130mph and, given the right conditions, would knock out 0-60mph times of around seven seconds.

There was nothing particularly subtle about the MG Montego Turbo - from its deep front air dam and turbo badging through to its prominent boot-mounted spoiler it was every inch a wolf in wolf's clothing. Beneath the bonnet there was a 150bhp turbocharged version of the O-series engine. The Garret AiResearch T3 blew through a single 1 3/4in SU carburettor, but at the fairly high pressure of 10psi, and it was this high boost plus an intercooler which made the Montego Turbo pack such a torquey punch, 169lb ft at 3500rpm. Drive through to the front wheels was via a close-ratio version of the Honda five-speed 'box. The suspension all round was stiffened up in comparison to the Montego EFi and an anti-roll bar was fitted.

ARG really went to town packaging this car. Not only did it have power steering as standard, but there was also a stereo radio/cassette system, tilt/slide sunroof, electric windows, electrically operated and heated door mirrors, central locking, split-folding rear seats, etc., etc. The company endeavoured to make the Montego into a high-speed executive express, going to the extent of giving buyers an MG Owners kit which included key fobs, a video of the car in action on a racetrack, matching tie and scarf and even a wristwatch which aped the shape of the original MG grille.

But while the car was undoubtedly strong on image it lacked engineering development and finesse. There was colossal torque steer, as the front wheels tried to cope with all the power unaided by a limited slip differential; the handling left much to be desired, and the ventilated front disc brakes took a hammering when driven hard.

Meantime, on the business front, plans to develop ARG's relationship with Honda had stalled. The two companies had been due to make an announcement about their continuing partnership in April 1985 at the ground-breaking ceremony for Honda's new UK plant near Swindon, but doubts about the government's future financial support had put the announcement on hold.

Both Labour and Conservative governments had poured billions into what many thought was a fiscal black hole, and it was obvious that the Tories were getting impatient at ARG's oft-promised recovery. A suggestion that ARG should lop at least £200 million off its £1.5 billion five-year investment programme was prompted by the group's 1984 losses. Furthermore this ongoing financial crisis was delaying production of ARG's first co-operative venture with Honda, the Rover 800. An integral part of ARG's planning for the Rover 800 was for it to be marketed in the USA through a joint venture with a North American dealer, Norman Braman.

Roy Axe's styling department had now grown considerably, but since the original media peek-a-boo a couple of years earlier there had been nothing of real consequence for them to show the world. Frustration was setting in and Axe started badgering Musgrove and others to allow ARG to produce a show car.

'This became even more urgent in my mind because, for one reason or another, Rover 800 was delayed. There was a fear of losing momentum because there was a lot of excitement in the press as to what was coming from the new company and its relationship with Honda. That's what drove me to want this show car.'

Although contemporary press reports quote Harold Musgrove as being totally supportive of the project, Axe, Sked and McGovern have a different story to tell. Roy Axe: 'There was a complete anti-feeling within the company against show vehicles, especially from marketing. The reason being the company had previously produced, show cars which had been raved about and the company hadn't built, resulting in the press coming back and saying, "There you are, what a bunch of dummies you had this thing, it could have done this and this and you never made it." People said it was worse to actually show something you're never going to make than it is to suffer the brick-bats of where you are at any particular time with nothing glamorous around.'

Gradually, Axe's persistence paid off and by November 1984 the project was underway. Although it was completed by the middle of the following year, some of ARG's senior management were still debating whether the car should be publicly displayed. Tentative plans had been made to reveal it at the 1985 Frankfurt Motor Show, but they weren't confirmed until the last possible minute. In fact Gerry McGovern recalls what he politely refers to as a 'very heated' discussion on the subject taking place in the styling studio between Axe, Musgrove and himself only days before the scheduled launch. But eventually Musgrove agreed.

Looking back on that September day in 1985 everyone, even the car's detractors, must have been delighted at the reception MG EX-E received when Harold Musgrove peeled back its Union Jack dustcovers. It was one of those rare occasions when the international press corps have spontaneously applauded, an event made even more remarkable by the fact that it hap-

The MG EX-E, which rocked the 1985 Frankfurt Motor Show with its daring shape and aerodynamics. It's a shame that ARG didn't have the confidence to produce what could have been a world-beater.

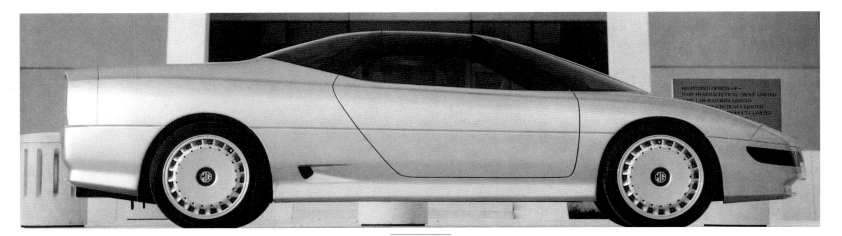

The MG EX-E, which later provided design inspiration for a future MG.

pened in that cathedral to the German motor industry, the Frankfurt Motor Show.

The MG EX-E (EXperimental and E to follow on the MG nomenclature) was quite unlike any car that had previously appeared from the UK, never mind from dowdy Austin-Rover. If it had worn a Pininfarina, Ferrari or ItalDesign badge few would have been surprised by its stunning lines. MG, though, didn't quite fit and the sad fact of life is that if it had been displaying one of those Italian signatures we might have been talking about a future production car and not simply a styling project.

MG EX-E was much more than just a sexy shape. The Austin-Rover team had, admittedly, looked into their technological crystal ball for headline-catching fripperies like credit-card entry and ignition systems, photo-electric cells that automatically dipped headlights and rear-view mirrors, Head-Up Display systems and a 'safe limits programme' that warned the driver of black ice, severe cross-winds and other hazards.

One person behind the project was senior product development manager Mark Snowdon, who could foresee EX-E boosting and exploiting the 6R4's technology. With this is mind, EX-E was based round the rally car's mid-engine, four-wheel-drive power train but stretched to give a long wheelbase; suspension was classic double

wishbones all round with the lower arms operating coil springs and dampers. At the time ARG were quoting a theoretical 170mph top speed

and a scorching five seconds for 0-60, thanks to the car's slippery 0.24 Cd and 250bhp from the de-tuned rally V6.

This car was no mere stylist's fantasy. ARG's Technical Centre had been heavily involved and, although there were some differences of opinion along the way between Spen King and Roy Axe, it was they who developed the lightweight bond-

The MG EX-E, with its distinctive Octagon-influenced twin cockpits.

ed aluminium space-frame chassis and the self-coloured polypropylene body panels.

Part of that development team, incidentally, was Roy Brocklehurst, who had taken over from Syd Enever at Abingdon when he retired and was then transferred to BL as MG wound down. Subsequently he had a hand in the development of the Metro, Maestro and Montego before becoming chief engineer at BL Technology at Gaydon.

Although Gordon Sked remembers that other configurations were considered early in the programme it soon became obvious that the show car had to be classic mid-engined supercar concept: 'The clincher was the 6R4 rally car that was beginning to prove itself and could be used as a basis for this supercar. . .that would meet the aspirations of the people who buy them. . .and would say "MG".'

The car's yardstick was the Ferrari 308 GTB, an example of which resided in Axe's garage at the time. 'That kind of car, but more rorty and certainly more futuristic,' says Axe. The dominant philosophy behind EX-E's design - which was led by Gordon Sked, with Gerry McGovern - was the F-16 fighter plane, says Axe, 'where the pilot was right at the front in a glass canopy so he's sticking up out of the plane and has this phenomenal view around and this powerful engine behind pushing him along; that's what we wanted.'

McGovern did many of the early sketches and Axe freely admits that the team struggled to get the proportions right. The early clay models looked 'too bulbous' and lacked its final distinctive stance. To Axe, who was strongly influenced by Ferrari's contemporary styling, the driver's view is all-important - he wanted to achieve the same distinctive muscular shoulders with the front wings rising out of a shallower centre section, almost like looking at a sprinter's shoulders when he's in the blocks before the starting pistol fires.

While the driver and passenger were encapsulated in a glasshouse produced from polychromatic panels with a graded tint, the panels were supported by hidden pillars linked directly to the main space-frame. This configuration combined with the car's flat rear deck afforded excellent all-round visibility, not always the case with mid-engined cars.

Gordon Sked was particularly pleased with the car's aerodynamics, as apart from its slithery Cd figure EX-E achieved zero lift without the aid of any spoilers.

Richard Hamblin's interior was more overtly MG, with strongly stylised octagonals throughout. The MG motif was featured on the carpets

EX-E, a mid-engined supercar if ever there was one.

and the Octagon's angularity was mimicked by a the fascia which resembled two top portions of an octagon. Hamblin achieved a twin cockpit feel to the interior with the passenger and driver separated by a deep central tunnel and all the controls and instrumentation focused towards the driver.

EX-E's tragedy was that it remained stillborn, despite the fact that its design and development team had made strenuous efforts to create a car that could be put into production - even the ABS-assisted ventilated disc brakes and electric power steering were production feasible.

There was much hyperbole from senior figures within ARG that the car might become a limited production reality, and much optimism from the EX-E team that this would happen. It was also mooted that it would take over from the Metro 6R4 as a Group S rally car replacement , even that Tom Walkinshaw's TWR operation would produce the car, but not even a running prototype was built.

Gordon Sked recalls the atmosphere at the time: 'I think the company was genuinely thinking about producing something like that. It was a difficult time, we hadn't launched Rover 800 and the engineering resources were hugely stretched producing Metro, Maestro and Montego, but on the other hand here was an opportunity to produce something that little bit different.

'There was a huge amount of engineering work done on it. With our knowledge of the chassis and body technology there was absolutely no reason why it shouldn't have gone on to the prototype stage. I think it should have worked and it's a damn shame that we didn't just go that next mile to prove it.'

However, as Axe points out, ARG couldn't produce EX-E: 'I think all of us realised that Austin-Rover wasn't the company to build EX-E. Today it would have been done with a partner, but that was anathema at the time.'

The EX-E project was finally abandoned in 1986, the same year that Rover 800 was launched. It still exists and looks as fresh and modern as it did then. However, as more than one commentator has observed, the irony of the EX-E story is that in 1989 ARG's partner, Honda, unveiled its own mid-engined two-seater, the NSX, and if you look carefully at the proportions and some of the styling cues.

Above all else, the EX-E project reinstated MG's credibility and instilled some pride back in the marque. It accelerated expectation of a real MG appearing. No longer was it a case of 'if' an MG sports car might appear but 'when'.

'Amongst many of us at that time,' recalls Axe, 'there was a strong feeling that EX-E would be the trigger that would enable some kind of proper MG to occur, but the Rover 800 launch got in the way.

Meanwhile the mandarins in Whitehall were tiring of ARG's sponge-like ability to soak up more and more government cash. Norman Tebbit, then Trade and Industry Secretary, was in favour of privatising ARG and there were lengthy discussions in 1985 with Ford executives about the American giant taking the company over. Then there were negotiations over selling Land Rover to General Motors. Both approaches fell apart in 1986 in the aftermath of the 'Westland affair', when it became known that a US company, rather than a European one, would take a major share in the British helicopter manufacturer. All talks with GM and Ford abruptly halted, leaving the government still nursing ARG.

Although the first major joint venture between Rover and Honda -the Rover 800 - had appeared, there was still concern over the company's long-term prospects. Eventually the government approved ARG's £1.8 billion five-year plan that would see it develop a replacement for the Maestro with Honda. The group would also design an all-new small engine, the K series, and build cars for Honda.

By 1986 improved sales from Austin-Rover and Land Rover had cut the group's operating losses from £66.5 million to £39.5 million. On paper Austin-Rover's performance had improved, with sales up 14 per cent to 479,500 units. Although this masked a loss of £6 million, it was a vast improvement on the previous year's

£26 million loss; moreover Austin-Rover was 99.95 per cent strike free.

The year still proved traumatic for the BL group when a new chairman was appointed by the government. Widely regarded as Thatcher's personal nominee, Graham Day was a dour-looking Canadian who had been running the loss-making British Shipbuilding for two and a half years. Despite having, in his early days, wanted to sing with the D'Oyly Carte, he had established himself as a ruthless, unsentimental manager, cutting back on manpower and facilities in order to 'save only the savable'. He wasn't a car man, as he readily conceded, but his motto of 'if you love your customer to death, you can't go far wrong' was to prove a vital part of his policy for the company. With its market share declining and rivals embroiled in a bloody and costly price war Day declared a strategy to set the tone for the future. Day's creed of quality products, service and profitability, not quantity and market share, provided another cornerstone alongside Edwardes's manufacturing revolution.

Day's attitude was quite different from that of anyone else within the group at the time. He reprieved the Mini from its 1988 death sentence, established an effective marketing department (something the company - amazingly - lacked) and reduced the amount of paperwork that flowed around at managerial levels. Perhaps his most controversial decision was to give the company yet another name. To him British Leyland was too impersonal, so he reverted to an identifiable prestigious brand name, the Rover Group.

While all this was for the good, clearly it was too much for some of the old guard. Men like Ray Horrocks and David Andrews were quick to depart, and they weren't the last. A poor first six months in 1986 saw Austin-Rover lose over £60 million and their share of the UK market decrease. At a press conference in late September, Day announced that Harold Musgrove was retiring, that he himself was to be the new chairman of Austin-Rover and Les Wharton, formerly of Leyland Trucks, the new MD. Mark Snowdon also left in this reshuffle.

MG's problem during this era was no different from when Edwardes abandoned it as an identifiable marque - there was simply nothing left in the kitty to develop a unique MG product. Even the Metro replacement, code-named AR6, was abandoned in favour of a face-lifted update.

Yet another corporate plan was approved by the government in early 1987. It included selling off the loss-making Leyland Truck and Freight Rover divisions to DAF, with Day persuading the government to write off £760 million of debts. This would free up capital for development costs, but development of mainstream products, not of MG. By this time Day was at least hinting that the Octagon should be more than just a badge on the back of a series of family hatchbacks and saloons. Whilst that sounded positive the fact that the Rover Group's net loss for 1986 was a thumping £892 million confirmed that MG was still some way away from revival.

By 1987 the MGB was celebrating its twenty-fifth anniversary and, while there were no positive signs of a successor on the way, speculation continued, fired by ongoing rumours of a revolutionary new lightweight engine that Rover had developed. During that same year, Rover re-entered the US market with the 800 badged as a Sterling. It seemed at long last that Graham Day's bitter medicine was beginning to work, especially as the first quarter's operating losses were down and production numbers were increasing as improved build quality and the effectiveness of more aggressive advertising and marketing campaigns began to filter through. There were hints that Rover's collaboration with Honda would become more intimate, and that future production and sales strategy would be based not on chasing Ford or Vauxhall, but on settling down to a more profitable 500,000-a-year bracket as exemplified by Mercedes-Benz or BMW. Meanwhile the spectre of privatisation

became ever more apparent.

There was even enough cash in the kitty to invest £8 million in Roy Axe's design department, trebling its staff to over 300, which must have encouraged him to pursue a number of internal projects. That and Graham Day's positive attitude towards design. Day might not have been a traditional petrol head, but that is not so say he lacked emotion for Rover products. 'I could never weigh Graham up,' says Axe, 'but I can't remember working with anyone else who was more consistent and supportive to what we were doing in design. His problem was the task he'd been given, which was to take the company out of public ownership and it was a company nobody really wanted. Could he concentrate on the product as well? Probably not. Perhaps his instincts were to support them, but the reality of the situation was that he couldn't,' says Axe, who is highly critical of Whitehall's interference at the time. 'There were a number of projects on stream that were going to happen, but were cancelled due to restrictions Graham had put on him by the government at various stages and were almost fatal to the company. It was civil servants trying to be businessmen.'

Nevertheless, things were beginning to look more hopeful. Sales and production were up, losses down. There was even the threat that

Rover might turn in a small profit for 1987. Under the circumstances, it was fortunate that Axe and his team had a free hand to develop their own themes and ideas. One of these was F-16.

Once again the principal players included Axe, Gerry McGovern and Richard Hamblin, who was in charge of the advanced studio now that Gordon Sked was more involved in current product development. According to Axe, the philosophy behind F-16 was different from that employed with the small red and white Midget of some years before: 'Instead of making body panels common with other projects running at

Rear view of the original F-16 shows the start of things to come.

the time, we decided to utilise components and build a unique body shell for it. We had the same difficulty working the shapes out, because at the time styles were still quite angular and I felt it should be rounded,' says Axe.

Although F-16 was purely an internal, design-studio project, Axe and his team lobbied senior Rover management and directors, showing them the car in the hope that it would become a reality, especially since it had been based round the chassis and running gear of the Metro replacement. Canning that project didn't help F-16's case and while Day didn't sanction F-16's development, neither did he say there'd never be another MG - just that it would only happen when the time was financially right for the group.

Seen in the cold light of day, F-16 is a more attractive car than the photographs would suggest. It has the beginnings of the muscular curves that the MGF eventually possessed, minimal overhangs front and rear - again like the MGF - and the stance of a car that's about to leap forward into action. Much of this is a development of themes first seen on EX-E, but softened and made more subtle, even the rear lights and the deck lid can be traced back to the mid-engined supercar, while the filler cap with its Allen-screw surround was to be resurrected in

The original F-16 shown in the Cowley design studio with (right) a convertible Rover 800 proposal.

years to come. Roy Axe talks enthusiastically about what might have been, especially in light of what emerged from Mazda, one of Japan's smaller players, in 1989: 'F-16 was nostalgic in its concept and its architecture was an MG of old, but its shape didn't hark back to any old MG. It was still recognisably an MG and I think that car would have been an absolute smash.'

Axe remembers that everyone from the company who saw F-16 'loved it', but no one could come up with a plan that could turn it from a styling concept to an engineering reality. The irony is, says Axe, that you can't make a sound business plan for a car like F-16. but what you can do is justify it in terms of the showroom traffic and the halo effect it has on your other products. 'Throughout that period we were demonstrating what could happen if circumstances allowed, rather than making any real progress.'

Graham Day's not-so-secret agenda was to privatise the Rover Group. It has to remembered that Margaret Thatcher had been returned to power in 1987 with a resounding parliamentary majority and the country was at the height of Thatcherism. Privatisation was a key word in her government's monetarist policies and the Conservatives had tired of feeding first BL's, then Rover's continuing addiction to injections of increasing amounts of capital. Since 1975 the

company had lost £2.9 billion and cost the taxpayer not much less. It is also said that Thatcher was particularly displeased as successive BL/Austin-Rover bosses had milked funds from the government's coffers with promises of turning the group round, only to return cap in hand year after year.

However, when privatisation came, its manner and the money involved was a surprise to one and all. The first real signs that Day's policies were beginning to take effect appeared in spring 1988, when Rover posted a modest £27.9 million profit before interest and tax. It's doubtful whether even that would have triggered a takeover battle if it hadn't been for a chance meeting earlier in the year between Graham Day and British Aerospace chairman Professor Roland Smith at a cocktail party. It was then that the possibility of BAe buying Rover was first mooted. Once BAe had approached the Department of Trade and Industry to talk the deal through, negotiations progressed rapidly and in March 1988 it was announced that BAe would be buying Rover from the government for a paltry £150 million. It was tagged as the 'sale of the decade' by DTI secretary Lord Young. The government also injected £800 million into the group to eradicate Rover's debts. In return BAe agreed not to sell Rover's core businesses or trademarks for at least five years and accepted various other financial restraints.

At last the government had shed itself of Rover. The question was, would BAe be an equally indulgent parent? There was much talk about the synergies between aerospace and the motor industry, but that was so much PR hype. At the time one thing seemed certain - if Rover couldn't generate the £300 million a year it needed to invest in new products, then BAe would increasingly look to Honda to provide the engineering bases for future generations of Rovers.

The Rover-BAe deal might have been grabbing all the headlines in early 1988, but the classic car enthusiasts were far more interested in British Motor Heritage's announcement that it had started manufacturing MGB Roadster body shells once again. The classic car boom, aided by a buoyant economy, had taken off in a startling manner. Suddenly people who had never considered wanting or owning a classic car were paying exorbitant prices for, in many cases, mundane vehicles. There was a resurgence of interest in MGBs - GTs and Roadsters - and prices were escalating. For some years BMH had been supplying numerous MGB components to restorers, but by early 1988 they had gathered together all the original body tooling for the car and decided to put the body shell back into limited produc-tion for those enthusiasts who wanted to reno-vate their MGB or, indeed, build a 'new' one from scratch.

At the other end of the performance scale was the MG Maestro Turbo. An amalgamation of the five-door Maestro body shell and the MG Montego Turbo's potent engine, it was launched at the 1988 Motor Show. This wasn't a simple engine swap. Rover called on the expertise of Tickford Engineering to fine-tune the chassis and add the macho body kit and sign-writing that adorned the car which was claimed to be the fastest production MG to date: 130mph and 0-60mph in 6.7 seconds.

The year had already been hugely significant for the Rover Group, but there was more to come. In November 1988 Graham Day handed over day-to-day responsibilities of the Rover Group to George Simpson.

For the MG marque, which had been fostered by more parent companies than it cared to count, it was the dawn of yet another era. Enthusiasts had grown used to seeing Octagons on Metros, Maestros and Montegos and had resigned themselves to the fact that 'the MG revival' would remain just a piece of opportunistic badge-engineering. Little did they appreciate that MG's dawn would break once more, but that first there would be the darkest of nights.

8

The new year, 1989, started off on a quietly optimistic note for MG. British Motor Heritage's success in reviving the MGB's body shell was such that production had more than doubled to fifteen a week since the project started in April 1988. There was even speculation that Heritage would turn its hand to building and selling complete MGBs but, nice though the thought was, nothing initially came of the proposition. Probably a good thing, too, as reviving a classic would have sent out all the wrong sort of messages from a newly privatised company that was doing its best to convey to the world that it was dynamic and forward-looking, not retrospective.

There were wholesale management changes going on following Simpson's appointment, including the emergence of John Towers as Rover's engineering director from his previous job as manufacturing director at Land Rover.

One black cloud looming on the horizon was Sterling's progress in the States. Sales in 1988 had slumped to not much over half the first year's 14,171. The US company also got its third boss, Graham Morris, and became a subsidiary of the UK operation rather than a joint venture with a local entrepreneur. On the surface this might not seem relevant to the MG story, but a Rover car presence in the US - Range Rovers were sold through a separate organisation - would have a

MGB bodyshells are still being built for enthusiasts the world over.

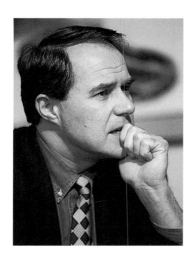

Gordon Sked played an integral role in developing Rover's 'British' styling cues as well as being a major influence on the MGF.

bearing on any future decision which might lead to an MG revival, as without Rover showrooms how would a new MG be sold in the States?

The really bad news, though, appeared at the 1989 Chicago Auto Show when Mazda launched its Miata (MX-5 in the UK) sports car.

'Absolutely and utterly frustrated' is how Gordon Sked recalls feeling when he first saw the Miata. 'On the one side we had tremendous respect and regard for what Mazda had done. They had the balls to do it, they got on and did it. As designers we all felt that, but on the other side, it should have been us up there.

When you look more closely at the MX-5 it's easy to understand why. For a number a years the Japanese had been playing at producing sports cars: the original Datsun 240Z with its straight-six engine was little more than an updating of the Austin-Healey legend, while Toyota's MR2 with its mid-engined configuration was a

bang-up-to-the-minute contemporary sports car. But the MX-5 was something different. It was instantly recognisable as an inexpensive, 'British' sports car from its chrome-rimmed instruments to its Minilite look-alike wheels. Its design unashamedly aped that of the Lotus Elan of 1962, while its layout was classic front-engine, rear-wheel-drive and its US price tag a meagre

Mazda's MX-5 showed what a revived MG might have been like.

$14,000, about £8000 at the time. Even when it landed in the UK twelve months later it was still an affordable £14,249.

There was nothing revolutionary about the MX-5 with its 115bhp twin-cam, 16-valve 1.6-litre engine, five-speed gearbox, independent suspension, all-round disc brakes and rack-and-pinion steering. It was steel bodied and no lightweight at 2150lb, but even so it would just about get to 115mph and hit 60mph in nine seconds or so - much the same performance as many hot hatches of the time.

In its very simplicity the MX-5 synthesised all the essentials of what British sports cars had once stood for. The treble irony of the MX-5 was that it took a Japanese manufacturer to produce the car, their Californian design studio to conceive it and a British company - IAD of Worthing - to develop the body-in-white engineering. The Japanese and Californians might sound an unlikely alliance, but when the Japanese love of traditional British style is combined with Californians' obsession with the car as an art form, is it any surprise that they should

Roy Axe has played a pivotal role in developing Rover's design strategy and now heads his own independent consultancy which worked on free-thinking Rover concepts.

have come up with a latter-day MGB, a Lotus Elan lookalike?

'Mazda had a problem,' says Axe. 'They had to bring out a car that awakened the nostalgic yearnings in the middle-aged - because that's where the market is - and that's what they were really after. They hadn't got a heritage and Tom Mantano who did the car always says that British design has been a major influence in his life.'

Looking back on the car, Axe thinks Mazda shouldn't have done such an accurate cover version of the Elan, as it 'could have been an opportunity for the Japanese to establish something of their own'. But even with that qualification he doesn't take anything away from them, 'because it's still right and successful'.

The MX-5's runaway success - it has sold some 370,000 worldwide since its launch - reinforced arguments by the enthusiasts within Rover that the sports-car market was alive and well and desperately awaiting new products, and that if MG were to be revived then it had to be with something more than the MX-5.

It was Don Wyatt's team which made the first tentative steps towards bringing the MG badge back on a limited-edition sportster.

Sked remembers using the Mazda to reinforce their arguments at 'every turn'. 'But, of course, the very fact that the MX-5 had been done demonstrated that if we were to produce a new MG, it had to be different, and that helped when we came to the Phoenix programme.'

While the eagerness to produce a new MG might have been growing within Rover, there was still the core business to worry about and that was on the point of undergoing yet another change. For some time the industry grapevine had been buzzing with rumours that Honda and Rover would get closer. That was confirmed in mid-July at a press conference announcing Honda's £300 million investment in its new assembly plant at Swindon. At the same time it was also revealed that the Japanese would take a 20 per cent stake in the Rover Group in return for Rover getting an equal percentage in the much smaller Honda UK manufacturing operation at Swindon.

Summer 1989 was significant to MG's revival in more ways than

Pragmatic enthusiast John Towers. He could see the potential of resurrecting MG - if it didn't cost a fortune.

one, recalls Don Wyatt, design manager of Rover Special Products based at Gaydon, as John Towers called a meeting to investigate the possibility of re-introducing an MG sports car 'from a stock parts/parts bin solution'.

Nick Stephenson, head of engineering and design at Rover, remembers it well: 'There was a whole bunch of us that given a spare few minutes would find the way of doing this car and financing it, but the business crises at the time didn't allow it to happen. I think one of the breakthroughs for the project was adopting some unconventional ways of thinking through how a business proposition would work. One or two of us in the project world always like to keep a cou-

Nick Stephenson, an out-and-out car enthusiast who helped champion MG's revival.

ple of extra programmes under review, because there's always a danger that you're only focused on the mainstream project and a vacuum occurs when you've delivered them - what comes next?'

In fact, what came next developed from a meeting held at Canley and attended by, among others, David Bishop from British Heritage and Roger Parker, who brought along his home-brewed V8-powered MGB Roadster. Part of that discussion centred round the possibility of Heritage putting the B back into production and the problems they'd encounter with homologation and type approval, but it was the sight of Parker's car which eventually rekindled the idea of a reborn MG.

In the meantime Rover had announced its replacement for the thirty-eight-year-old A-series engine that had first appeared in the Morris Minor and was still going strong in the Mini, Metro and Maestro. Three versions of the four-cylinder K series were launched in late August 1989: a 1.1-litre eight-valve 60bhp; a 1.4-litre, eight-valve 75bhp; and a sixteen-valve version producing 95bhp. The most novel aspect was its ladder construction comprising the cam cover, cam carrier, cylinder-head, cylinder block, bearing ladder and sump which were secured together by ten 16in bolts running from top to bottom. The bolt passages also helped crankcase ventilation and acted as oil paths for lubricant returning to the crankcase. The all-alloy engines were light and powerful and even at the launch there was considerable speculation that in the future a turbocharged variant of the 1.4 would appear, as well as bigger capacity and variable valve timing versions.

The announcement of a unique Rover engine that owed nothing to the group's partnership with Honda was just the fillip the company needed - it confirmed that Rover wasn't destined to become a badge-engineering operation for the Japanese. The first hints were also filtering through that MG would no longer be just a tune-up and tart job on existing cars, but a stand-alone marque in its own right.

Within Rover, there were some major upheavals going on. Gordon Sked took over the day-to-day running of the Canley styling studio while Roy Axe established a design/styling studio, Design Research Associates, on the outskirts of Warwick. 'I was still responsible for Canley, although Gordon ran it,' explains Axe. 'This office was established by myself at Rover's suggestion as a place where I could input into Rover some ideas I felt were pertinent without being too hung up by what was happening at the factory or in the company.

'The first task we took on was to look at

Britishness, although there had already been a lot of work done at Canley on this, with bringing back the Rover grille on the 800. There was also the American viewpoint concerning Sterling as they wanted a grille and more wood inside the car. The thing that European manufacturers have and the Japanese don't, is heritage. If you can play on that we have an edge that the Japanese can't compete with.'

Given a very open brief Axe, and his team decided to produce two cars, one a Rover 800-sized saloon and the other a sports car: 'They were purely and simply to illustrate the Britishness thing and how you could get a modern car that looked recognisably British to anybody.'

As Roy and his team began working on their 'Britishness' theme a proposal was being put to the Rover board to establish Rover Special Products, headed by Richard Hamblin, Steve Schlemmer and John Stephenson. The aim was to explore future niche cars based on Rover products. When it was eventually formed in 1990, RSP had a staff of forty, representing all the major areas of the company with offices located at the main Rover sites, Gaydon, Longbridge, Solihull and Cowley.

RSP's brief was to develop projects in one of three ways: firstly to explore potential business opportunities and, perhaps, even produce full-sized prototypes although they may not go beyond that; secondly, to develop products and then hand them over to mainstream engineering; and thirdly, to engineer specialist products through to launch in alliance with the appropriate Rover business unit.

By the end of 1989 or early 1990 all the ingredients were, seemingly, in place for a serious attempt to reinstate MG as a marque in its own right. Roy Axe and his team were working on a British sports car project in Warwick. RSP had been tasked to look at niche products within Rover. Sterling in the USA, the American dealers and public were all clamouring for an MG. In Nick Stephenson there was a determinedly enthusiastic engineering director who wanted to see MG reborn. Gordon Sked led a design team that was champing at the bit, just itching to design something that might become a classic, and in John Towers there was a pragmatic enthusiast. All that was needed was for someone to give the go-ahead but, as Towers, says that was easier said than done. 'In a business contest, MG versus sorting out the 800, then the 600 and so on, didn't stand a chance, objectively.'

The only thing the enthusiasts within Rover could hope for was that commercial objectivity would be overruled by passion.

9

The formation of RSP played a key role in what happened next, as it created a facility outside Rover's mainstream engineering programme - the beginnings of Rover's own skunk works.

Combine that with Nick Stephenson's unbridled enthusiasm and the determination of people like marketing director Kevin Morley to make MG more than just a badge-engineering exercise and the marque's rebirth begins to look almost inevitable. While this is recognised by John Towers, he admits his view has the benefit of hindsight: 'It's a fundamental fact of life that you don't take a valuable asset like MG and badge-engineer it on to ordinary cars, even though you try your best to make them extraordinary, which people did.'

Although Towers agrees that Rover in its various guises had ignored the marque, he does so with 'the humility to recognise that I've said

F-16, the Gerry McGovern-designed MG which never saw the light of day beyond this styling clay. Its links with EX-E are many and obvious.

that very much in hindsight, as someone who actually wasn't involved in the pressures at that time. The resources and the skills there to do it. The fact of the matter is that the business had a huge amount of core top priority it had to do in order to get in line with building an image that would connect properly with Rover.'

Despite the growing undercurrent of desire to see MG back in production in its own right, there remained the questions of how, and, the biggest stumbling block of all, where do the engineering and financial resources come from? Rover's senior management decided on a twintrack approach. Spurred on by the BMH meeting and the almost accidental viewing of Roger Parker's V8 Roadster, RSP was tasked with developing an MG Roadster revival as well as investi-

The designer's 'storyboard' where MG's rebirth started, this time as a V8.

One that didn't make it past the drawing board. Don Wyatt penned this MGA clone using Metro parts and a Heritage Midget shell as its basis.

gating the feasibility of producing an all-new small MG. Project Phoenix had begun.

The starting point for the B's revival, says Don Wyatt, was 'Where would that car be today if we were still producing it?' The precedent for that, according to Wyatt, was the evergreen Porsche 911: launched in 1963, it has been completely re-engineered yet is still recognisable as the car that first appeared more than three decades ago.

The early RSP sketches from late 1989 depict a car heavily influenced by the Stuttgart classic, although it is recognisably based on a chromeless MGB bodyshell, but with new bumpers, headlights and flared wheel arches. With its EX-E cloned rear spoiler it is not a particularly subtle treatment and the only link with the 911 that remained in the completed car were the headlights; as Wyatt says of their sourcing, 'We won't discuss where those came from, but if anyone can't figure that one out they're not much of a car enthusiast.'

BMH had meanwhile been building a one-off V8 Roadster to use as a base for the project. Once this had been completed in March 1990 it was handed over to Geoff Matthews at Styling International together with the renderings, for his team to interpret into a full-size model.

Wyatt remembers that debates over the

An early concept drawing. Note the Porsche 911-style headlamps and the EX-E style rear spoiler.

Another interpretation, this time with a front grille treatment which radically updates the hideous black bumpers of the last MGBs.

grille's design were often time-consuming and intense: 'It was a long discussion as to whether we make it a split grille as per the MGA and B, or whether we make it one opening with just a little indentation in it, because if you look at how Phoenix developed....'

During this period Rover were heavily involved in mainstream projects such as the 600 saloon and convertible and coupé versions of the 200; there was also considerable activity on the Land Rover side, which constantly forced the possibility of a new MG on to the back burner, as Nick Stephenson remembers: 'John Towers and I had various conversations as to how we could get MG started and I've always had a clear view that the best way to get something started is to have some product in the cupboard, because getting programmes off the ground in a large organisation is always a challenge.

It's a risky policy, warns Stephenson, as someone will always ask who authorised it, made more so by the fact that no one really knew what constituted a modern MG, although 'John [Towers] was always very clear that it had to be a small car, he'd cut through all the market research and did it have to be a big car, etc.? His emotions told him that MGs are small cars.'

To get a feel of what a 1990s' MG might be like, Stephenson suggested building a number of different concept cars, which was fine by Towers as long Stephenson spent no money - 'the usual problem'.

Stephenson recalls how he escaped the financial straitjacket: 'I came up with a scam to use outside contractors. I've long been personally intrigued as to how these small organisations, the TVRs, Morgans of this world, succeed in doing cars when we need armies of engineers. We occasionally skirmish into this world to make sure we're not missing any tricks.

At the same time, Stephenson was talking with Howard Dermott, who used Rover mechanicals for his Midas coupé, and Stephenson had it at the back of his mind that Midas could 'knock up a car for us'. Although that didn't come to pass, the seed had germinated and, in early 1990, Stephenson recalls phoning John Towers to sound out his proposal for getting a trio of outside contractors to build three different MG prototypes at a fixed price. 'I remember calling John up in his Range-Rover saying we'd got the breakthrough, but we needed X thousand pounds. The benefit of that was that I could give John a figure and he'd know I didn't need any more. He said "fine" and bought right into it, so we went ahead and did it and that's where PR1, 2 and 3 came from.'

In March 1990 - the same month that BMH

started worked on its V8 Roadster - Motor Panels, Reliant and ADC, an independent design and engineering consultancy, were given a brief to produce three different MG prototypes each with their own power-train configuration. Brian Griffin, who worked for Nick Stephenson at that time on the Rover 100 project, recalls Ron Cook, one of his engineers, disappearing on secret missions which, it subsequently transpired, involved these three companies: 'I wasn't involved at all, I only knew who was going out for a particular day. I didn't know what he was doing, where he was going, who he was talking to.'

The reason for all the cloak-and-dagger stuff was that Rover was suffering from a lot of press leakage to motoring magazines and there was a distinct feeling that it was coming from within the company.

Don Wyatt recalls those early days as a band of enthusiasts determined to make MG happen again. They really had no idea of the route to take or what would be required in order to produce a profitable sports car and a viable business plan to convince Rover's board that MG was worth reviving: 'We knew RSP could never have supported a manufacturing programme if it were into the 75-100,000 a year figures, but 5000, then low-cost tooling makes the whole thing quite possible. That was always a conundrum, we didn't know

what numbers we needed and wouldn't find out until we had a closer look at it.'

There was enough debate raging about 'What is an MG?' The issues didn't need to be clouded with questions of, 'What does a modern MG look like?' Fortunately this problem was solved relatively easily by unearthing Gerry McGovern's F-16 sports-car prototype. Three identical fibreglass bodies were taken off the car and one each presented to the outside consultants. That way, when the cars came to be judged, their dynamic and engineering concepts could be fairly assessed without any emotional baggage about styling cluttering up the debates.

BMH completed the B Roadster conversion into a V8 by June, when it was driven for the first time at Gaydon. Like most mules it's a pretty rough-and-ready-looking machine - it even has rubber bumpers - with tacked-on wheel spats to house the fat 205/65 tyres and 15in rims. There's a pagoda-like hard-top covering a ghastly interior, while the bonnet had developed an unsightly blister to clear the engine. Over the years the Rover-Buick V8 had grown to 3.9 litres and sprouted fuel injection; despite the catalyst it now thumped out 190bhp compared to the MGB GT's V8's 135bhp and there's a locomotive-like 242lb ft of torque at only 2400rpm. All this in a body shell designed when most of the engineers

developing the car were probably going 'brrrrrrmmmm, brrrrrrmmmm' with their Dinky toys on Mum's newly polished dining-room table.

The old GT V8 suffered from severe traction deficiencies thanks to its leaf spring rear axle, so Rover developed the new Roadsters. But since the whole project was allocated only a £7 million budget, they didn't spend much time. The rear geometry and componentry were retained, but augmented by a pair of anti-tramp rods secured to the bottom of the axle and forward spring hangers. The insertion of a Quaife limited slip differential also helped calm the rear axle down so it didn't buck like a colt trying to throw its rider when full bore take-offs were initiated.

Thankfully, more time was spent at the front of the car, where the lever-arm dampers were binned in favour of a double-wishbone set-up with Koni dampers and Goldline ball joints.

There was enough positive feedback from that first June assessment for the project to continue and by the following month Styling International had finished its first clay. Project Adder, so christened by a dewy-eyed engineer with aspirations of producing MG's answer to the feared AC Cobra, was on its way.

Simultaneously, ADC, Motor Panels and Reliant delivered their offerings to RSP for evaluation. It was going to be a busy summer.

Early clay modelling being done on an MGB at Styling International. The flared wheel arches and Porsche 911-derived headlamps are apparent even in these early days.

10

There was a considerable amount of pressure coming from outside for MG's rebirth. Mazda's surprise announcement of its MX-5 had reawakened the public's desire for cheap, fun sports cars after a diet of hot hatches.

The first semi-official confirmation that Rover was seriously considering an MG came at the 1990 Detroit Show where Graham Morris, admitted as much to Car magazine, mysteriously adding that 'it wouldn't be another Miata'. Although Morris had been very circumspect, the fact that he was prepared to make any hint at a new MG confirmed to the press that it would be available in the States and therefore built in quite large numbers and with a low(ish) sticker price.

The initial conclusion to which the media jumped was that the new MG would be based on the front-wheel-drive Rover 200 platform, launched the previous autumn. Power, it was

claimed, would come from a 1.6 Honda engine or a turbocharged 1.4-litre K series.

Car again set the cat among the pigeons when it ran a campaign in its April 1990 issue, urging readers to write to George Simpson asking him to sanction a new MG. Car was still pursuing the front-wheel drive/Rover 200 theme, but hedging its editorial bets with suggestions that a V8-powered MGB Roadster was on the stocks, as well as a Reliant-chassised special. Their remarkably good sources must have concerned Rover's management, but John Towers says that they didn't feel under any particular pressure: 'The nature of the correspondence, the conversations, the communications that we had were quite positive. It was a case of "We'd love to see you doing one."'

Neither did Rover feel as if they were coming under pressure from the Mazda MX-5 or Toyota MR2, or that the Japanese had usurped MG's territory. 'It was only frustrating,' recalls Towers, 'if you happened to be in a conversation that focused on the issue itself. So, you'd come up against conversations which said there was a terrific heritage and a huge business opportunity here - which, in fact, there isn't, there's not big business, not in the context of the mainstream car and Land Rover business - but that was always the sense of it. A huge business opportunity the Japanese had taken away from us. "What are you going to do about it?" "Not telling you!" So there was that frustration as well.'

The first management ride 'n' drive of the Project Phoenix cars came late one August evening at Gaydon in the ember hours of an English summer's day

The three prototypes, which still exist, are distinctly different animals.

PR1, the Motor Panels concept, is the most professional, as the company invested the time, money and effort into producing soft-tooling off the F16 fibreglass buck and then building a metal-bodied car. It is based on a Maestro floor-pan with 2 3/4in chopped out of the wheelbase behind the front seats and powered by a 138bhp, 2-litre M16 engine. Front suspension was Maestro-derived MacPherson struts. Ignoring the car's tatty interior PR1 has a very square feeling to it, from its open flat-floored cockpit to its overall plan view, which makes it feel like a front-wheel-drive car from behind the steering wheel. Apart from the fairly high door line, which comes almost to shoulder height, it does not feel as intimate as a sports car should, a shortcoming accentuated by the distance between driver and

PR1 from Motor Panels was probably the most professionally finished of the three prototypes. Powered by a twin-cam, 16-valve engine and based on existing platforms, Rover was concerned that it wouldn't be seen as being modern enough.

PR1 again

passenger and the low screen height which, if you're tall, means you end up craning your neck to see over the screen or hunching your shoulders to see through it. Other features which show that Motor Panels had put some thought into their prototype are a flush rear deck and solid tonneau covering the collapsed hood. It is not a styling tour de force -you need to sit lower and further back, and the windscreen base needs pulling forward to enhance its cab-forward design, but as Wyatt has pointed out, the car's aesthetics were secondary. It was dynamic brilliance the team was looking for.

'There was a lot of interest in this car, but there were two big problems that we could perceive. Firstly, would people see beyond its Maestro underpinnings? Despite the fact that it would be totally updated, we were unhappy that it would carry the Maestro's negative image with it. Secondly, could a real MG buyer live with a front-engine, front-wheel-drive layout?' It would obviously have been relatively easy for Rover to spin the car off a more contemporary front-wheel-drive platform, as Car had theorised, but would that overcome the front-wheel-drive image barrier?

According to Wyatt, there was a considerable amount of debate centred on that.. It was argued that although front-wheel drive might

deter the more traditional, i.e. older, MG buyer, there was a whole new generation of young car buyers who had been brought up on an exclusive diet of front-wheel-drive cars and this new generation of owner/drivers were the new, cheap MG's potential purchasers.

The front-wheel-drive sports-car revolution had, controversially, been started by the Lotus Elan launched twelve months earlier and was subsequently, and successfully, taken on by the 1995 Fiat barchetta and Alfa Romeo Spider. In hindsight, Rover's decision was probably the right one - the likelihood is that a front-wheel-drive MG would have been viewed as an expedient route for Rover to follow. It would need to have been very carefully designed and engineered not to betray the archetypal front-wheel-drive characteristic of safe, predictable understeer. Unless it instilled the car with some sporting characteristics it could have done the reborn MG more harm than good.

Reliant's offering, PR2, was a totally different concept based on a stretched Scimitar chassis with heavily modified Maestro front suspension grafted on and a Rover 3.9-litre V8 power train shoe-horned under the bonnet. McGovern's original F16 design had been stretched over the chassis, giving the car a hint of the classic British sportster, long bonnet and short passenger cell

PR2 from Reliant is the most ungainly of the trio, but displayed all the brutish characteristics and appeal of a classic front-engine, rear-wheel-drive sports car.

The ADC mid-engined concept is cute, but lacks the styling cues that identifies it as an MG.

Still wearing its F-16 badging, the ADC mid-engined concept is the most compact of all, especially when compared to an original MG Midget. It is well packaged, but looks too Japanese ever to be a real MGA.

with seats practically on the floor and minimal boot space; in truth it's more hairy-chested Austin-Healey 3000 than MG.

Once behind the wheel it feels more of a sports car than PR1, the long bonnet sweeping away from you and the stubby tail behind while the extra length slims the cockpit, making it feel narrower than it really is. The driving position is less saloon-like as well, straight-armed, straight-legged and less sit-up-and-beg - and that was probably at the same time its biggest strength and its biggest weakness: 'It's a brute,' grins Wyatt, obviously relishing memories of driving it. 'It's absolutely gorgeous in terms of when you fire this sucker up, the sound you get, a little bit of shake and all that sort of thing. You feel like you're in a real sports car.'

Finally, there was PR3, from the now-defunct Luton-based design and engineering consultancy, ADC. Tiny compared to the others with its minimal overhangs, intimate cockpit and a transverse power train located right behind the driver and passenger's shoulders, it's an audacious concept: a mid-engined, rear-wheel-drive convertible as the next MG. The only other manufacturer to attempt such a configuration was at the other end of the price scale, Ferrari with its Mondial.

Crudely put, PR3 was a mid-engined K-series Metro; a heavily modified Metro floor-pan was used for the centre section with a Metro sub-frame and suspension at the front, while the mid-engine location was achieved simply by transferring the power train, complete with gearbox from the front of the car to the centre and in doing so converting a front-wheel-drive set-up into a mid-engined package. On paper it sounds simple, but in reality it threw up several shortcomings and the overall packaging - boot, fuel tank, etc. - was unacceptable. But the concept was intriguing.

As might have been expected, everyone involved in that early exercise has slightly different memories and interpretations of the results. Don Wyatt: 'Out of that came the general direction for the future of MG, which was not MGF. At that time the priority was seen as being the PR2 direction, which was more towards a V8 sports car. PR3 was very well received and everybody loved it, but it was a very small car...somewhere between a Midget and a B. It was a very difficult time because everyone was spoilt for choice. Nobody wanted to let go of this PR3 thing, yet at the same time, particularly in terms of the States, everyone saw the V8 solution as perhaps the way to go.'

Nick Stephenson sees it far more clearly: 'We were looking for the glint in people's eyes when they came back from the test track and

there's no question about it that the one which brought a smile to everyone's face was the mid-engined car. The front- and rear-wheel-drive cars had their attractions and were very different in character: the V8 was the most exciting and PR1, because of its configuration, the most dull to drive. The mid-engined car...produced this small package and very taut handling - but the potential was there.'

For John Towers, PRs 1, 2 and 3 finally brought the realisation that MG could be reborn: when we were doing the ride and drives with the different mules - PRs 1, 2 and 3 - we recognised there was a lot of new potential that would mean we could recategorise all the things people remembered as MG: an affordable, exciting sports-car experience. But we'd actually do something that other people hadn't done by creating a sense of value in the product through the combination of mid-engine, rear-wheel drive and the adoption of what is a very special form of Hydrolastic suspension.'

While the debate over PRs 1, 2 and 3 raged, with the front-wheel-drive concept gradually losing ground to the others, the Adder programme was progressing. By August, Styling International had completed its buck and RSP was ready to present the car to Kevin Morley. As Wyatt recounts, it wasn't an altogether successful preview: 'Kevin says, "Yeah, great car and I love the idea of the V8, but I don't buy it. You haven't excited me and as of that I don't see a programme there."'

It says much for the determination of RSP's core players that they didn't give Adder up there and then. There were a number of people within RSP who felt the project had potential. Typically, David Wiseman from finance saw the car's future as a limited-edition product which could make RSP some money as well as raising the ante on MG. Undeterred by Morley's comments, RSP dispatched the styling buck to ADC together with their own stylist, Dick Barton, who was under strict instructions to get the car right for another viewing.

To a large extent the Adder programme was driving Project Phoenix as well. There would have been no point in launching a born-again MGB as a one-off and then letting the marque slip back into oblivion. The desire to get a proper MG back into production was strongly evident, but the debate still hadn't been settled as to what constituted a contemporary MG. On the one hand there were those backing PR3 and on the other there was the US sales potential of a PR2 development. The argument would be settled soon enough, but perhaps not in the way Rover envisaged.

11

Roy Axe's design exercise resulted in two distinct cars: one a Rover 800-sized saloon and the other - perhaps predictably, knowing Axe's love of British sports cars and the fact that he penned an MGB rival, the Sunbeam Alpine - a two-seater sports car. Having started the MG ball rolling it would have been churlish for Rover not to include Axe's car in these clinics as a parallel exercise, with one eye focused on the lucrative North American market.

Taste in car design is a very personal matter although there are some cars which can unite all sides. Few would argue that a Ferrari Daytona wasn't a superb piece of design, or a Jaguar E-type for that matter, and if it had ever come to fruition Axe's DR2, with its drop-dead looks, would have had similar unifying qualities. As it is, DR2 currently languishes beneath dust-covers in a corner of Gaydon Technical Centre, a largely forgotten relic of what might have been the sexi-est British sports car this side of the original E-type.

From the moment the dust-covers are drawn back, you can't help but be overwhelmed by the car's looks. It needs a little finessing: the MGA-cloned grille is heavily chromed and none too subtle for European tastes, though it would probably have appealed more to the US market, and the stainless steel windscreen surround is, likewise, a shade too bulky. But the overall form of the car has a British signature on it as much as Ferrari's Pininfarina styling bears an Italian one.

The front grille and bonnet echo the profile of the rubber-bumper MGB; the stainless-steel surround, which cleverly disguises the stout windscreen with its integral roll-bar, again suggests the MGB, whereas the side view is a mixture of MGA and Austin-Healey 3000 with its swooping swage lines and rear haunches. There are little touches of brightwork outlining the rear lights and the flush fuel filler, complete with its racing-style Allen key surround.

Ignoring the interior fixtures and fittings, you feel quite exposed in the cockpit with its low waistline - 'All the better for posing in,' explains Wyatt. The muscled form of the bonnet and wings' is echoed behind the driver with its high rear end that could be interpreted as anything from a 1950s Ferrari or Maserati to a Jaguar XKE convertible.

'We felt very strongly that it had to be front-engined, rear-wheel drive,' says Axe of DR2. 'We were in an era of mid-engined sports cars, people had moved away from front-engine, rear-wheel drive. That's why the car had a V8 and is larger than we perhaps wanted to produce as an MG...it was more appropriate to call it a Healey.'

It's plain that DR2 would have immense appeal in the USA. It is very much a boulevard

Roy Axe and his team at DRA came up with this beautifully proportioned two-seater with its distinctive Austin-Healey hip line. The angular interior is straight from a TVR, around which the car was built, and not as Axe would have intended. Power comes from a Rover V8 - what else?

cruiser in the mould of the original Cobra, complete with the threatening burble of a V8 and the promise of tyre-smoking acceleration from the stop lights. But its format created problems for Rover, who didn't have a front-engine/rear-wheel-drive platform on which to base the car. Nevertheless it was decided to pursue the concept further and at the same time to continue PR3's development.

The only readily available candidate for a donor chassis was a Rover V8-powered TVR, but RSP could hardly go to the Blackpool-based sports-car maker and ask them to fabricate a special chassis or buy one from them.

Consequently Don Wyatt went on a TVR hunt posing as a private buyer. Eventually he found what he was looking for at a Midlands dealer and returned a few days later to collect the car. 'It was all spiffy and nice,' recalls Wyatt; as the seller had spent the previous evening valeting it. 'The engineer took the car home over the weekend and drove it to Canley on the Monday morning. No sooner had it come to a stop in the workshop than guys with chainsaws set about stripping the body off. I'd love to have seen the owner's face.'

Which is why DR2 has an outdated, angular TVR fascia, instrument pack, steering wheel and column assembly rather than the plush interior Roy Axe and his team had envisaged.

By now Rover's number-crunchers were coming on the scene, trying to establish the financial viability of a sports-car programme and especially a product like DR2. To make economic sense, any larger sports car almost certainly had to go to the States, which could add 20-30 per cent to the cost of an engineering programme, according to Stephenson: 'Some of the additional cost is designing different things for the USA, but a lot of it is quite simply down to their incredibly demanding homologation requirements, so you have to run a very large number of additional cars simply to meet their legal demands.'

One way of reducing the investment would be to embrace the policy envisaged for PR1 and develop the car off an existing platform already homologated for the USA. Plans were already being formulated within Rover to productionise the Rover CCV coupé, which had wowed everyone at the 1986 Turin Motor Show, and sell that as Sterling's prestige model in the USA; so why not follow the same policy for MG and base that on the R17 (Rover 800) floor-pan powered by Honda's 2.7-litre V6?

DR2 had also been very well received at customer clinics in the States, where it had been viewed alongside McGovern's F-16 at a private

Rover's CCV concept coupé never made it into production, but whetted many appetites when it was unveiled.

investigative routes: a classic convertible in the British style and a more contemporary-looking roadster, christened Adventurers 1 and 2 respectively.

PR3, meanwhile, hadn't been abandoned or forgotten. In fact, the 'pocket rocket' had left such an impression following the management's August ride 'n' drive that its development was continued too.

Developing the front-wheel-drive R17 platform into a good-looking convertible worthy of carrying the MG Octagon was not an easy task. A key styling cue for any well-proportioned front-engined/rear-wheel-drive sportster is the distance between the wheel arch and the A post/leading edge of the door. Look at any classic British, or Italian for that matter, front-engined sportster from the 1950s and '60s and you will see that they all betray the same proportions. Ferrari, Alfa Romeo, Jaguar, Aston Martin, MGA - they all possess a long bonnet which seems to be pulling the rest of the car forward, while the driver, passenger, fuel tank and boot are tacked on behind, almost over the rear wheels.

showing. None of the public who attended knew the cars were Rover products or maybe future MGs, but they immediately identified DR2 as being British. F16 fared less well in the eyes of the Americans, who were unused at that time to short overhangs - large bumpers and long front and rear overhangs were prevalent on their domestic products. Nevertheless the clinics' results indicated to Rover that they were on the right design track.

The R17 policy got the go-ahead in October 1990, and at the same time DR2 was given the internal code of PR5. From there sprang two

The RSP team's early two-dimensional

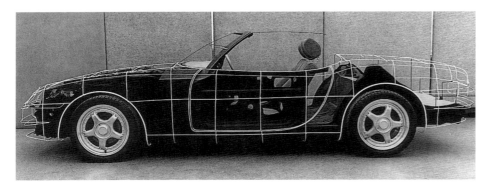

Using the front-wheel-drive Rover 800 floor-pan prompted this wire-frame model. Note the short distance from the front wheel arch to the 'A' post.

Stretching the panel between the wheel arch and the leading edge of the door creates a longer, thrusting bonnet line, as shown in Wyatt's second rendering (right).

the wheelbase by nearly 5in was a step in the right direction, but tended to accentuate the car's hard-edged wedge profile.

The solution was arrived at when John Stephenson - who, in a previous life at Rolls-Royce, had helped create the Project 90 concept coupé which influenced future development of the Bentley marque -suggested adding a second firewall to the 800 10-12in aft of the original and hanging the instrument pack and steering column to that. Relocating the windscreen at the new firewall and removing nearly 8in from the car's wheelbase altered the proportions radically and transformed a typical front-wheel-drive-looking car into one which looked as if it had a traditional front-engine/rear-wheel-drive power train. All the classic ingredients were there: long bonnet with restricted front overhang, small, well set-back passenger compartment and short boot. It's an ingenious piece of engineering and design deception.

By this stage, February 1991, the momentum behind MG's renaissance seemed unstop-

attempts to recreate that sense of proportion on a Rover 800 platform didn't succeed. Chopping off the roof only created a featureless convertible with a short bonnet and a large flat section behind the windscreen not dissimilar to many contemporary American convertibles, but definitely not one with a British signature. Reducing

Wyatt's rendering shows touches of MG-ness around the front grille.

procedures and put weight behind it rather than it being a skunk engineering project.' Nick Stephenson had gathered round him a core team of Brian Griffin and John Doyle who had both worked on the K-series powered Metro - renamed Rover 100 -to start work on the feasibility of a new small MG. Doyle's role was manufacturing and project management, while Griffin was product engineer.

'Our role then,' says Doyle, 'was to take this PR3 concept and see if it could be made into a

pable as PR3 and the Adder programme were also gathering pace. The debate about PR3's production numbers was still going on and Nick Stephenson believed that while RSP could cope with the low-volume Adder and Adventurer development and build programmes, PR3 would be too much for their resources. 'In truth I had more leverage in the company and at times they struggled to get the right level of leverage. It became clear that the project possibly wouldn't go anywhere and it was actually John Towers who said that if it's going anywhere it needs to get back into the mainstream and not be an RSP project.

'At about that time we were able to insert it into plans below the line and debates started about if we could afford it, had we got the resources, etc. Then we could get it into formal

PR3's concept was stylised in these early renderings from Rover Special Products, which show allegiance to the EX-E at the rear combined with a 'shark' snout.

realisable proposition.' Gradually over those early months of 1991 they started to gather other people on board, like Don Kettleborough and Martin Abba, as other programmes finished or

John Doyle (left) and Brian Griffin (right) were in right at the beginning of MG's revival.

were terminated, 'and that's when we started to play around with the concept of PR3 and what it could be'.

Brian Griffin takes up the story: 'We had a running prototype -Sim(ulator) 1 - that was mid-engined, but it was a 1.4 K series and we started to explore whether that was appropriate for the market and its engineering and manufacturing feasibility, the cost and numbers involved. Sim1

was based on a Metro van and was little more than a mid-engined version, built simply to demonstrate the feasibility of a mid-engined Metro concept.'

While that was going on there was a relook at the exterior with ADC and MGA, located a few miles down the A45 from the Canley design centre, contracted to style two mid-engined convertibles.

At the same time the first links were being established between the PR3 team and Rover's power-train department, who were busily engaged in designing a larger-capacity version of the K series as well as taking the first steps in developing an ingenious variable-valve control version. It didn't take the PR3 team long to appreciate that both would be ideal for the new small sports car.

However, in March, the ADC's 'pocket rocket' ran up against some cooling and exhaust problems. Originally the radiator was located between the engine and the bulkhead immediately behind the rear seats, with the result that it simply didn't get a sufficient flow of cool air, which in turn led to engine overheating. Furthermore those testing the car at Gaydon were suffering from fumes being sucked back into the cockpit from the vents located on the rear deck. Both problems would have to be

PR3 begins to take shape. Its mid-engined configuration is obvious from the air scoops just forward of the rear wheel arches. Even so, with its bland, over-long front bonnet line, it lacks the true MG style.

This simple MGB body shell was the basis for RSP's development of a new-look MG, which was gradually transformed over months of clay modelling at ADC.

addressed urgently if PR3 was to stand a chance.

About the time the MGA and ADC styling bucks were delivered to Canley. Both developed the mid-engined convertible theme but, as Gordon Sked points out, neither achieved what Rover was looking for: 'The MGA design was simply too big, it was a 2.2-litre engine car, not what we were aiming for; secondly, it looked Japanese and not British. You could imagine a Toyota badge on it, but not an MG. What it did show, though, was that a mid-engined car of roughly those dimensions worked.'

The ADC design was if anything too small and feminine-looking. Like MGA's, it confirmed Rover's belief that they were heading in the right direction, but that to achieve the unique MG

qualities it would have to be styled in-house.

Adder had gone through a major face-lift in the months since it had been at ADC. The front of the car was beginning to gain a more recognisable face with meaningful links back to the rubber-bumpered MGB's profile. The wings were also beginning to gain more form and character with a distinctive crease flowing down the flanks to emphasise the wheel-arch extensions which had been teased out to house the wider wheels and tyres. The headlights had yet to be resolved, but Wyatt and his team had at least managed to convince the money men that they would have to tool up for unique rear-lamp assemblies. 'We tried a lot of things with tail lights, trying to get a carry-over unit from another car, but we just

As the project progressed the clay was built up into an identifiable car with a modernised rendering of the last B's black bumper. At this stage two headlamp configurations were under-consideration: faired-in on the left-hand side and a sloped back 911 headlamp on the right.

*Still in its clay form
but now in British
Racing Green. RSP
remained undecided
about the headlamp
and rear configuration.*

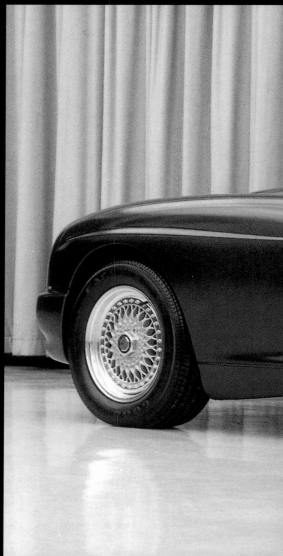

couldn't make it work. We sweet-talked the financial guy and got a new tail light, which is very, very expensive to tool up for in relation to the overall cost of the programme.' There was also the unspoken danger that the press and customers would indulge in a game of 'hunt the donor car' which inevitably happens with any car produced on a tight budget.

Delivery date for the completed Adder clay was March, when a major RSP presentation was due. However, the team was worried that a clay wouldn't portray successfully the finished car, so they gambled on taking a glass-fibre buck from it, thereby destroying any base reference they might need at a future date.

Luckily the gamble paid off. Kevin Morley declared himself happy with the car, bought into the programme and was ready to sign off the required budget later that summer. The first stage in MG's revival had been completed. Once that budget was signed off in July 1991 there was no turning back for Rover. The Octagon was back.

For all the public knew, MG and the Octagon had been laid to rest in the April of that year, when MG versions of the Metro, Maestro and Montego ceased production. Graham Day, George Simpson and the rest of Rover's hierarchy appreciated the value of brands and could see MG slowly becoming another moribund marque like so many before - Riley, Wolseley, Austin, Morris. But if enthusiasts mourned the passing of MG, Rover's executives were secure in the knowledge that the marque hadn't gone and certainly wasn't forgotten. 'And to some extent that's why we decided to go ahead with the MG R V8,' says Towers, "because we felt there was a need - and we knew we could do that programme quickly and relatively cheaply - to revitalise the sense of MG in people's minds as a sports car, not as a badge you stuck on a mundane saloon car.'

A secret consumers' clinic was held in Manchester during June with the MGA and ADC cars, plus DR2/PR5 and Adder, on view. Once it was explained that Adder was a celebration of MG's thirtieth anniversary and that it would only be available in very limited numbers, but at a higher price than usual for an MG, the 'customers' accepted and understood the logic behind it. Likewise DR2/PR5 immediately found favour, its looks being especially appreciated, but they said it wasn't an MG or even a Rover. Those questioned saw it as a £40,000 sports car in the Jaguar or Aston Martin vein, whereas the MGA and ADC styling studies, yes, they were small, compact, cheaper fun cars - they were what MG was all about.

If the Manchester clinic was a severe blow to

Finished. The faired-in headlamps and spoiler are gone. And Adder's swooping lines win over Rover's bosses, a modern rendition of what the MGB could have become if it had not been abandoned years before.

PR5, then August's news delivered the knock-out punch: it was announced that Rover would withdraw from North America for the third time in twenty years. Sterling's US sales record had been dismal since it had re-entered the market in 1986. The following year sales were a respectable 14,171, but disastrous results in the all-important J. D. Power customer-satisfaction index, poor build quality and an inadequate dealer network saw sales slide to only 4015 in 1990 and a miserable 1878 in the first seven months of 1991. To make matters even worse, the US economy took a nose-dive and luxury imported cars were hardly flavour of the month. Not even taking over the running of the operations themselves and offering a stately home as an incentive prize to potential Sterling 827 owners was sufficient to turn the tide.

That withdrawal effectively spelt the end for Roy Axe's DR2/PR5 project, but equally left the door wide open for PR3 to become the all-new MG.

12

Sterling's failure in the USA spelled the end of any presence in that market for Rover or any of its car-based products. The only representatives the company now had in the States were their successful Range Rover and Land Rover Discovery four-wheel-drive leisure vehicles. 'We no longer had a natural home for the cars, ' says Nick Stephenson and that continues to be the case, for the time being, according to John Towers: '.We couldn't create a single product franchising with all the marketing, advertising and overheads that would entail. It wasn't a business proposition, unfortunately.'

Don Wyatt, not unnaturally, was sorry to see work on PR5 stopped: 'I mean, what can I say? I'm the funny Yank. I love that kind of car...if I was putting my money down for a car to be seen in, I'd want to be seen in that one.'

However, Rover were still in the luxurious position of having two MG projects on the way.

There would have been no point in confirming the V8-engined Roadster programme if a contemporary MG wasn't in the pipeline.

The V8 programme filled the MG void, says Stephenson, and was a 'nice little tool' for keeping the conversation about MG alive. 'But what were we keeping MG alive for? It helped in turn create credibility for being more serious about getting an MG proper back into the plan.'

Although PR3 had still to become a mainstream engineering programme, work on the concept was growing in intensity. The first in a series of mid-engined Metro van simulators had been built and was being used for early development work on the chassis, brakes and transmission just to assess the feasibility of the concept.

What did emerge was the first PR3 car to be crash-tested. Brian Griffin's team used it for the first front-end crash: 'Just to get an understanding of how it would perform without an engine at the front, it just helped confirm the sort of performance we were trying to get out of the seals, for example, on the

Early crash tests at the Motor Industry Research Association's facility were performed using heavily modified Metros.

A posts.'

At the same time as the executive committee meeting, marketing was beginning to take an interest in the project. Research in Japan had confirmed Rover's twin-track approach of the classic, retro-look V8 Roadster as well as an ultra-modern two-seater.

With this in mind an informal clinic was held, drawing forty-eight people from different parts of the BAe operation to assess what they demanded of a modern performance car. Those chosen were all identified as theoretical MG owners, mainly because of the cars they already drove. Each was asked to drive a selection of cars perceived as potential MG rivals - from a Honda Beat through to VW's Corrado G60 - over a 15-mile route, to assess various aspects of the driving experience and establish which were the most important to them.

The engineering team was trying to assess what potential owners look for. Is it style, ride and handling, economy or performance, refinement? If these parameters could be locked into early in the programme then the car would be engineered to achieve the genuine desires of customers, not the perceived ones.

The exercise threw up some interesting conclusions: while the specialist motoring press might be obsessed with 0-60mph times and balls-out handling, owners were more concerned about mid-range performance. Fuel economy wasn't particularly important, nor was maximum speed, but a good gear-change - as exemplified by the Mazda MX5 - was vital. Having established these goals it was now up to the engineer-

Potential MG customers were asked to rate the most important aspects a sports car should possess.

POWERTRAIN QUESTIONAIRE INDEXED IMPORTANCE RATING

Throttle response

Performance at low revs

Performance at mid revs

Performance at high revs

Gearchange quality

Cruising refinement

Idle quality

Acceleration refinement

MPG

0-60mph time

Max engine power

Max speed

Max engine torque

0   10   20   30   40   50   60   70   80   90   100

ing team to achieve them.

The results of this ride 'n' drive stressed some of the feedback that had filtered through from the Manchester clinic - where the original PR3 had been lined up against the Mazda MX5 and Toyota MR2 as well as its internal rivals - that a 1.4-litre engine, with a 1.6 as a high-performance derivative, simply wasn't going to be powerful enough. The car had to be 1.6-2 litres, and even then the smaller engine would be at the bottom end of the credibility spectrum. It wasn't top-end power or performance customers craved, but mid-range flexibility - that reserve of power which is instantly accessible for quick, safe overtaking manoeuvres.

What all this told Brian Griffin and his colleagues was that likely MG customers didn't want an engine that had to be kept in a narrow power band by constantly changing gears. They wanted instant access to a wide spread of mid-range torque and responsive acceleration.

Griffin recalls that 'As we understood better the car's weight, it was obvious that the 1.6 engine wasn't going to deliver the kind of performance aspirations we were looking for: 0-60mph in 8.5 seconds and a 120mph top speed. We had to deliver something really quite extraordinary in terms of throttle response. Basically what it gave us was the objective definition of the things that we had to deliver in PR3. That's when we said what levers can we pull to deliver those customer requirements?'

There was now enough general confidence in the PR3 programme for it to transfer from RSP into Rover's mainstream engineering schedule. It still had to be signed off as a programme which would see the light of day, but it was generally felt that despite the good groundwork which RSP had done, and what they had achieved on minimal resources, it was time for PR3 to make the transition from a limited production-run special to a product that would be built in its thousands. As Wyatt admits, it was difficult to let go of the project: 'It was always understood that because of the volumes involved it wouldn't be us, and then the Phoenix team started to come on board and they had full latitude to take that work and do anything with it. They could have turned round, I suppose, and said, "We don't want to do a mid-engined car, we want to do front-wheel drive." But the consensus was that PR3 was the right direction to go.'

Everyone at RSP, says Wyatt, 'was quite pleased' with what they had done And they could console themselves with the knowledge that they would be upholding MG's honour with the continuing development of the V8 Roadster.

As soon as PR3 was in the mainstream

Stephenson's greater leverage within Rover started to pay dividends, especially when it came to increasing engine power: 'We were looking to the future and were already planning larger swept volume versions of the K series, that was no mystery. Just a case of looking into other programmes and saying, "This will do the job." If the MG programme had had to carry the development costs of those power units that would've been a nail in its coffin, but no, the work was going on elsewhere.'

That isn't to say that alternative power units weren't considered, so it was not surprising to learn from Nick Stephenson that forced induction was seriously contemplated. There were numerous rumours going round the press at the time that prototype PR3s were powered by supercharged or turbocharged 1.4-litre K-series engines: 'We did consider pressure charging and had virtually every type of pressure charging you can think of on a K series,' says Stephenson, and although Stephenson won't confirm it, other engineers have talked about conventional turbochargers as well as a Sprintex screw-type supercharger and a version of VW's scroll-like G-lader system. All Stephenson will admit to, with a grin and a hearty laugh at the memory of it, is a very powerful Metro: 'We had some very exciting little test products, but we were never too certain whether the 180bhp Metro was sensible.' (The most powerful current production Metro has 102bhp under its bonnet.)

The critical concern was to keep costs under control and pressure-charged engines by their nature tend to be more expensive than high-performance derivatives; They presented other problems too, but the one which did survive led a useful life in another part of the programme.

Brian Griffin was constantly adding to the Phoenix team: Bob Butterworth became a team leader for the first time, responsible for most electrical items - although, strangely, not alternators, starter motors or wiper mechanisms; Dave Ovens took on the responsibilities of trim and hardware team leader - 'everything that isn't body, electrical, chassis or power train'.

Even though the programme had yet to be fully signed off to become a production car, outside suppliers were being contacted. One of the main contracts was hood development and for this Rover went to the Italian coachbuilders and eminent design house, Pininfarina. Ovens and Griffin already had a good picture of what the hood packaging would be like from ADC's 'pocket rocket' and they knew the stack height was going to be the major problem. The only mid-engined convertible on the market at the time was the much larger Ferrari Mondial whose 2+2 configuration meant that some of the hood-stowage space could be robbed from the back-seat area. Rover didn't have that luxury. PR3's hood would have to stack virtually on top of the engine, behind the two seats. Furthermore, the folded hood mustn't look like a camel's hump on the car's rear deck.

It was during September 1991 that responsibility for PR3's styling came in-house from MGA and ADC. The two outside contractors had been retained primarily to augment RSP's limited resources. With only forty staff RSP was fully stretched on other programmes which included the Mini Cooper, CSK Range Rover, the Mini and Metro Cabriolets and the Rover 400 Tourer as well as the V8 Roadster.

By this time Roy Axe had left Rover to concentrate on running DRA and, though he regrets not being directly involved with PR3's final evolution, likes to think he laid some of the fundamental foundations for the programme: 'I was sorry I wasn't there when the final thing came round, but I've played my part in it. It took some pretty hard hanging in to a board that wasn't totally sympathetic to it [MG] at all.'

Gordon Sked, who had taken over full-time responsibility for Rover's styling, had very clear views on what a new MG should be: 'I think that while one or two people saw some benefits in the alternatives, I don't think there was any doubt which was actually going to be built. Had the MX5 not existed things might have been different.

'PR3 had to be different, so that accusations that it lined up against the MX5 would be minimised. From an engineering standpoint the components existed, we knew how we could do it, we knew how we could deliver it, we used the subframes from the Metro, we knew the positioning of the engine, the orientation of the gearbox, all that sort of stuff we knew how to do. I felt there were tremendous technical problems doing it, particularly gear-change quality and weight distribution, but I felt it ought to be delivered. From a design standpoint we could change the proportions, make it longer at the tail with a slightly higher deck, to emphasise that the car was mid-engined. Maybe it's not a latter-day MG Midget or MGB but it needed to be a latter-day MG. It must be modern, must be British, must be MG.'

Sked and his styling team had to set their own parameters, a process that happened on several levels: 'It happened with me individually, thinking it through. It happened through myself talking to my inner team, people like Gerry McGovern and Geoff Upex and one or two other people and it happened on a greater level within the PR3 team as a whole. As far as inputs were concerned we had MGs of the past and, indeed, current sports cars which were likely to be competitors. I felt we had to achieve extraordinary levels of storage, I thought that was very important and with a mid-engine, rear-wheel-drive layout that was beginning to look risky, so we had to find ways of overcoming that as a problem and make a benefit of it.

'In the teams' minds we believed that the drivability of the vehicle had to feel very different and to be almost in a class of its own.'

Sked admits that creating 'the world's most exciting car to drive' was arrogant and ambitious but, as he says, 'Unless you set a fairly ambitious target, you'd never achieve anything. So that was the target we set.'

The MGA and ADC programmes showed Sked and his team what not to do. 'What we had to do was move on to the next stage and basically start again. Gerry and I sat down and sketched around various ideas and eventually came up with the solution of taking EX-E - because it was modern, because it had some exposure and because it was a mid-engined MG - and work from that.'

Sked had already decided in his own mind that EX-E needed softening off a little - 'It's too crisp and doesn't acknowledge some of the

design trends since its launch. Design had become just a little bit softer, but I still believed in the tautness.' But he didn't want to influence McGovern's thinking. Fortunately, he agreed with Sked: 'Just soften the tail off and the character lines.' McGovern immediately started reworking the MGA and ADC concepts: 'Really they were studies in proportion to see what you'd end up with when it came to packaging the car. Purely from a design point of view what they did was stop us from doing investigative work in style terms. We knew, for example, when we looked at those cars that we didn't want to do what was

Gerry McGovern had been involved with reviving MG since his early work on EX-E. Under Gerry's guidance, the design team turned the bland MGA and ADC cars into the definitive PR3.

there. They hadn't really styled the car in detail, they had alluded to certain forms that we knew wouldn't ultimately be right for an MG. For example, the MGA car had pop-up headlamps and it didn't have a face. Because it was a contemporary design we knew this car had to have a face and it had to have an element of MG in it but, more importantly, an element of Britishness. Both the MGA and ADC cars didn't display that and that was very important to us. They both looked very Japanese, especially the MGA one, and because it had got pop-up lamps it had a very severe wedge, was too bulbous and didn't have the tautness that we wanted.

'The ADC one was probably more realistic but, again, had pop-up lamps. Because they'd seen the work we had done on the F16 and EX-E it had got this split line running all the way through and because of the balance of the car it wasn't dynamic enough. The resolution of all those problems... really became the objectives for a new design.'

The simplest styling strategy for Sked and his team would have been to don sepia-tinted glasses and clone as many styling traits as possible from MG's heritage. However, if one goes back through successive post-war designs, MGs have done exactly the opposite: the MGA doesn't reflect the TF any more than the B takes cues from the A; being mid-engined, the EX-E was as different again as PR3 is from any past MG.

Subsequent sports cars, especially the Fiat barchetta, lean heavily on past emotions, something which Sked and McGovern were determined not to do. 'From the start we decided not to go down memory lane,' says Sked. 'We didn't really want to do that at all. The first thing we did was to proportion the car out, to get the masses to look right because the car should look modern. The second thing was to try and find a design rationale for the car and the third thing was to inject the British/MG-ness into it and I believe it's there. It is certainly there in terms of the front end; the bonnet surface, the headlamp area, the grille, the line across the front are directly from the MGB.

'This car is potentially closer to a rubber-bumper MGB than it is to anything else. So why not build on that? If you can make it look good, and I think we have, there's no real problem at all. We'd taken the decision to build the design very much round the back of the EX-E and extend it all the way to the front end; the design of the rear lamps, the bumper and centre section are lifted straight off the EX-E. Maybe there are those people who say, "Well I'd have preferred just a little bit less EX-E and a bit more TF", which would have been easy to do. But how many people remember the TF? We're dealing with customers of today.'

Gerry McGovern was also very mindful of the 'incredible pressure on us' because this was the first new MG in thirty-three years. 'A lot of pressure,' he says, 'was coming from the MG Owners' Club and people like that, and as a consequence we didn't want to fall into the retrospective trap. So we were very careful about how much we looked into the past.'

McGovern emphasised that he wanted this to be a thoroughly modern concept, a thoroughly modern car, '...and part of that comes out in its execution, the fact that it's quite innovative, quite advanced with its mid-engined layout. To a certain extent form follows function, so we've got those elements to work on and then we recognised the heritage through the execution of its detail. When you look at the exterior of the car, for example, you will see a very deliberate execution of detail around the Octagon on the shield plinth. The general robustness of the forms on the bonnet, the exposed lamps and the simplicity of the body side section. Those elements of MG-ness, and fundamental Britishness evolved through the programme.

'We were starting to develop a design philosophy for MG in the same way as we've evolved one for Land Rover.'

Trying to meet the demands of both styling and engineering was Trevor Holdsworth, chief engineer concept engineering. With more than thirty years' experience in the motor industry Trevor's job was to try and fit all the mechanical components within the body shape that McGovern and his design team were evolving while trying to satisfy the demands of Brian Griffin's engineers as well as ensuring that once built the components would be easily accessible for maintenance requirements: 'We work through to style ratification. In other words we're trying to prove out the overall package of the vehicle, not just the power-train applications, but also how do we relate to the hood stack or the body contours? The issue here is if Gerry is defining the exterior shape of the vehicle and, because he can't get the bulk of the vehicle right, he starts to shave an inch off the back of the vehicle - which he did at one stage - I've still got to get all the components in. I am fighting for every millimetre I can get.'

In the early PR3 days Holdsworth's job must have been like trying to squeeze jigsaw pieces into an ever-shrinking puzzle. His task was made a little easier when the car's wheelbase was increased 3.9in to help accommodate a larger fuel tank as well as ease the interior packaging. One of the early requirements identified during the market-research stage was initiated by press comments that long journeys in sports cars were marred by having to refuel more often than every 300 miles. PR3, it was decided, was not going to come in for that criticism.

Lengthening the wheelbase had the added benefit of further improving the car's handling, making it less prone to sudden rear-end break-away. An imperative feature that had been identified early in the Phoenix programme was benign handling; PR3 had to be a car that any-

Left and below left: Even before the styling had been signed off by Rover's senior management, the development team was working out how to package all the components into the very tight dimensions to which McGovern was working.

body and everybody could enjoy, irrespective of their driving skills. Such a policy was in the MG tradition, but mid-engined cars aren't best known for their forgivingness.

Although all of PR3's masses - power train, fuel, passengers, luggage - are contained within the wheelbase, weight distribution is biased to the rear, 45/55. Normally this means that once the car reaches its cornering limits, the rear wheels and tyres break traction first as the inertia takes over and the car starts to spin off backwards unless opposite lock is applied rapidly. The problem is usually exacerbated by lack of warning.

As the PR3 team were struggling with styling, packaging and engineering, the roadster V8 team over at RSP were making steady progress

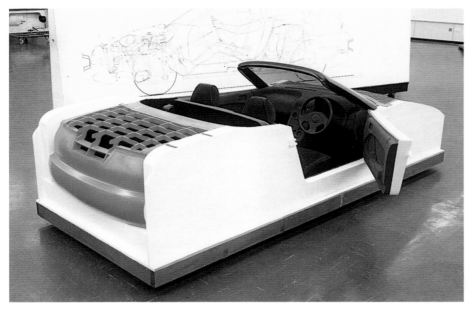

with their role in MG's revival. But they too were having their problems. The major heartache was over the body itself. When the glass-fibre buck was being digitised for the press tooling to be manufactured, there was found to be a 0.8in bend at the front which threw the whole programme into the air for a while. The only solution Don Wyatt and his team was to rejig the body on the computer as best they could and then finish it off by hand once the full-size buck had been cut.

Following the Manchester clinic most of the questionmarks over the design had been answered. They'd done away with the split grille but agreed on the Porsche 911 headlights and a small raised block on the bonnet and grille to mount the MG badge. RSP tried to mount the windscreen further back, but the budget just didn't stretch to such modifications. The original MGB's hood stack had to be retained, but the windscreen surround was fabricated from a single pressed-steel section rather than four separate aluminium ones as in the original. This, combined with very careful body-in-white production, improved the car's torsional rigidity

Tickford were contracted to fabricate a new double-skinned hood, which meant the stowed hood wouldn't sit flush with the rear deck and thwarted any plans to develop a flush-fitting tonneau.

The interior, with its swathes of Connolly leather, veneer fascia and door cappings, is very un-MG like. The comfy leather seats tend to push tall occupants above the windscreen's header rail and though Wyatt and the RSP team wanted lower squabs, seat-belt legislation dictated otherwise. There was also an efficient heater fitted - something of a novelty for an MGB - and the pedals were repositioned to aid heel 'n' toeing.

Component spotters could have a field day with the V8 Roadster's interior, with its VDO instruments, as used by TVR, the interior door handles are Jaguar XJS, the control stalks are Rover 800, the door mirrors come from the Metro and the steering column is Land Rover Discovery. In a departure from the original MGB GT V8, the new V8 roadster has a five-speed gearbox which, with 29mph per 1000rpm in fifth, means very lazy high-speed cruising. Behind the Alloy Wheels International mock spoked rims are 10.6in ventilated discs at the front with four-pot calipers and good old-fashioned 8.9in drums at the back.

Far removed from the intricacies of ride and handling or packaging was Nick Boneham, who was appointed finance manager for the Phoenix programme, the bean counter who would have to

various alternative routes as to how the vehicle could be manufactured to become a profitable product were being explored. The issues we were looking at were target costs and sales -commercial were exploring that, and we had potential retail prices. The bones of the programme were pulling together the financial viability of PR3. The whole concept surrounded the MG marque: what demand was out there for MG? The product came second.'

Echoing what John Towers has already said, Boneham continues, 'We had to develop the product to fit the marque, whereas in the past we had produced MG Metros, Maestros and Montegos, which we wouldn't do in the future.'

By the time Boneham arrived on the scene, the team had identified a sector for the product, eliminating on the way concepts like DR2/PR5. So the key question left was, 'What sort of volumes are we likely to sell in the particular segments? There was a big difference between the V8 Roadster and PR3. The V8 volumes were 2000 in total, plus a medium-volume sports car which, nevertheless, is low volume to Rover.'

The PR3 programme was unique within Rover as it was developed on a low-technology/low-cost basis, says Boneham: 'What we've tried to do during its gestation over three or four years is that we've picked up technology

Left and right: *Just a few of the hundreds of renderings which the Rover design team produced on their way to the car's definitive style.*

argue for more funding if needed. 'There were six core people when I joined at the end of '91. The project had passed through the feasibility stage, the concept had been developed and as it's advanced within other programmes.' He cites as examples the transition from 1.4- to 1.6- and finally to 1.8-litre engine. 'As and when we've seen these opportunities to put them into the car at no incremental cost to the project we've done it, because the up-front development costs, start-up costs and investment costs for this programme had to be kept to a minimum.'

Boneham could be echoing John Towers' words when he says PR3 isn't a mainstream product for Rover - 16-20,000 a year isn't. It is highly prestigious and, like any product, at the end of the day, 'It still has to return a profit.'

In late September an even closer collaboration with Honda was announced when Sir Graham Day (as he now was) and George Simpson revealed a strategy that would see all of Rover's mainstream products being developed jointly with Honda, certainly until the end of the century. The differences between the two ranges would be in the detailing. Rover would continue to utilise its home-grown K-series and new T-series engines, both petrol and diesel, and the Land Rover range of products would continue to be developed by the Solihull specialists. When it came to styling and design, matters were less

clear. It was obvious from these early days that Honda would be responsible for the floor-pans and overall body concepts, but with Rover input.

This process of Rover tuning the suspension to its own demands, re-equipping the interiors with leather and veneer fillets, adding chrome grilles and Viking badge-embossed kickplates went under the dreadful title of 'Roverisation'.

The announcement probably didn't come a day too soon, as giant industrial/electronics/aerospace conglomerate GEC put in a bid for Rover's parent company BAe. The question was, if GEC won, what would they do with Rover? In an effort to stave off the hostile bid, BAe launched a £432 million rights issue which was coolly received by the City. All it seemed to do was push Rover reluctantly into the arms of a potential new senior partner - Honda.

13

The next twelve months were going to be make or break for the Phoenix programme. If the engineering, styling, financing and marketing strategies weren't in place by the end of the year then PR3's future would be doubtful. As a manufacturer, Rover might have been locked in to the V8 Roadster programme, but the investment required to bring that to reality was tiny. Phoenix would demand a greater financial commitment from Rover and BAe.

There was always a suspicion that BAe didn't fully understand the complexities of - or the financial commitment demanded by - a car manufacturer. While on the surface designing, developing and manufacturing aircraft and cars might not seem to be that dissimilar and both involved huge financial sums, in reality they are very different. Aeroplanes cost huge amounts in R & D but don't - relatively - need a lot of investment in

factories. Components are made by outside contractors, bought in and assembled in vast hangars. Cars need robots, factories, paint shops, a new car invariably demands a refurbished factory for production. That was part of the message Rover was constantly having to get across to BAe.

The notion held by many press observers - that BAe wasn't always supportive of Rover - is refuted by John Towers: 'It's often said that Aerospace were not car people, but Dick Evans loves cars. My experience of car programmes submitted to BAe is that they got approved. The difference between then and where we are now [early 1996] is the size of our corset. It's changed dramatically as we've doubled our engineering and capital expenditure.

'Within the business plan there were assumptions on how much money we'd spend on engineering and how much on capital expenditure and within that framework I can't think of a proposal that was turned down. I didn't get a particular sense of "Um, my goodness we must do this", but there was no problem in getting approval.'

Nick Stephenson remembers it being somewhat tougher: 'I don't in any way want to do BAe an injustice, but it was tough justifying new product programmes, which was part of my role. You could see it was a shock to their system, because cars are very capital intensive and aircraft are not. And that was a very big learning point for me. What we thought were quite mundane programmes, we were actually asking for huge sums of money in their terms.... Therefore, maybe there was an element of us having to fight quite hard for marginal projects like Phoenix. Nonetheless, they were supportive at the end of the day.'

The need to persuade BAe to support the programme spurred Stephenson and the Phoenix team to be as inventive about its financing as they were being about the engineering and design challenges they would have to meet in the coming months. 'It led us,' says Stephenson, 'to present a case that was more palatable. Rover had been very cash hungry and BAe had supported our mainstream projects, so something that might look a little peripheral we were very sensitive about.'

Nick Boneham takes up the story: 'In early '92 we were looking at problem issues such as funding, which was significant for a small programme. If you look at it from a strategic point of view we had to see what other products we had going on at the time to appreciate there wasn't sufficient funding for an MG roadster, so we had to look at alternatives to finance this programme. Fairly early on we appreciated that we needed

additional backing for it to carry through.'

Boneham and his colleagues then undertook a series of brainstorming sessions to try and plot a route by which PR3 could become a production reality. Their task would have been simpler if it could have been done in isolation, but that was an impossibility: 'We had to look at the company strategy and how we could maximise our resources on the programme and a strategic fit between the parts of the car we could do and had the resources to do, and those parts where we needed help because we hadn't got the resources available. For argument's sake, the more you put outside, the more expensive the end product is. If we could use the costs we were already incurring to help us with this programme, then it would be cheaper than putting it all outside and get the money from another source as well.'

Getting a third party to build the car on Rover's behalf would have pushed costs up, especially to the end buyer, and MGs have always been known as good value for money sports cars. On the other hand, raising capital from the City wouldn't have cured any of the manufacturing bottlenecks which Rover had at the time: 'There were certain areas of product development where we felt we couldn't cope with the manpower we had at the time. We had to fund the mainline programmes, the bread and butter for

MGR V8s are a rare sight: only 2000 were built and most of those ended up in MG-mad Japan.

the company.'

At board level, says Boneham, it wasn't a question of whether Rover did Phoenix or not, but when and how. 'There was always the drive to move the product forward, it was just finding the way.'

Boneham wasn't even concerning himself with the problem of where the car would be built - 'It could have been anywhere in the company, Cowley, Solihull, Longbridge.' The answer to that question, like the answer to the problem of funding, would eventually present itself.

Don Wyatt and the RSP crew were having their own headaches as they built up to the announcement of the V8 Roadster. Because of the delays caused by having to hone the buck by hand, they resorted to photographing a glass-fibre model for the original teaser brochure: 'You'll notice there are things not shown in any of the pictures, there's nothing on the turn indicators because they were changing on the dye-stack. We had no badges on the car, they were photographed separately then dropped in place on the pictures. And the tonneau cover was just rendered in as well. The car was fitted with a hard cover and we knew we couldn't run with that, so the photograph had to be faked.'

British Aerospace boss Dick Evans and George Simpson saw a completed car for the first

Out on the open road, the MGR V8 is great fun, powerful enough to provide thrills without the spills.

time in March and both fell in love with it, especially Evans, who ordered one of the first production cars for his own use.

On 13 March 1992 Rover's external affairs department issued a one-page press release announcing a 'Special edition MG to mark thirtieth anniversary'. We learned from the release that the V8 Roadster had been christened MG RV8, that fifteen a week would be built, that it had a 135mph top speed, a 3.9-litre engine and would go on sale in September. Apart from that, nothing.

Rover were going to milk MG's rebirth all they could over the coming months, and who can blame them? That would, at least, distract some of the media flak the company was getting.

Given the age of the tools from which it was produced, the MGR V8's fit and finish were of a very high order.

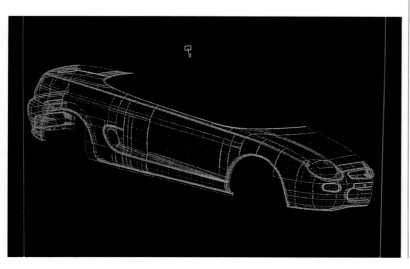

Despite the cautionary line in the release which read, 'Rover is still assessing the possibility of returning to volume sports car production'.

A month earlier, Gerry McGovern's team had started surfacing the car's exterior. Between September 1991 and February 1992, PR3 had been gradually taking shape within the confines of the Canley styling studio. The days when engineers, stylists, production experts, etc. all worked in separate cells trying to do their jobs in isolation are long gone within Rover. Now they all work in unison, interacting so that no one is going off on a tangent and developing a component or system that is out of tune with the rest of the team. It is the same with styling. McGovern was leading the clay modellers, ensuring that they kept true to his original concept of a taut, almost pugnacious style for the car.

It was during this period that PR3 developed its final shape - the rear deck height diminished considerably, for instance. It was always going to be a packaging nightmare trying to stack the hood assembly practically on top of the engine. The engine itself couldn't be lowered any further, not only because it would minimise ground clearance beneath the sump and gearbox, but also the angles of the drive shaft would have been compromised. Undeterred by the technical problems, Holdsworth came into the styling stu-

Clay models are painstakingly sculpted by hand to ensure every nuance of styling is captured. Note how the design team has experimented with two differing nose profiles.

Computer modelling played a key role in surfacing once the clay modelling had been completed.

dio one Monday to find that the boot height had been shaved down by 3in. Worse was to come later when McGovern lopped 4in off the bonnet to shorten the car's nose line and front overhang.

For Holdsworth and his team, 'the largest task we had was getting the petrol tank, power train and doing something that nobody else had ever done, which was to package a hood on top of the power train and to put a hard top on that and still make the engine accessible for servicing. At the same time as doing that achieve a driving position that was good for ninety-fifth percentile drivers. Gerry was trying to get the proportions right, so while he was trying to knock weight off the vehicle we were trying to package everything.'

Moving the radiator location to the front should have been a help to Holdsworth, and it was until the car lost that vital 4in. 'He didn't talk to me for a week,' recounts McGovern, who justifies his action by saying that he needed to 'take Holdsworth's guys out of their comfort zone'.

For Gordon Sked it was a question of balancing out the masses, it's 'dead easy to sort of sling the front end right down because you're not putting anything in there, a spare wheel, and the minimum height for the headlamps, those are the sorts of criteria for the front end of the car. We actually lifted all of that up to get a bit more

presence in the front so that   so that people would recognise it as an MG.'

According to Holdsworth, McGovern also dug his heels in over the shape of the doors. It would have been the easiest thing in the world to cut a pair of vertical lines for the doors, they would have been cheaper and easier to manufacture than those on the finished car. 'Trevor and Brian used to gang up on me,' McGovern mocks. 'If there had been a weaker person on the job, they would have got their way on all those points.'

The fact that he didn't give way isn't a reflection of weakness on either Griffin's or Holdsworth's part. For Holdsworth it was a business debate: 'There were obvious cost issues - when doing vehicles it's far cheaper to have a square door and far easier to make because a pinch radius at the bottom of a door is expensive, but Gerry stuck his heels in - it was a styling cue that he wouldn't let go.'

But that is typical of Rover's attitude towards this project. The easy option would have been to develop an MG off an existing floor-pan. After all, Fiat has done it very successfully with both its Coupé and its barchetta, but Rover's determination, some would say bulldog stubbornness, led it to produce one of the most, if not the most, technically advanced products in its price and class range.

14

Project Phoenix is a rich mixture of technology: Hydragas® suspension, the option of variable valve timing and electric power steering. If that had been the specification from a Japanese manufacturer we'd have been none too surprised -after all, it is the free-thinking and free-spending manufacturers from Japan who have led the motor industry's technological race.

But for Rover to come up with such a sophisticated and technically challenging confection was something of a revelation. Although Land Rover products had been developed independently of any partners, there hadn't been an all-new Rover car since the Montego in 1984. Subsequent new products had all been engineered and developed in partnership with Honda.

For Nick Stephenson it was an obvious route to pursue: 'We've been very pragmatic about engineering the car and taken components which worked very well for us and assembled them into a rather fun vehicle. After all that's very faithful to MG, every MG was created that way.'

Stephenson has no time for those who think it perverse for Rover to pursue such technological challenges when it would have been cheaper, simpler and easier to go for a front- or rear-wheel-drive package. 'We'd just done the Metro with Hydragas® suspension, so it's what we'd been living with, it wasn't alien to us. Secondly, front-engined rear-wheel-drive cars for us at that time in the corporation were difficult to do, because all our cars were front-drivers and we hadn't got small rear-drive transmissions, axles, etc. Putting the engine where we did was very straightforward to do, because in essence we lifted the whole front end of a Metro drive train and placed it in the centre of the vehicle. So, from a parts bin point of view it was very logical and we had no concerns about getting sensible levels of existing component utilisation and making sure we actually created a new product. As for the electric power steering, we happened to have a research programme going on, so it didn't appear from nowhere. We feel it's got a lot of potential merit for small and lighter vehicles.'

John Towers acknowledges that 'it would have been cheaper for us to create a different configuration and do what many people have done, which is to take a bag of components and sling them together with a new subframe and body and call it a sports car', but for him the Phoenix programme 'is an excellent example of making sure that you create value first and then you examine how to do it most effectively, efficiently and productively. The fact that we chose not to go the easy route I think has two implications: first of all the cost of the programme and the material cost of the product, but also a major implication in terms of how it's been received.'

Towers is obviously not impressed by rival manufacturers taking the easy route, but. at the same time pleased that Rover has been able to produce a unique product. 'People who have done that type of car on a reasonable volume base,' he reflects, 'have tended to concentrate heavily on how they can avoid engineering. So they've come up with a configuration that if you examine it closely is connected to lots of bits and pieces that happen to be available and is compromised as a result of that.

'Our objective varied during the course of the programme, but the intention was to create a world first, a premier league position epitomised by the phrase "The most exciting sports car in the world". It probably meant it cost another £1500 a car to do it that way. If it had cost another

£10,000 more we'd probably have had second thoughts, because you can't move too far away from the MG marque position of being affordable, that's really important. It would have been so easy, and I am sure marketing could have created a rationale, to do a front-engine, front-wheel-drive approach. Of course it wouldn't have had anywhere near the handling characteristics PR3 has.'

The car's combination of a supple, well-controlled ride and very high levels of cornering ability came not overnight, but as a result of an intensive development schedule that was pursued throughout the programme.

Remember MG's slogan? 'Safety Fast.' That's what drove the ride and handling team at all times. PR3 was meant for Mr/Ms Average to enjoy. It wasn't destined to be a week-end fair-weather-only sports car, but one that would be equally happy pottering down to the supermarket for the weekly shop, cruising in the South of France or being taken for exhilarating drives across deserted moorland roads.

Creating a car for all driver abilities wasn't going to be easy and highlights the work done by Don Kettleborough, Philip Turner and John Cooper. Kettleborough and his team were responsible for building the simulators, while Turner, Cooper and colleagues spent endless

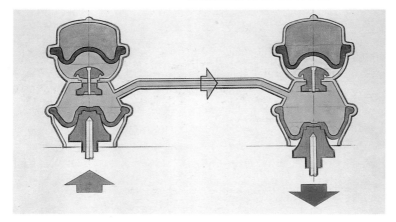

Hydragas® is a simple, but highly effective suspension system promoting a fine balance of ride and handling.

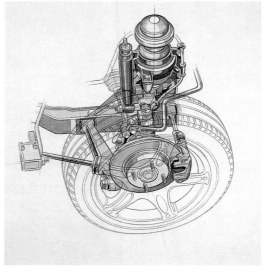

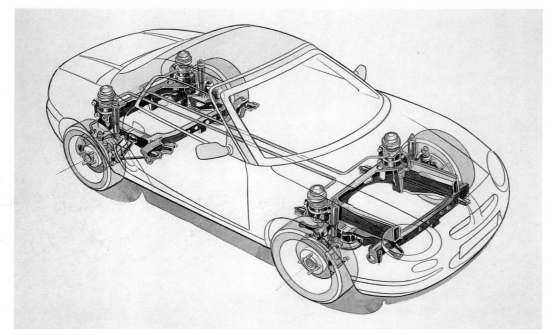

Both the front and rear set-ups are augmented by conventional struts to improve ride control even more.

The Phoenix team went one step farther with Hydragas® and interlinked the front and rear systems.

hours - usually under the cover of darkness -tuning and constantly refining the car's ride and handling.

The essential ingredient in PR3's handling performance is its suspension system. Dr Alex Moulton's Hydragas® suspension appeared some thirty years ago on the Mini and, despite having been fitted to 10 million cars since, has never quite made the transition from quirky but brilliant solution to everyday application. A history that includes Moulton bicycles and the Austin Allegro might have something to do with its lack of wider acceptance, yet anyone who has driven a modern Hydragas® car will vouch for its comfort and control levels. Stylists love it because the system is so compact to locate. Its installation in PR3 is the best yet and, hopefully, points the way to further use.

Unlike conventional cars, one fitted with the Hydragas® system would, ideally, have no springs, dampers or anti-roll bars, but that has yet to be attained. So, as in PR3's case, anti-roll bars and conventional Monroe dampers are fitted.

The Hydragas® system essentially comprises two spheres - one on top of the other, rather like a wide-waisted hour-glass - at each corner of the car. A displacement strut sits up against a diaphragm, which seals in a non-corrosive water and alcohol fluid in the bottom chamber, while the other end of the strut is located on the lower wishbone arm. The upper hour-glass chamber is filled with nitrogen, a rubber membrane separating it from the fluid. In the waist between the

two chambers is a two-way valve which controls the passage of fluid in either direction. In very simple terms what happens is that when a wheel moves up, so does the strut, and since nitrogen, unlike the fluid, is compressible, the movement is absorbed.

This is essentially how the early Mini and Allegro systems worked, though for a number of

Don Kettleborough was a key player in Project Phoenix. He is pictured here with a race/rally version of the car he and his colleagues developed after hours.

reasons - including the fact that neither had a robust subframe - they didn't work particularly well. The other shortcoming was that the Hydragas® units all acted on their own. In PR3, as on the latest Metros from which the system is derived, they are interconnected front to back. Now what happens is that if the front wheel is pushed up by a bump, fluid from the front Hydragas® unit is displaced down the pipe to the rear unit, pushing the rear wheel down so as to keep the car level. It gets better; if both wheels on the same side encounter a bump simultaneously, fluid is displaced into the upper spheres where it compresses the nitrogen. The big advantage of this refinement is that it controls bump and pitch, i.e. fore-and-aft movement.

Additional, conventional dampers regulate movement over small bumps, which allows the spring rate to be backed off to improve ride further, while the front and rear anti-roll bars control body movement, especially during high-speed cornering or lane-changing manoeuvres.

ADC had already built Sim1 back in 1991, to test out Phoenix's

theory in very general terms, but by the time Kettleborough and his team became involved the simulator programme had moved on. Sim2 was built in March 1992, with Sim3 following shortly afterwards.

Whereas Sim1 had been a highly modified Metro, Sim2 was more like a pick-up, but with a clip-on rear section to make it look like a van. In fact, to try and disguise it further from the prying lenses of scoop photographers (not entirely successfully, as the May 1992 issue of Car revealed), a set of detachable panels promoting a fictional

Car magazine was one of the first publications to to break pictures of the MG prototype with shots of the RTC 'pizza' van.

pizza delivery service were made for the simulators. Both Sim2 and Sim3 had a lowered steering column and driver's seat to try and emulate what PR3's driving position would be while Sim3 had the longer wheelbase that had been defined because of the packaging problems encountered by Trevor Holdsworth's team.

When Turner and Cooper first got their hands on Sim1 in August 1991 they were unimpressed with its dynamic qualities. 'It had very poor steering and straight-line stability,' remembers Cooper. 'It felt as if it wanted to swap ends all the time and there was a very tail-heavy feeling to the car. The major problem we had throughout this time was the effect of lifting off the throttle in mid-bend which needed instant correction. We were very aware of that and the people who were likely to buy this car.'

The problems were caused not so much by the theory being wrong as by the way Sim1 had been built. For speed and cheapness a Metro subframe had simply been moved from the front to the rear of the car and grafted on. This had the effect of converting the Metro's anti-dive front suspension into pro-lift rear suspension, just what wasn't needed. The situation was further aggravated by the Hydragas® system not being interconnected.

'Over the next four or five months we did a lot of changes,' says Turner, 'and made some improvements, particularly in straight-line stability, by changing the geometry and putting some more damping up front, as well as getting more weight and feeling into the steering, but the lift-off oversteer was still present.'

There was a difference of opinion over whether or not the Hydragas® spheres should be interconnected, but Cooper and Turner eventually got their way. Linking them up led to an immediate reduction in pitching, as Cooper explains: 'Metro front-suspension geometry is designed to stop the car dipping under braking, so when you put it unmodified on the back it actually helps to lift it up, so we had to get rid of that. Nevertheless we persevered with it for four to five months, doing subtle changes and making some improvements. But it became clear we were going to have to do something radical to the rear suspension to achieve the level of performance we were after.'

The ride and handling team also confirmed what had been found in early wind-tunnel testing, that the original rear-mounted radiator wasn't man enough to cool the engine - even the 1.4 - so a second radiator was jury-rigged to the front of Sim2. Apart from being more efficient, despite the pipe runs to and from the radiator and engine, it helped weight distribution, packaging

Greg Allport (left) was responsible for a lot of the early research surrounding PR3's market potential. Mike Ferguson joined the Project Phoenix team at a later date, taking over Allport's role.

and styling.

By this stage in MG's revival the marketing and commercial process was up and running. Announcing the MG RV8 and establishing a special telephone hot line had created a surge of interest in the marque and the car, with some 250 firm orders soon taken. There was also a degree of interest from a number of European markets, principally Belgium, Holland and Germany, but Rover were hoping that the bulk of sales would come from the UK.

Unfortunately, RV8 sales never took off quite as Rover might have hoped. The car was eventually unveiled at the London Motor Show in October 1992 and went on sale in spring of the following year, with the promised fifteen cars a week being built at Cowley. In the interim, though, the UK economy went into another tailspin and the hoped-for takers dried up, frightened at the thought of spending £26,500 on a 3000-4000 mile a year week-end plaything. The high price tag also pushed the car into TVR territory - both were Rover V8-powered, front-engined two-seaters - and led to inevitable comparisons.

While the RV8 was aimed at a limited number of buyers who probably wanted to relive their own times in an MGB, or wished they'd always had one, the media lined it up against a car targeted for younger buyers. TVRs aren't based on a 30+year-old chassis; almost to a man the specialist press accused the MG RV8 of being old-fashioned and overpriced, many even saying it handled no better than the last rubber-bumpered Bs, which was patently untrue.

In hindsight Rover will privately concede to making errors with the RV8. It should have been cheaper, to avoid the comparison with TVR, and the message that it wasn't a new MG should have been emphasised more strongly. 'We hoped we

Fiat beat MG to the market with its front-wheel-drive barchetta

would get across that it takes a macho sort of person to drive a TVR, it's not the sort of car you want to give your mistress for the week-end unless you want to see her biceps and triceps increase. The RV8 was a more sophisticated vehicle, that wouldn't be out of place in Park Lane...it was seen as more elegant, the TVR as more brutal. I think Rover tried very hard to get that message across, but people out there writing articles didn't listen to it,' said one insider.

Gordon Sked was never the RV8's biggest fan, believing that it was 'a very compromised product...an indulgence....that it didn't actually move the marque forward. I felt it wasn't good enough in any area and could, in fact, have knackered it for what was to come.'

In hindsight he thinks, 'There was a need to communicate that this was an additional vehicle, not part of the total MG plan...and basically to pinpoint precisely who the MG RV8 purchaser was. Because it was nothing to do with PR3, whose prospective buyer is not the guy who would go out and buy an MG RV8. Something along those lines was said, but it wasn't said strongly enough. Had it [PR3] been a year earlier or eighteen months, RV8 wouldn't have been needed.'

Thankfully, though, once the car made its début at that year's Tokyo Motor Show, the

Japanese loved it. The combination of the Octagon badge, veneer and Connolly trim in an updated B Roadster body shell finished in a contemporary British Racing Green was too much for them to resist and within weeks the order books were full.

Greg Allport was charged with the task of being Project Phoenix's brand manager after having handled the later stages of the RV8 programme. It was his job to establish if there was a market for an open two-seater sports car badged as an MG - the answer to which must have been obvious - and, if so, how many could be sold, where and at what price?

From being virtually non-existent before the MX5's arrival, the sports-car market was gradually expanding from about 1.5 per cent of total UK car sales in 1989, to double that in 1991. 'The market is heavily driven by new product coming into it, which grows the sector,' says Allport. Preliminary research also suggested that PR3 would win sales from other market sectors as well; the hot-hatch phenomenon had just about peaked in 1991 when insurance levels started to rise markedly, so there could be some transfer of allegiance from those owners; there were also potential sales to be accrued from the coupé market, then dominated by such products as the Vauxhall Calibra, Rover's own 200 Coupé and the

Honda CRX, as well as more marginal competitors such as the BMW 3-series Compact and Coupé and the Audi Coupé. Other rivals flagged by Allport were the cabriolet offerings based on the VW Golf, Peugeot 205, Vauxhall Astra, etc. He and his team were also keeping a weather eye on news of forthcoming rivals from Fiat, Alfa Romeo and, further down the line and at a higher price, Porsche, Mercedes-Benz and BMW.

The question remained, will the UK and European markets -principally identified by Allport as France, Germany and Italy - be able to absorb all the new product?

Fiat, when they launched the barchetta ahead of PR3 in 1995, forecast that the European sports-car market (segment H in marketing speak) would reach 205,000 - about 1.7 per cent of total new car sales -in 1995, with Germany taking about a quarter of the total. In those terms the limited MG production numbers Allport and his team were talking about account for less than 5 per cent of the European sports-car sector. Beyond Europe there was the Japanese market beckoning, and fringe sales in New Zealand, Australia, South Africa and the emerging Pacific-Rim nations.

Despite the confidence surrounding Allport's predictions, he also sounded a note of caution: 'MG branding is perhaps a mixed blessing. While on the one hand it will give the car many PR opportunities, the downside is that no car, no matter how good, can possibly live up to the current expectations. It is therefore important that all positioning is forward- rather than backward-looking, and that it concentrates on PR3 the product rather than the MG marque.'

This really was Rover's dilemma. The car had to appeal to that generation who had fond memories of MG and to a totally new car-buying public who either had no recollection of the marque or, even worse, had only negative recall from the last days of the rubber-bumpered Bs.

The matter was further complicated by how the car was perceived/remembered at home and abroad. Awareness levels varied greatly from market to market. In the UK a survey revealed that only 1 per cent of the general public had never heard of MG, compared with 47, 49, 54 and 38 per cent for France, Germany, Italy and Spain respectively. While 29 per cent of the British public admitted to 'knowing well' the marque, those figures dropped to 8, 3, 7 and 10 per cent for the countries listed above.

However, the Japanese awareness of, even obsession with, British heritage came through when a survey on unprompted awareness of open-topped cars placed MG third with 31.8 per cent behind Eunos (Mazda) at 61.4 and

Mercedes-Benz at 34.8.

To try and establish some guidelines as to how much 'MG-ness' the car should have, an 'MG Design Day' was held in March 1992 with 452 invited 'associates' (Rover-speak for employees). On display were ten MGs from different eras - TCs, TDs, As, Bs, etc. - as well as videos and old film footage of MG's heritage, all to the accompaniment of music going back to the 1950s and '60s. The one car that was absent was PR3 itself. What the Phoenix team were trying to establish was what styling cues should and shouldn't be included in the new car.

The idea for the day came from Graham Morris, who at that time was Rover's commercial director, in a conversation with Brian Griffin: 'What we decided to do, rather than get the board along as a group where they might gang up on us, we got them along one at a time. Not inviting them to change it, only to show them what we were doing. We got very, positive feelings from the likes of John Towers, George Simpson, Graham Morris and Kevin Morley, which is how the idea for the MG Day arose. Graham Morris said the one thing we'd better do is make sure we haven't missed any MG cues or all the MG enthusiasts around the world would criticise us for it.'

It took Griffin and his team about three

weeks to filter down all questionnaires, but in the end they arrived at a series of guidelines which

CUE	ADOPTION
Distinctive exhaust	*yes*
MG Grille	*vestigial*
Sports filler cap	*yes*
Wire wheels	*no*
Bonnet badge on shield	*yes*
No model badges	*yes*
Cream and brown badge	*yes*
No Rover logo on key	*yes*
MG on instruments	*yes*
Treadplate badge	*yes*
Ivory instruments	*yes*
Sports gear knob	*yes*
MG steering wheel	*yes*
Interior chrome	*yes*

could be incorporated into the style that Gerry McGovern's team was evolving:

'One of the things that came out really strongly,' says Griffin, 'was that MGs didn't have badges other than the marque badge. They didn't have loads of words written on them that said it's this model or that, and one of the things that came out was that we weren't going to put a name badge on the car. Other details that were deemed important were items like the ivory

dials, the style of the seats, the shield mount on the bonnet which in turn forced us to look at the colours in the badge itself.'

Over the years the Octagon's ivory background and rust-red lettering had been watered down, so it was now redesigned to distance it from the Metro/Maestro/Montego days and lend just a hint of classic nostalgia.

The Canley design studio had also by this time finalised the interior concept. As with the exterior, the styling team took its initial cues from EX-E, as McGovern explains: 'We wanted the interior to reflect a feeling of security and felt

Early renderings for the interior show a far more radical treatment than the one eventually settled on.

This clay model clearly shows the 'bird-bath' in front of the passenger and the sill bins which were later abandoned.

With an open car, the interior styling is as much part of the vehicle's total architecture as the exterior.

very strongly there should be a robust-looking fascia, solid A pillars and header combined with a rising waistline so that people felt cocooned in the vehicle's dual cockpit. In turn that promotes interaction between the driver and the controls.'

Although the theory is that exterior and interior styling run in parallel, the reality is that interior is always a tad behind, according to McGovern: 'In the past we had separate studios for interior and exterior, but this time we had the same group looking after both. So the interior was led by the exterior on the rising waistline and the substantial screen surround came from the wish to use a high-tensile steel frame to give the car more torsional rigidity. I thought it'd be very heavy, but it gives the car a feeling of integrity.'

Again, ADC did some of the early concept work on the interior, but for McGovern it was 'too Alien, too Star Wars - we wanted an element of heritage.' So they had to start again.

Whereas EX-E incorporates heavily stylised octagon shapes for its interior, these are absent in PR3, although the feeling of sitting in twin cockpits with the transmission tunnel separating the passenger and driver survives. 'PR3 takes some of EX-E's elements and brings them into a more modern era which is more sculpted and softer,' says McGovern.

Originally, the deep one-piece fascia had

what McGovern describes as a 'birdbath' facing the passenger, scooped out of the upper surface. The idea behind it was to avoid producing 'handed' fascias for left-and right-hand drive markets. All that would be needed was for the instrument binnacle to be transferred to the left when required. However, the realisation that many customers would expect the car to have both driver and passenger airbags meant the 'birdbath' would have to be filled in and used to house the safety device.

The cascading central binnacle is also an update of an EX-E theme, with overtones of mid-60's Corvette, perhaps, although at first it was too wide, which narrowed the seat squabs. The seat frames themselves are a carry-over Rover item, but the use of piping and the pleated inserts are throwbacks to MGB days. Early days PR3's interior buck also had Rover 200 grab-handles on the doors and Rover 800 storage bins on the inner sills, ideally located for storing the inevitable detritus that gathers in a car, as a substitute for door pockets.

As with the rest of the car, there are a number of carry-over items from other Rover-Honda products - Honda Civic stalks, modified -cream, red and black - instrumentation from the Rover 200 and odd switchgear from the 800 and 200 ranges. With all this input from earlier cars, it is

a tribute to the expertise of the styling team that PR3 doesn't look in the least bit cobbled together.

It would have been easy to festoon the interior with MG badges and Octagons - Graham Morris's attempts to inflict MG Octagon material on the seating were stoutly rebuffed by McGovern - so there are logos on the speedometer, tachometer and steering wheel, and, controversially, moulded into the top of the dashboard. McGovern says that it is there to indicate that the car has a unique fascia moulding which, because they are notoriously expensive to produce, many manufacturers are too eager to carry over from one model to another. But it also helps identify the car when people walk by and look down through the windscreen and, whether McGovern realised it at the time or not, continues a theme established on the MG Metro, Maestro and Montego.

Car interiors are particularly difficult to create when they're part of a convertible. In a closed saloon, they are seen by no one but the occupants. But when the hood is folded back, the interior becomes open to view for one to view, becoming just as important visually as any part of the exterior.

Both Sked and McGovern have voiced some reservations about the interior's final looks. 'I wished we had kept some of the quirkier touches,' says Sked, with McGovern expanding on his comments: 'Originally we had more retro cues, brightwork on the heater controls, on top of the gearshift knob, the ashtray and hand-brake button. But a number of issues reversed the decision; the trim engineers had problems keeping a chromed insert in place on top of the gear knob and marketing said they weren't getting the right message through from clinics.

'Gordon and I look back on that with regret. You fight battles to protect design all the way through. Sometimes with certain issues you have to prioritise or let go or accept you'll not always get your own way. I was torn. It would have been nice to have the details, but I suppose in the final analysis they were superfluous.'

If, at a later stage in the programme, the marketing department became nervous about the brightwork, then it was adamant from very early on that power steering must be included in the specifications. A leading campaigner for this was Rover's Japanese subsidiary, who made it plain there was no option - it had to be fitted. Philip Turner and John Cooper weren't at all convinced - after all, the car had a light front end and it was a sports car - but marketing were determined. 'Look where our customers are coming from,' they argued, 'hot hatches, cabrios,

coupés and GTis and, at the top end of their product ranges, power steering is the norm. If it isn't available, a lot of people won't even consider the car.'

Which was all very well and good for marketing to demand, but engineering had to deliver. A conventional, hydraulic system had immediate drawbacks in that the pump would be a constant drain on engine power, even with the car cruising on a motorway with minimum steering inputs. It would also require a convoluted pipe run with lots of joints, leading to possible concerns about reliability, and could even demand a pressure reservoir at the front of the car.

The first solution was a park-assist steering system that would make the car easy to park and then disappear altogether once it reached a set speed, but that didn't satisfy anyone. An earlier experiment on a Metro had involved a conventional, hydraulic rack powered from a remote accumulator which was pressurised by a pump driven by an electric motor. Although it worked well the cost of modifying the Metro's subframe and the difficulty of packaging the whole system led the chassis department to consider an electrical system.

This wasn't Rover's first dalliance with an electrical power-assisted steering system (EPAS)

greatest assistance during parking and low-speed manoeuvring and gradually tails off so that by about 60mph the electric motor is practically idling. Unlike hydraulic systems there's no pump whine or characteristic hiss when parking; it doesn't rob the engine of any power and is therefore more energy-efficient.

It might have been feasible to test this sort of technology on the early simulators, but the Project Phoenix team were still taxed with the difficulty of putting some real road miles on the engines and transmissions that would eventually power the car. Don Kettleborough's Metro hybrid simulators were good up to a point, but they were hardly roadworthy. They spent most of their working life within the confines of Rover's own Gaydon test track or at the Motor Industry Research Association facility at Nuneaton, and there's only so much that can be learned from a test track. The searching questions are answered out on the open road in everyday motoring conditions. The problem for the Project Phoenix team was that the programme hadn't been signed off to build prototypes, which they couldn't do anyway since the styling buck had yet to be digitised. So, how were the team to know if the K-series power train could survive a mid-engined application? Fortunately, a rival manufacturer had just the answer.

Left and right: *Still with the 'birdbath' clearly visible, this finished clay has sporting and classic MG cues, such as the chromed gear-lever knob and ashtray, which were eventually abandoned. It lacks, though, the cream and rust red instrumentation.*

- remember the EX-E? - but wasn't fitting it to a mid-engined two-seater diluting the intimate relationship between man and machine? No, all Rover was doing was following in the wheeltracks of Mazda, Fiat and Alfa Romeo which all have power steering fitted to their two-seaters, never mind thoroughbreds like Honda's NSX.

Additionally, as the ride and handling team discovered, there are benefits in that power steering allows wider tyres to be used and the suspension to be tuned for optimal handling and steering without drivers needing to develop Schwarzenegger-like biceps. EPAS gives the

15

Toyota had launched its original mid-engined MR2. Its most attractive feature to Rover was the power-train location; as well as being approximately the same size as PR3. What better home, then, to act as a host for testing out the K-series power train in real-life conditions?

There's a Toyota specialist somewhere in the Midlands who must be slightly puzzled by one man's obsession with blue MR2s. Within the space of about six months John Doyle, PR3's project manager, purchased four MR2's. The purchases were made 'through a friend of a friend' and must have upset Rover's accounts department no end, as Doyle had to buy them on a personal cheque: 'We couldn't hand over cheques for X thousands signed on behalf of the Rover Group, as that would give the game away. A personal cheque was the only way we could do it, company security insisted.'

Originally the plan was to install PR3's rear subframe assembly and engine in the MR2s, but because of major differences in body structures and the extra weight that idea was abandoned and the power trains were simply bolted to fabricated mountings, with appropriately modified drive shafts and exhaust systems fitted. Even the standard Toyota cooling arrangement was retained.

An added bonus on a project with PR3's financial constraints was the MR2's low cost. Doyle reckons each car cost about £7-8000, 'which is damn cheap for a prototype', and by the time it was converted, £20,000.

Doyle takes up the saga: 'The idea was to use them every day. Emissions, for example, could use them and develop the engine tune in real-life situations. So they were driven as a normal owner would; cold starts in the morning, short drives down to the shops to pick up a paper, all that sort of thing.' Furthermore, the MR2s allowed the Phoenix team to work on the power-train's drivability to reduce engine movement and driveline shunt and start development of the gearchange mechanism.

When originally conceived the K-series' capacity wouldn't stretch beyond 1.6-litres, but some clever lateral thinking within Rover's Advanced Power Train Division, led, incidentally, by Nick Stephenson's brother, Alex, meant a bigger capacity and more power could be achieved.

Increasing the engine from 1.4 to 1.6 litres entailed the relatively simple task of enlarging the bore diameter from 75mm to 80mm, but this couldn't be achieved by retaining the original wet cylinder liner. Instead, a stepped 'damp' liner was developed, combining a wet liner at the top where the greatest cooling is required and a dry liner in the bottom portion of the cylinder. A new crankshaft was designed to increase the stroke from 79mm to 89.3mm with modifications to the main bearing ladder casting to provide the necessary clearance.

Unlike the original 1.4-litre K series, which has simultaneous operation of all four injectors, the 1.8 has grouped fuel injection with two pairs of injectors operated alternately controlled by Rover's own Modular Engine Management System, which was specially upgraded for the engine.

Other improvements include ultra-light-

The ingenious wet and damp (right) liners developed for the 1.8 K series.

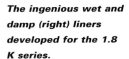

weight pistons weighing less than 7oz each, a new dry ignition coil mounted directly to the engine, a smaller and quieter alternator and an advanced plastic inlet manifold and throttle body.

Although a generation apart, the K-series engine shares virtually the same bore/stroke dimensions of the original B series - 80.26mm x 88.9mm for the B and 80mm x 89.3mm for the K - although the power outputs are very different: the original twin-carburettor B produced 94bhp at 5500rpm and 107lb ft torque at 3500rpm, while the DOHC K series develops 118bhp at 5500rpm and 122lb ft at 3000rpm.

Originally tagged as 'variable valve timing' but rechristened Variable Valve Control in time for its launch, this was a new multi-cam version of the K-series engine that boosted power to 143bhp at a heady 7000rpm and 128lb ft at 4500rpm.

Under the code-name 'Hawk', Rover had started looking at variable valve timing in the late 1980s, during the course of which they came across a lapsed patent once held by the piston-makers AE, which they thought worthy of development.

Variable valve timing isn't new; Honda's VTEC system, which switches between two inlet-cam profiles at a predetermined engine speed, was the first on the market, but has been followed by BMW's VANOS technology, which employs cam phasing, and Fiat's timing variator, which advances and retards inlet valve opening. All have been developed to increase power at high engine speeds and torque at low and mid-range rpm without affecting fuel efficiency and emissions. Despite the effectiveness of these systems they all suffer from the same shortcoming in that they only operate from a given, preset engine speed. Rover wanted to go one better and develop variable valve timing that worked over the complete rev range - the difference, if you like, between an electric light on/off switch and a dimmer control.

The K-series 1.8 VVC has been described as the world's first five camshaft engine and its effectiveness is down to detailed development work by Peter Parker and the availability of an advanced micro-processor engine-management system. Effectively each cylinder has its own inlet cam. Looking at the engine from the front there is a cam operating number one cylinder's inlet valves (8); running through the centre of that camshaft is an independent shaft which operates a camshaft acting on the second cylinder's two inlet valves (9) &

(10). The inlet cams themselves are driven at half crankshaft speed by a toothed rubber belt (11). A gear-driven rod runs the length of the engine and its action is turned through 360 degrees so that the inlet valves on cylinders three and four can be activated (6).

An uprated engine management system, MEMS 2J, controls a pair of solenoids (1) & (2) which activate a small hydraulic piston (3) linked to a miniature rack-and-pinion(4) that is meshed

Affectionately known as the 'Very, Very Complicated' engine, the VVC produces a seamless stream of torque and power through the rev range.

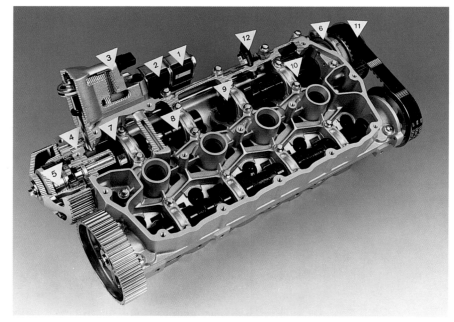

on to the control shaft. According to signals from the black box, the hydraulic piston moves up and down. This in turn rotates the control shaft one way or the other (5). The control shaft is geared into a drive disc (3) that is eccentrically mounted from the camshaft; within that drive disc are a pair of guide blocks that move up and down a slot and transmit power to the camshaft itself.

As the hydraulic piston moves up and down, it activates the rack and pinion against the control shaft which acts against the drive disc; because that is mounted off-centre the rotational speed of the guide blocks varies and, because they power the camshafts, so the turning speed of the cam alters.

The VVC provides infinite variation of the inlet-cam period between 220 and 295 degrees with a constant lift of 9.5mm. The corresponding variation of inlet/exhaust valve lap is between 21 and 58 degrees. When this is combined with bigger valves - inlets are up from 27.3mm to 31.3mm and exhausts from 24 to 27.3mm - it means that above 4000rpm the inlet valves are held open for longer, which allows the engine to breathe more freely and produce more power. It's not difficult to see why even Nick Stephenson refers to it affectionately as the 'Very, Very Complicated' engine.

The MEMS 2J black box also controls full sequential fuel injection with adaptive control and a distributorless direct-ignition system with one coil per cylinder.

PR3's mid-engined location also meant that Rover would have to overcome the problem of mounting the transmission and producing an effective gear linkage that would equal the MX5's; this had, after all, been identified as a core value for the car.

Originally the R65 transmission was going be used with the smaller - 1.4- and 1.6-litre - engines, but as the power outputs grew they quickly outstripped the 'box's 109lb ft torque capacity. Derek Jones, who didn't actually join Project Phoenix until later in the programme, paints in the background details: 'The early prototypes were built with R65 gearboxes in mind, but it soon became obvious that we'd have to use a more robust transmission, so we decided to adapt the PG1 'box.'

PG1 is a higher torque capacity - 160lb ft - Honda gearbox that Rover manufactures under licence and has used in diesels as well as the

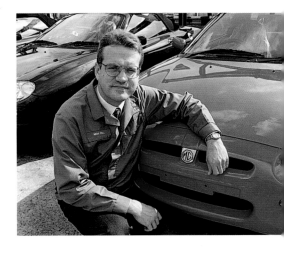

Nick Fell, who led the Phoenix project team after Brian Griffin's early work.

Montego and some Rover 800 applications. 'The difference was,' says Jones, 'that we never had any experience of rear-wheel-drive cars because, obviously, it's the first K-series PG1 application as well as the first time this combination has been used in a rear-wheel-drive car. Also, PG1 was always designed for rod actuation, not for cables, so we had to design a new cable linkage that went over the top of the engine. Not only that, but a new bell housing had to be fabricated so it would mate with the K series.'

Installing a cable change on the R65 prototypes wasn't that much of problem since its linkage faces forward and it was relatively easy to route, but the PG1's linkage had to go over the top of the engine, which meant fabricating a cantilever mechanism that reversed all the inputs from the gear stick. This caused all sorts of reliability headaches in those early days as Andy Bailey, the emissions team leader, discovered driving an MR2 from his home on the outskirts of Birmingham to the Gaydon test centre in the dead of night: the linkage failed and jammed the 'box in fourth. Despite that - and despite all the roundabouts and traffic lights - Bailey completed the journey safely, which at least goes to highlight the 1.8's flexibility.

During their working life the MR2s proved invaluable to the Phoenix team, but they had their shortcomings: their different architecture meant the team couldn't assess what underfloor or underbonnet temperatures would be like in a PR3, never mind how the gear linkage would operate.

It was getting to that stage in the programme where some big decisions had to be made. For the likes of Nick Boneham, Brian Griffin and John Doyle, 1992 was proving to be a nervous year. Not only were they trying to develop a new generation of MG that would see the marque's rebirth, but they were doing so against the backdrop of a deep recession. Nick Boneham recalls the steep learning curve they all went through: 'We spent the first six to eight months going through all the opportunities for a funding route...discussions with the City to find capital, etc. And then in March-April time we pulled together a strategy - a quotation to tender for the whole programme was put out to seven or eight companies. We went about it in finite detail, the only parameter we were working to was for someone to come in to at least part-fund the programme, what they wanted out of it and what they could contribute to it was left open for them to tell us.' This had the important benefit that Boneham and his colleagues could pick things out of the tenders, forming their own opinions of the best route forward and assessing each of the options.

The team had done their sums and decided against getting a third party to build the car on Rover's behalf. They had also discarded the idea of trying to raise funds from the City. What was needed, they had decided, was a limited partnership which would allow Rover to concentrate their human and fiscal resources on developing and, hopefully, assembling the car, while a third party provided expertise of another sort and, possibly, financial assistance too.

Nick Stephenson remembers that summer well: 'We modelled virtually every way of financing the project and then tested them both in theory and practice. Theoretically we might have been able to find a merchant bank who wanted to back it, but then in practice we had to find one and make things happen. We used a degree of theoretical best fit and then pragmatism as to the various organisations we'd go and talk to, to see how it would come together. A measure of enthusiasm for the project was going to be the key. Finding a partner whose eyes lit up and said, "Wow, we want to be involved." We knew it was going to be tough to deliver, these programmes always are.'

Pininfarina were already developing the hood mechanism for the car, so why not take it one step further and get a coachbuilder to fund and assemble the bodyshells?

Eventually the selection process whittled the choice down to three and, although Rover are reluctant to talk about them, they were Italy's Pininfarina, Germany's Karmann and Coventry's Motor Panels. For John Towers the final decision 'boiled down to two issues: one, this was going to be complicated enough without having the added geographical complexity and, secondly, if we could create the revenue and added value within the UK - which happens to be the most important economy from a selling point of view - then all the better.

'The issues of building an MG abroad were debated, but not considered seriously. At the end when the emotion was sieved through and the objectives sieved through, our business sense was that we had the same marketing potential irrespective of whether we pressed and welded the panels together somewhere else or in the UK.'

'There were quite a number of organisations that on the enthusiasm scale scored quite heavily and, indeed, the final decision came to two organisations,' recalls Stephenson, who goes on to say that it was a tough decision and finely balanced, 'because they had both presented very strong cases. Both had the enthusiasm factor.

'It was hard breaking the news to the losing party. There were two right down to wire. Both

Project Phoenix finally gets the go-ahead from Rover's main board. Here the finished styling model is on view in the design department's outdoor viewing area.

had strong merits, different characteristics and we could have probably achieved the car with either of them. I am pleased to say there's no bad blood and we'd happily work with them in the future.'

'Them' is rumoured to have been Turin-based Pininfarina, considerably further away from Rover than the successful candidate, Motor Panels, just half an hour down the A45 from Longbridge.

Rover and Motor Panels already had a relationship: the Coventry company produces major components for both the Land Rover Discovery and Defender ranges and the Rover 200 Coupé. Established for seventy-five years, Motor Panels has a portfolio of clients which includes some of the most illustrious names in the British motor industry, among them Rolls-Royce, Jaguar and Aston Martin, so the new MG would be in good company. In winning the contract Motor Panels had really come full circle - it had built the front-wheel-drive Maestro-based PR1 prototype for Rover Special Products when Project Phoenix was initiated.

Hugh McKenzie, Motor Panels' sales and marketing director, was intimately involved in the negotiations: 'After building that prototype we heard nothing for two years, until Brian Griffin and John Doyle visited us in April '92.

They told us about Project Phoenix, explained their requirements and asked if we could respond to their needs. To put it crudely, the country was in a deep recession and Rover's funding and resources were geared to their core products and they didn't have the ability to fund non-core products, even though they really wanted to revive MG.

'Brian and John's task was to find any avenues that would help get the programme launched. They were being extremely creative about ways that might be achieved and said they were looking for a partner. They even raised the issue of us building the car for them.'

Once Motor Panels had reviewed the situation they concluded that they couldn't fund the programme and that their expertise lay not in vehicle assembly, but in body-in-white production.

Meetings continued throughout the summer months, but negotiations proceeded slowly, as McKenzie explains: 'We proposed a route whereby we part-funded the body-in-white programme and Rover made the car. Although that was quite a good plan, from a Rover point of view it wasn't - they needed the programme funding from outside. We were getting closer, but there was still a big gap.'

October proved to be a crucial month for the

discussions: Terry Whitmore joined Motor Panels as chief executive of its automotive division. Whitmore had previously run Rover's Cowley operation and in McKenzie's words added fresh impetus into the programme: 'He believed it was a great opportunity to develop Motor Panels, he thought it was a great product and was able to act as a catalyst to bring everyone together to get a solution.'

Over the coming weeks the austere-looking Posthouse hotel on the A45, where most the discussions took place, was host to many late-night sessions as the two sides negotiated and argued, with the deal almost falling apart on more than one occasion as one side or the other dug in its heels.

'The idea of Motor Panels building the car had been abandoned, it had to be a Rover Car company programme, so it all added up to whether we could stretch ourselves on funding,' explains McKenzie. 'Our parent, Mayflower, supported the project, but there wasn't a drawer full of money we could call on. It was more a question of raising lots of money - how much would the deal cost, how much could we raise? There was also the profit-share element - there's no point in spending money and risking things if you can't make a reasonable profit out of it.'

By December a heads of agreement docu-ment had been signed; Motor Panels had agreed to find £25 million to finance PR3's body-in-white development and production.

For John Doyle there seemed to be a natural synergy in the deal: 'The nature of the collaboration was such that we were taking a discrete part of the programme, the body, out of it. You could take the body and say, "There we are, in conjunction with Rover Body and Pressings, who did the production tooling, you will produce the body and we'll go on from that."'

That December proved to be a pivotal month for PR3. Not only did the Motor Panels deal come together, but on the 22nd Don Kettleborough got an early Christmas present: 'Sim7 was built especially for the rear-end barrier tests, as there were concerns about having a fuel tank sandwiched between the rear engine and the passenger compartment. Sim7 was based on a Metro front end and half a floor with a very early hand-built PR3 rear end welded to it. It was crash-tested at MIRA just prior to Christmas with great success.'

But the best news of all came when the Rover board gave the go-ahead for Project Phoenix to move into the final pre-production and development phase. Now it seemed that only an unforeseen disaster would prevent MG's rebirth.

16

British Motors plc were reeling under the cudgel throughout 1992, so Rover's decision to continue with the MG project was particularly brave.

Hidden within the doom and gloom, though, were occasional glimpses of hope and recovery. The leisure 4x4 market was still strong and Land Rover enjoyed its best sales year since 1948 with Discovery sales up almost 25 per cent to 10,427; while the Rover 800 had a mini-boom all of its own with a 19 per cent sales increase to 28,500.

But overall it looked as if 1992's total new car registrations wouldn't equal the previous year's. That is, until December, when the Rover 200 topped the sales chart with 7415, the first time a Rover product had headed the list for eight years. What is more Rover as a group sold a huge 67 per cent more cars in December 1992 than it had managed twelve months previously. Enough to edge the UK's new car sales 0.08 per cent over 1991's total, to 1,593,601.

When it came to adding up the Rover Group's bank balance for the preceding twelve months it wasn't good news. Despite the success of the Discovery and 800, Rover still lost £49 million in 1992, £3 million less than the previous year, but that was on sales of 405,000 - a decrease of 15,000 over 1991.

It is little wonder, then, that speculators were questioning Rover's long-term future within BAe. The aerospace giant had picked up Rover for a trifling £150 million back in August 1988, a deal made all the sweeter by some surreptitious inducements from the government equivalent to about three times the purchase price. What made the analysts and pundits particularly nervy about the BAe-Rover relationship was a stipulation that BAe would have to hand some of that money back if it sold Rover within five years.

The end of that five-year period was looming in 1993 and BAe was looking none too healthy itself. Its military and commercial aircraft sector was in a mess. What is more, its property company, Arlington, which had gained handsomely from disposing of many of Rover's land assets, was in a pickle and so was Rover. The car company still had a voracious appetite for cash - £300-500 million a year to invest in new models.

Would BAe keep its nerve, and faith, with Rover or would it cut and run?

Most observers thought it would hold on. It was reckoned that BAe would bide its time waiting for economies to pick up and car sales to

Honing the car's aerodynamics was done on a full-size model at the MIRA wind tunnel.

climb. Since the Michael Edwardes era, Graham Day and George Simpson had transformed Rover into a much leaner, low-cost production facility. Those qualities might prove very tempting for a producer from a high-cost manufacturing country such as Japan or Germany. No, Rover was safe - for the time being.

Over at Canley, Gerry McGovern's styling team were putting the final touches to the car's exterior surface and including any modifications demanded by wind-tunnel developments or experiences gained while testing. The most significant of these was the addition of louvres on the rear deck. Originally McGovern had envisaged a narrow vent with the warm air being drawn along the top of the boot and out through a slot in its leading edge. Visually it showed allegiance to the EX-E's rear wing, but there was insufficient aerodynamic pressure to draw the air out. As a result the warm oily-perfumed air tumbled back into the cockpit. A number of solutions were attempted on the wind-tunnel buck, including a suggestion by Trevor Haynes, principal engineer aerodynamics, for a pair of corner vents in the rear haunches. Efficient though they were, the body-in-white engineers couldn't accommodate them and the boot hinges, while the vents also upset the car's sensitivity to yaw, especially with the hood in place. The possibility of locating extractors in the rear wheel arches was also investigated and though feasible, the pressure was too high to draw out all the hot air from around the engine successfully. Haynes and his team even went to the trouble of fixing a perspex engine cover on the buck and putting traditional wool tufts on the engine so that they could study air movement around the engine bay while the car was in the wind tunnel to ensure the final solution was effective.

Ever since Audi launched the trend-setting 100 saloon in 1983 with its slippery 0.30 Cd, manufacturers have paid more attention to their cars' aerodynamic tuning and stability. Although some fuel economy is gained from a clean aerodynamic shape and minimal frontal area, it is only apparent when the car is moving at a reasonable speed. Refined aerodynamic balance and contours make cars quieter, with reduced wind noise and buffeting; they also help to keep the glass clean and assist stability. Every motorist must have noticed their car being buffeted by side winds as they pass a lorry or emerge from a motorway cutting. In extreme circumstances this can upset a car's balance and force the driver to make steering corrections to counter the yawing effect.

Usually aerodynamic fettling starts early on with one-fifth scale models but, because the Phoenix project was so time-restrained, Trevor Haynes and his colleagues were presented with a fait accompli and had to do most of their work on a style that was already signed off. Unless there was something disastrously wrong with the car, all they could hope to do was fine-tune it and hone detail areas.

A smoke lance is used to determine that fumes from the engine are vented away from the passengers.

Initial doubts that the side vents wouldn't provide sufficient cooling proved unfounded.

Fortunately for Haynes PR3 turned out to be a well-balanced car once it was put in the wind tunnel. The longer rear deck helped to pull the fumes away from the cockpit and the boot's abrupt trailing edge reduced lift at the back. But that isn't to say there weren't any concerns.

Initially, however, there were doubts as to whether the side intakes would feed enough cooling air into the engine bay, especially as that on the left is practically blanked off by the fuel tank, but these fears were quickly discounted. There were also some early concerns about front lift, as Haynes elaborates: 'We flagged up there was quite high front lift, although rear lift was good and, together with the rear-biased weight distribution, there might be a problem.'

The cooling team were also concerned there might not be enough through-flow of cold air to

the front-mounted radiator to keep engine temperatures down. This led to a small bib spoiler being added to the underside of the car at the front to direct more air through the radiator. Like so many aerodynamic cures it had an added bonus as the bib helped reduce front lift and gave the car additional stability during cornering by reducing oversteer.

If there is one major concern to all manufacturers these days it is safety and protecting a car's occupants in a crash. Globally, legislators are imposing more rules and regulations on producers for frontal impact, rear impact, side impact, roll-over protection, seat belts, airbags, interior safety, low-speed accidents, pedestrian safety. The list of demands is, seemingly, never-ending. Though the pursuit of reducing accident injury and death is one that should be followed vigorously, the manufacturers' task isn't made easier by local governments. What the USA - never mind California, which often goes out on its own - might demand is usually different from what Europe wants, which is different again from Japan. There are few global standards and to make matters even more complicated there are often national demands created by peculiar local conditions. Furthermore, manufacturers need an ability to see into the future so they can predict what might become law during a car's life-

time. Safety has also become a marketing and sales issue -think Volvo - so, in some instances, manufacturers might include a safety-related feature or test not because the law demands it, but because it endows their products with a higher perceived safety level than those of their rivals.

This is the sort of background that any manufacturer has to contend with, but it's one that is made even more complicated when it comes to producing a sports car. Don't forget that it was Ralph Nader's 'Unsafe at any Speed', published in 1965, that eventually led to the rubber-bumpered MGB and effectively killed off sales of open-topped sports cars in the States.

Adding a small bib spoiler at the front greatly enhanced the car's stability during high-speed turns.

Little wonder, then, that the Project Phoenix team had been working on the car's crashability from day one. The extra elements required to make the car crashworthy have to be designed into its body structure right from the start.

One of the original targets the Phoenix team

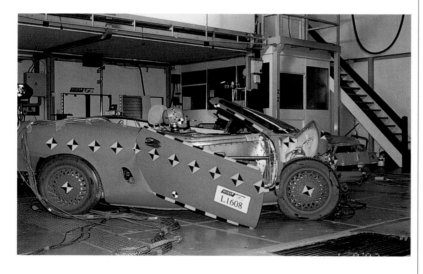

It's not as bad as it looks. The front section has deformed well and the windscreen and 'A' posts are virtually untouched.

set itself was to have an exceptionally rigid body shell, which is always a problem with a roofless car. A car's torsional rigidity, i.e. resistance to twisting along its axis, is vital for good handling as it means the chassis engineers know they have a solid platform to work from. They don't have to concern themselves with compensating for any

unnecessary and confusing inputs from a body shell that is flexing.

The other constant bugbear of convertibles is scuttle-shake, typified on those that have it by the fascia and instrumentation vibrating.

A car's roof plays a big role in helping to counteract these shortcomings - take that away and you immediately start to have problems. Without a roof bonding the two ends together, PR3 was about as structurally rigid as a pair of empty margarine tubs glued to either end of a playing card, while all the doors do, as long as they're shut, is prevent the whole assembly from folding in half. There is some lateral restraint from the windscreen surround which helps to tie the two sides of the car together, but not much.

Martin Abba, who was responsible for PR3's airbag and its safety systems, picks up the story: 'When we looked at some of our past models such as the Midget, Rover 100 and 200 Cabrios, we realised that in terms of body stiffness we'd got a range of vehicles that weren't particularly stiff. Our target competitor car was the MX5, that was considered our benchmark, and that has a torsional stiffness of around 6000 Newton metres (Nm) per degree, so that seemed like a sensible target.'

From that the team started looking at increasing the sill sections and introducing a boxed central tunnel. These features were built into the first crash prototype. 'The Pram' was essentially a roofless Metro with a modified rear incorporating an engine block, so the vehicle dynamics were similar. It was subjected to a 30mph full-frontal impact at MIRA in October 1992 and if it didn't pass with flying colours it created sufficient optimism for the team to know they were working in the right direction. At that time the car didn't have a front-mounted spare wheel and there was some toe-board intrusion, but nothing the team wasn't confident about curing.

From there they successfully moved on to Sim7, which was subjected to the North American Specification 30mph rear-end crash at the end of 1992. 'We were looking to examine what really happened in worst case conditions and, again, the initial results were very encouraging in as much as the engine bay remained fairly secure and there was no intrusion into the fuel-bay bulkhead area,' says Abba.

Although that simulator was doorless, Abba and his team fitted struts to replicate the load paths - only to discover that the crash pulses ended up pivoting the A post round the sill and folding them up, so stronger sills had to be engineered.

By this stage the programme was passing from the simulator phase into the 'D Zero' stage - the final engineering development countdown, prior to quality prove-out and the build-up to production.

Just to confuse matters, the first trio of D01 phase cars were classified as Sims 8, 9 and 10. These hand-made metal prototypes were built at Rover's Drews Lane plant, so for the first time PR3 looked like the real thing and not a glass-fibre buck. The first torsional stiffness tests on Sim8 produced figures of 7116 Nm per degree, well in excess of the target.

The team now had more representative cars which they could subject to the punishing durability testing all new products must go through, in addition to further impact testing and the chance for the ride and handling boys to see if the early work they had been doing would translate on to prototypes that were much closer to the real thing.

Now that Project Phoenix had received notional board approval, and there was a heads of terms agreement between Rover and Motor Panels, more personnel were coming on board. People like Steve Garrett, who was responsible for engineering the hood and hard top; David Lloyd, principal engineer for the console and bulkhead; and Nick Fell, who took over as project director.

Fell is unstinting in his praise for the work Brian Griffin and his team achieved with such severely restricted resources: 'It's important to understand that the project spent a long time in a kind of genesis until it got to board approval stage. Basically, Brian kept the project alive and kept the development of the concept going through to the end of '92, when we had something that looked like a business and technical proposition for the car.

'I was appointed then to see it from the approved stage through to project delivery. At that point we hadn't actually got as far as signing the agreement with Mayflower, but we had the heads of terms. So, my first task was making sure that we turned those heads of terms into a contractual agreement between Mayflower and the Rover Group.

'My second task was to run a so-called DO event which ratifies the commercial and technical feasibility of the project, so we know that the details stack up to deliver a commercial proposition.'

As Fell continued to negotiate with Mayflower, Garrett was beavering away with Pininfarina to make their hood work. Since they had originally been commissioned to develop the hood mechanism the Italians had been largely left to their own devices, so that by the time Garrett came on the scene they had engineered a beautifully neat folding hood with a lower stack height than anticipated. Unfortunately, when erected it wouldn't seal satisfactorily against PR3's rear deck.

The hood design, like that of the optional hard top, was done by Gerry McGovern's team while the body was being styled and is the reason why both look so homogeneous with the car.

The glass-fibre hard top fits snugly in place, transforming the car into a two-door coupé.

Many convertibles never look quite as good with the hood up or the hard top in situ; these elements tend to look like afterthoughts designed once the body has been signed off - which they usually are. But not in this instance. Sked and McGovern demanded that the car should look equally handsome with the hood up or down or with the hard top in place. While the lower-folding Pininfarina hood would have allowed Rover to engineer a rigid tonneau cover and have a flush rear deck, this was never in the game plan, according to McGovern: 'We wanted to keep the car simple, and having a solid tonneau cover complicates that. So would an electrically powered hood, as well as increasing costs.' Sked agrees, adding that 'a folding hood like PR3's means it's dead easy just to unclip it from the header rail and fling it back when the sun comes out and equally simple to erect when the weather clouds over.'

The tonneau cover was developed in conjunction with local specialists, Callow & Maddox, who with Steve Garrett developed a system that was secured in place without using the traditional press studs. 'I had my hands tied by the stylists,' says Garrett, 'because the first statement on our product design specification was "No exterior fittings".' A combination of press studs hidden in the door jamb and tensioned piano-wire beading that runs along the rear edge of the tonneau keeps it from coming loose and flapping about.

Development of the glass-fibre hard top didn't begin until the end of April, but as with so many aspects of this project Rover were working in the dark. It was so long since they, or anyone else, had offered a hard-top as an optional extra on an open two-seater that they had no real idea of what sort of customer take-up they were aiming for. In the end they decided on about 1300-1500 a year and then looked round for the most cost-effective supplier. There was some initial thought of making it from aluminium, but that was quickly rejected on grounds of cost, weight and the difficulty of pressing such a deep shape; they opted for glass fibre.

Express Plastics in Norfolk were eventually contracted to produce the hard tops. They used a combination of nickel-plated tooling to provide the glass-like finish and hand lay-up, but Garrett's problems had hardly started. The detachable roof had to be redrawn to match the moulders' capabilities, so that the top ended up with a single-piece outer shell and four smaller, inner mouldings. 'We couldn't and haven't compromised quality,' says Garrett. 'The hard top had to fit in the same location as the soft top, it had to be easy to plug in the heated rear window and there couldn't be any risk of misalignment between the windows and the hard top's seals.'

From Norfolk the part-finished shells were transported to Paint Box in Tipton, who spray-painted them, and then to Automotive Industries, who trimmed them out and put in the heated rear window and other components,

Sked and McGovern worked hard to blend the hard top into the car's overall profile.

before shipping them to Rover.

At one stage there nearly wasn't a roof at all. Each tool face has a 5-6mm layer of electro-plated nickel on it which takes about eight to ten weeks to build up. Each tool is immersed in a chemical bath with an electric current running through it that is constantly being agitated. Unfortunately Express Plastics suffered a power cut the week their back-up generator was being serviced, which caused the plating to delaminate. That lost them two weeks, but by working virtually twenty-four hours a day they managed to make up the lost time.

Although the roof weighs only 40lb, it would still be a bit tricky to install single-handed. However, once in place, thanks to its proper roof-lining, it makes the car feel as snug as a genuine coupé; the only thing driver and passenger might be aware of is a slight increase in engine noise.

One idea that was vetoed by the rest of the Phoenix team at this time was Nick Fell's suggestion that the MG Octagon logo be outlined in the heating elements.

Reliability is taken for granted with modern cars. Thanks to sophisticated design and development, exhaustive testing under the most arduous conditions and precise manufacturing and assembly techniques, contemporary cars last much, much longer than their forebears of even

fifteen years ago and with even less maintenance. This is especially so of engines, which now benefit from sophisticated, electronically controlled injection systems, synthetic oils and platinum spark plugs that don't need cleaning and require changing only every 66,000 miles. It won't be long before engines are truly 'sealed for life', although it might be some time before the customer accepts that philosophy. It was an argument which was used within the Project Phoenix team as they discussed service accessibility of the power unit.

By their very nature mid-engined cars are awkward to service, and so it is with PR3. There were some quite extreme suggestions about how to ease this problem, including a proposal that the whole rear end of the car be designed as one piece and hinge upwards from just behind the hood stowage area. Apart, says Dave Ovens, from the sheer weight of this body section and the difficulty of engineering sufficient structural rigidity, there was the problem of designing hidden hinges and developing sturdy enough supporting struts.

It was even proposed, and rapidly dismissed by the service engineers, that because the engines were so reliable there could be quick-release fixings to drop the power train out for major servicing. Eventually the current solution

was arrived at: (limited) engine access is via the boot lid which opens virtually all the way back to the hood stack. The boot compartment - large enough to take a couple of sets of golf clubs plus Gerry McGovern's sports kit-bag - is sealed off from the engine bay and there's a removable grille atop the power train.

The thorny question of where PR3 was going to be built still had to be resolved by Nick Boneham, but it all started to gel in March '93. When the Phoenix programme started nothing grander than a low-tech assembly process had been envisaged - anything more would start to increase investment to such an extent that PR3 wouldn't be viable. But by the time PR3 became a real programme and Motor Panels were on board, Rover were already producing niche cars like the 200 Cabriolet and Coupé, and Longbridge was about to undergo a massive revamp to accommodate the forthcoming 200 replacement.

Such limited run cars would disrupt the daily flow of mainstream production. The ideal solution would be a unique production line that could accommodate all three niche products. Longbridge had just such a facility that had been standing idle since the demise of the Honda Ballade project seven or eight years previously: Car Assembly Building 2 was available, if not

Engine accessibility is not one of the car's strong points.

ready and waiting.

But as Nick Boneham points out, 'It wasn't by luck. A lot of work had to go into making the bits of this jigsaw come together. We've been very inventive in finding new solutions, the whole senior team here at Longbridge rolled into the task of working out how we could produce three vehicles with the resources of two, but without cutting corners or compromising quality.'

Rover and Motor Panels might have signed an agreement at the end of 1992, but there was still plenty of serious detailing to go through before a final contract was signed in April. Hugh McKenzie says Rover were 'exceptionally open', sharing all the market and sales forecasts it had

gathered. They even went so far as to show the styling model to Motor Panels' key investors - 'unheard of in any industry', according to McKenzie.

Essentially the deal that was finally struck means that Motor Panels are purely involved in manufacturing PR3's bodywork and delivering them to Rover's accepted standards. They are also responsible for supplying the computer programmes from which Rover manufacture most of the tooling at Swindon, with the balance coming from the Japanese engineers Miyazu. Rover paint the body shells and do the final assembly of the cars.

On the strength of this, Mayflower went to the City and launched a rights issue which raised £35 million. Of this £24.2 million was invested in the Phoenix project for uprated manufacturing facilities and the tooling necessary to build upwards of 20,000 new MGs a year.

The news of that deal broke in the national press on 15 June 1993, confirming what many had suspected: that Rover were developing a new small MG. Even so, the company were being very coy about the whole subject, trotting out the usual line about 'not discussing future products'.

Not that that mattered to the MG enthusiasts. To them it was just a case of ticking off the months until MG's all-new sports car arrived.

17

Quality and reliability. Prime virtues that any car must have if it's to succeed. It doesn't matter a jot if a car has stunning styling, explosive performance and pin-sharp handling if it's not well built and isn't reliable in service.

It's a lesson that Western and American manufacturers learned the hard way from the Japanese. Japan's manufacturers might not have turned out some of the world's best-looking, best-handling or best-performing cars, but what they have consistently produced over the years is boringly reliable ones.

To compete successfully European manufacturers, had to raise the level of their game. For Rover it was perhaps easier, as they could learn directly from their partners, Honda, and adapt Japanese techniques to suit their own style. The exercise has patently worked, as Rover's build quality and reliability are equal to, and in many cases better than, their rivals.

Although Land Rover had engineered its own products without Honda's assistance, PR3 was going to be Rover's first all-new, independently created car since the 1984 Montego, so its engineering quality and durability had to be right. 'We'd got a bit dismayed,' recalls Nick Stephenson, 'that within the Honda products so far there was far more Rover engineering than we were ever given credit for. So it was important to get cars on the market that we could say were ours. It's an important statement of engineering in the UK, we've got superb engineers in the UK and it allows us to shout about them when we do cars like the MG.'

Talk to any member of the PR3 team and there's an overwhelming enthusiasm for the car, far beyond the emotion usually attached to a new product. Although most claim that this keenness is the same whether it's a new MG or an 'ordinary' Rover 200, they aren't wholly convincing. Every member of the team, now scattered throughout the Rover Group working on a myriad of new products, will continue to have a special affection for the time they spent on Project Phoenix. They were all aware of playing a small role in automotive history and that spurred them on, perhaps unwittingly, to ensure PR3's quality was 100 per cent, though they would claim that to be the case with all their programmes.

John Towers might hold a different view and attribute it to the way new car programmes are structured: 'The way we do programmes these days, long before we get anywhere near the production stages, there's a large amount of detail put to bed in terms of fundamental engineering, styling, systems, specifications. The way we front-load programmes now is very much the fastest and highest quality way to do it. The detail we put into that means the programme doesn't have to be running very long before it's put its stake in the ground.... It's this question of continuously focusing people's minds on the quality of the output, achieving value through that output; not just in the key areas of manufacturing, engineering and marketing, but whatever you do.'

Nowadays meticulous attention to detail throughout the design and engineering process by everyone involved, combined with improved lubricants, means that in many cases service intervals have quadrupled. Take, for instance, two generations of MG: the B required a visit to the garage every 3000 miles for an oil and filter change at the very minimum - that's without the recommended weekly/250 mile lube check. A ritual that demanded that the owner scrabble around under the car with grease gun primed ready to lubricate all those swarf-encrusted grease nipples.

Thirty years on and as a PR3 owner you'll never need to own a grease gun and servicing is required only every 12,000 miles. For the average driver, that translates to a couple of hours in the MG dealership about once a year.

Such quality and reliability isn't achieved overnight. It takes years of radical changes in the employees' attitudes - from the CEO downwards; huge investment in new manufacturing technology and minute attention to detail in the design, development and production processes. Despite all of that it also takes plenty of testing - rig-testing in laboratories and thousands of miles of punishing driving. Not just pounding around secret facilities like Rover's own at Gaydon, but also the high-speed bowl at Nardo in southern Italy. Testing in the most extreme climatic conditions, from the frozen wastes of the Arctic Circle to the searing badlands of Arizona via the dizzying alpine routes of the Stelvio Pass. As well as midnight forays on to deserted public roads in prototypes swathed in disguises.

It would be physically impossible to replicate a car's real life cycle. Just imagine how long it would take to imitate faithfully a car's 100,000-mile life and the different types of usage and abusage cars are put through.

To make testing quicker, easier and less costly, manufacturers put their products through approval programmes. Even then, they will differ according to the model involved. So, for instance, within Rover, Land Rover has its own test routines demanded by the 4x4 ability of their vehicles, test programmes that would be wholly inappropriate for a Rover 200 (even if 95 per cent of all Discoveries and Range Rovers are owned by Fulham farmers whose idea of off-roading is putting two wheels on the kerb). However, the 200's validation programme would be more relevant to PR3.

The testing obviously starts right at the very beginning of a car's life and continues through to its launch and beyond. All the components go through constant updating until they meet the specifications the development team has laid down for them. So, in the early days of Project Phoenix, the Toyota MR2 mules were used to validate the power-train package and help the electronics engineers map the Modular Electronic Management System for optimum performance while meeting the various emission regulations and other restrictions such as pass-by noise. It was during the MR2 testing period that the engine was upgraded from 1.6 to 1.8 litres and the gearbox specification changed.

But once the prototypes had reached the later stages of the Simulator phase and were maturing into the DO programmes, the product validation became more intense in its nature. Durability cars were pounding around the Gaydon test track, undergoing Rover's G11 structural tests. It might be only 6800 actual road miles over varying surfaces, but it is such a punishing routine that by the time it's completed the body and chassis have been subjected to the equivalent of 75,000 road miles.

At the same time another DO car was undergoing the most arduous test of all - Belgian Pavé. In the old days test drivers would have to subject themselves to days on end driving cars over these bone-shaking cobbles. Nowadays a chassis is mounted on to a computer-controlled electro-servo hydraulic rig that is programmed to simulate what a car goes through over these tortuous surfaces so that at the end of just 1000 miles, the chassis and body have been subjected the equivalent of a hundred times that mileage.

Rig testing has a number of advantages over more traditional types of endurance tests. For a start they are cheaper and take less time - ten to twelve days compared to three to five weeks - and, because they are computer simulated, they are exactly repeatable time after time. Neither are they influenced by climatic conditions or different drivers.

Programmes like these throw up any structural durability problems a car might encounter in real life. In PR3's case they showed weaknesses around the spare wheel housing and the general front-end structure. The testing also led to modifications to the rear subframe damper mounting so that when it came to final production this differed substantially from the original Metro one with which the car had started out.

To ensure all problems are dealt with and cured there needs to be a 'closed loop' system. At Rover this is called a 'Problem Status Report'. John Doyle explains: 'If you're going to resolve problems adequately you have to have extreme attention to detail. Therefore, for every single problem that you find on a car, you raise what's called a Problem Status Report. The reports cover everything - for instance, a bill of materials should have contained an M8 nut and it didn't and I need one for this application. Similarly, if you had a problem where, for example, the subframe wasn't marrying with the mount, there would be an extremely detailed description of the mount and subframe.

'So that process actually delivers several hundred Problem Status Reports at that level of detail, because what you're seeking to do is eradicate the problem - and good problem resolution is only brought about by adequate problem definition.

'We have a structured code that says we have identified the problem. Then we identify an owner for the problem; we then get a solution that we believe will work. Then you release the drawings, get the part made and at the next build phase demonstrate the proposed solution. And at that next build phase the cure can only be cleared by the person who originally raised the PSR. So there's a closed loop system which says, "I saw it at this build phase and at the next build phase I saw the solution." Only then can he sign it off.'

The PSRs are backed up by what are known as 'Gebber' meetings, a name that is an amalgam of German and Japanese terminology. It's at Gebber meetings that all those who have raised PSRs demonstrate their solutions, and the necessary modifications to tooling, etc. are signed off for the next build phase.

An example of this project management occurred in mid '93 when Sim8 underwent the Level Two 50 per cent offset barrier test. The team had been sufficiently concerned that the Metro subframe wouldn't collapse particularly well in an offset test that they commandeered BAe's Cray supercomputer one weekend to run eleven simulated crash programmes. This resulted in modifications to the buttress which runs from the front of the Metro's subframe to the top of the damper tower. Although this was partially successful there were still floor deformation during the crash. So, with help from Terry Strong of Mayflower, a new design of stronger and stiffer longitudinals was fitted to the floor, together with stronger sills; the brake servo was moved across the bulkhead from in front of the driver to a new location on the left of the car (and vice-versa in left-hand-drive cars). Basically what had been happening was that the servo was pushing back high up into the car and forcing the steering column aside into a position Rover didn't want.

Identifying the problem early and effecting a quick resolution prevented a major engineering concern later in the programme. However, moving the servo also meant that those responsible for developing the braking system had to engineer a remote linkage between the brake pedal and the servo, which didn't deny the driver any sensitivity or response from the brakes.

Come September, they were ready to repeat the Level Two crash. This time the car passed both that and the side impact and roll-over tests with ease.

The roll-over test is another instance of meeting world standards. Although there are no legislative requirements for open-topped cars, even in the States, Rover engineered the PR3's windscreen surround to comply with the USA's

semi-static roof crush standard for saloon cars. There were some early thoughts about engineering a fixed roll-over hoop, but these were quickly abandoned on aesthetic grounds, and the trend in more expensive convertibles from the likes of Mercedes-Benz and BMW for pop-up roll-over bars would have been too costly a solution for PR3.

In spite of all the simulator rigs and accelerated validation programmes and the hours spent pounding round Gaydon's and MIRA's ride and handling circuits, there comes the inevitable time when the cars have to be taken out on the open road and driven in real-life situations. 'We obviously believe that at the end of the day the only real way to test a car in terms of its dynamic

Body-in-white assembly is done by Mayflower, just a few miles down the road from Longbridge, where the car is assembled.

Non-reflective NATO green paint made the prototypes harder to photograph under the cover of darkness.

qualities is on the road. You can't judge it properly on a test track, a test track is totally false,' says Griffin.

Which immediately poses the problem of how do you prevent unauthorised pictures of the car finding their way into the motoring press before the car's official début?

The easy answer is to disguise it and we've already seen some ingenious examples of that with the Metro delivery van and pick-up. But even that didn't prevent the car appearing in some motoring publications, even if they did get their editorial wires crossed at times.

Rover employs very strict security on all their new products, and PR3 was no exception. Any PR3 that left Gaydon for Longbridge or MIRA went in the back of a covered wagon - though that didn't prevent a couple of fitters driving a prototype out of Longbridge to Bartley Green one day to buy a newspaper!

When Brian Griffin, Nick Fell and the rest of the PR3 team were out on management ride 'n' drives to assess how the car was developing, elaborate precautions were taken to try and lessen the risk of being spotted. Details of the test routes, usually in remotest Wales and Lincolnshire, and the final location were given out on a purely 'need to know' basis only hours before the drives, which were usually conducted under the cover of darkness.

The most effective forms of concealment, though, are the elaborate body kits fixed to the cars to confuse any observer about the shape beneath. Brian Griffin and his team used the talents of trainee stylists over at Canley to create the weird and wonderful body kits that bulk up the car's size and distort its shape. In turn, though, these create their own problems as Griffin explained: 'One of the disadvantages of the camouflage is that it puts an awful lot of weight on the cars, about 60-90lb, so the chassis boys have a bit of a task when they want to do dynamic work. So we had to remove things like the engine lid, armatures out of the bumpers and trim to compensate and try and get back to the original weight.'

Even Trevor Haynes got involved, trimming the aerodynamic balance of the car with its disguise on so that it matched the unclothed car.

Security was equally tight when the cars went overseas for hot-weather testing in Phoenix, Arizona, and cold-weather testing in northern Sweden. For the States the cars were fitted with 'bra kits', fabric bags strapped to the nose and bonnet. Those, combined with heavy random taping on the bodywork, which breaks up the light lines, certainly disguised the shape of the car, but also had their drawbacks as the 'bra kits' blew up like parachutes across the bonnet, affecting stability. Taping is very effective as it means the size and shape of windows can be altered and feature lines completely distorted. The car for Sweden was, naturally, painted white.

To confuse onlookers further Rover used registration numbers from anywhere except the Midlands and painted the cars matt NATO green, which helps prevent night-time and infrared photography.

Don Kettleborough doesn't remember anyone showing much interest in the cars even when they were spotted out on the open roads: 'I don't ever recall a great interest in any of the prototypes because they looked so ugly. They obviously drew interest from certain people, but the average man in the street didn't take a second glance.'

Rover weren't totally successful in keeping PR3 away from the prying lens of scoop photographers like Hans Lehmann, but what pictures did appear were only of heavily disguised prototypes. 'What really pleased us,' says Griffin, 'was that nobody got a picture of the genuine car or its shape until it was practically launched.'

But that was still months away. As 1993 progressed the combined Mayflower/Rover teams were transforming Gerry McGovern's style into sheet metal, ensuring the panel gaps were a constant 4mm and that the 320 panels which go to make a single body would be just as Sked and McGovern intended - which they almost are.

The critical point in this process is the surfacing, when the final body shape is scanned and turned into digits so the press tools can be machined. The problem is transforming the subtle shapes which have been created by hand and eye into a numerical sequence. The computer can't always capture all the delicacies of curve and radius that a skilled coachbuilder can, and both Sked and McGovern feel that PR3 lost something during this process. 'The cord line down the flanks went a little bit soft. You need eyes in the back of your head, there are so many programmes involved in development and you need to look at every little detail. But, you know, I don't think there's a any car where you can say, "That's exactly the way I wanted it",' reflects Sked. Gerry McGovern agrees: 'That's one of the things where it lost some of that finesse. Companies don't want to do hand finishing on tools, so it's all being done on screen, but instruments with a mechanical basis for a memory haven't always got the sensitivity to achieve that same finesse that can be done by eye and hand.'

It might be assumed that by this time PR3 was secure, but there was still a questionmark hanging over the choice of engine. The Project Phoenix team had established that the 1.6-litre K series wasn't going to provide the sort of performance which marketing said the car needed. Now that the DO programme was underway and Nick Fell and his team had a better idea of the car's probable weight, the apparent lack of performance was even more obvious. To complicate matters further, the concept of a potential alternative, a high-performance supercharged 1.6, hadn't been ratified. Nick Fell takes up the story: 'We lived through the summer of 1993 on the assumption that the Rover 200 programme - which used the 1.8-litre K series - would approve the power train we were working on to deliver PR3. Clearly you don't generate a power-train

family based just on a sports car application of, maybe, 350 a week. So, in a sense, we were on borrowed time and the point where Aerospace approved the 200 programme was a moment of colossal relief to me because it meant all the development work we were doing was valid.'

British Aerospace's approval of the Rover 200 engine programme came just prior to PR3 moving to its DO2 phase at the beginning of November. As with so many activities within the car's development programme it at first ran parallel to the DO activities, but gradually assumed more importance as the months passed by.

For the first time in the programme Motor Panels supplied bodies they had manufactured. Some were off production tooling but the majority, says Fell, were pressed using prototype tools. 'Those cars largely drove our development programme and, I guess, one of the big things that came out of that was the torsional stiffness.' Or lack of it.

The team had set themselves a target of at least equalling the MX5's torsional rigidity and the Sim cars had easily exceeded that with figures of 7000 to 7100 Nm per degree. 'We felt we had a fair margin of confidence in that. In fact, by the time we'd moved from the concept to the productionisation of the panel design, we'd squandered an awful lot of the torsional stiffness

Computer-controlled assembly is a long way from Heritage's hand-built 'B' bodyshells.

and we were down to about 5000 Nm per degree.'

This looked like a major calamity for Project Phoenix and must have caused a few sleepless nights, but Nick Stephenson is philosophical about the whole episode: 'It was probably no great surprise. We'd done all our sums and built quite a few prototypes and a standard danger to any prototype phase is that unless you do absolutely everything to the manufacturing process you can lead yourself astray, even if the parts are the same.

'As we started to move into building cars in the manufacturing process we started to find we had a body that wasn't as stiff as we'd hoped. But we were able to modify it and restore the torsional rigidity we were looking for. In a perfect world we'd have got that from day one, but there isn't such a thing as a car-development programme that doesn't have these problems. It didn't feel like a failure.'

One anonymous observer from outside Rover has been less charitable: 'There wasn't enough work done at concept in terms of Finite Element Analysis, so the analysis programme was always behind where it should have been in support of engineering, and the failure should have been predicted through the FEA programme. Any engineering programme is always dealing

with those compromises and it is always more difficult when you haven't got a lid on the box because you've got to put more effort into the base of the structure. PR3 wasn't the first programme of its type.'

Brian Griffin attributes some of the losses to the manner in which the early cars were hand built: 'With a hand-built car you've got almost total freedom to put it together, you can put all the welds exactly where you want them. But when you actually come to look at production tooling, there's a limit to tool access and you end up having to change the way you joint it. You end up with less favourable joint conditions, panels whose forms are compromised or changed by the process they've been through. So, cumulatively and to our alarm and despondency, that added up to a very severe dilution of the car and you could feel it in the way the cars drove.'

Over the next six months, until June 1994, the team worked frantically to regain the high levels of torsional stiffness they had lost. They were not only striving to compete with and, hopefully, better the MX5's performance, but potential rivals as the Fiat barchetta, which recorded 8554 Nm per degree when it appeared.

Nick Fell explains: 'That triggered some fairly rigorous work in creating a dynamic computer model of the DO2 design and we used that. By modelling what we'd actually done, we used that to make sure the computer model worked properly. We then went through forty-eight proposed design changes on that computer model to improve its torsional stiffness and it will come as no surprise to learn that we eagerly sought patch pieces and lots and lots of minor changes round the car. It was quite clear from the modelling work that we were, frankly, pissing in the wind if we were going to do anything minor.'

The single most important change to the car's structure was to box in the floor section between the door sills. 'Although the sills were very stiff,' says Fell, 'they could move relative to each other by flexing the floor pan. So what we did was lock the sills together by this box which actually sandwiches the floor.'

The quest for additional stiffness was aided by the car's mid-engined layout, as Fell elaborated: 'Because it's mid-engined you don't have a prop-shaft to contend with, so we completed that box section and the centre tunnel section by having a big bolt-on panel that could be fitted after the service pipes and cables had been routed.'

Structural adhesives were also used to supplement the welding of major body components together and thus enhance rigidity further. These modifications resulted in PR3 finishing up with an impressive 8500 Nm per degree.

Instigating these changes had a knock-on effect in other areas of the car's development, according to Fell: 'That meant quite a big tear-up on carpets, harness routing, seat-harness brackets, sill bins - they disappeared at that stage - to deliver that performance.'

Part of Gerry McGovern's interior concept had included a pair of bins located between the seats and doors, but they couldn't be accommodated with the new structure. 'In theory these changes shouldn't change the style as it's been signed off,' says McGovern, 'but in this case it did. It affected the packaging and the fact that we had these bins was a nice touch, but we had to take them out.'

To ensure the programme kept on schedule the first phase of DO2 cars didn't incorporate the major structural changes, as this stage gave the various teams a chance to validate the electrics, cooling systems and other items not directly affected.

Stiffening the car did seriously influence its on-road behaviour. The ride and handling characteristics changed markedly as did the bodyshell's behaviour in crash testing. But all that was still to come, later in 1994. In the meantime there was an announcement that would send shock waves throughout Rover and, indeed, the British motor industry as a whole.

18

After years of struggling it finally looked as if Rover had turned the tide of misfortune. 1993 hadn't been a wonderful year, but the company had made a £56 million operating profit, although it still ended up with a pre-tax loss of £9 million after £65 million in interest charges. Overshadowed by these statistics was some genuinely good news for the group. In a recession-strangled year, Rover had made a leap forward in European sales, increasing its market share from 2.5 per cent to 3.2 per cent or 361,000. It was heartening news for everyone and boosted hopes for the future.

That all changed on Monday 31 January 1994 when it was announced that British Aerospace had sold Rover to BMW. To say this was a surprise would be an understatement. It was well-known that BAe's then chairman, John Cahill, was uneasy at the lack of common ground between BAe's core military aerospace businesses and Rover's car business, but hints that a sale of Rover was even being contemplated had always been firmly and swiftly denied.

Led by its new chairman, forty-five-year-old Bernd Pischetsrieder, cash-rich BMW - which had £2 billion in reserves at the time - paid £800 million for an 80 per cent stake in Britain's last remaining independent mass car producer. The sale effectively signalled the end of an autonomous British motor industry, except for a few specialists like Rolls-Royce, TVR, Morgan and Reliant. Ford owned Jaguar and Aston Martin, and Vauxhall was part of the GM empire.

Motoring historians were quick to point out the irony in the purchase: BMW's first car, the Dixi, built in 1928, was an Austin 7 manufactured under licence and Rover was all that was left of a conglomerate that once embraced Austin, Morris, Wolseley, Riley and a host of names that made Britain a dominant force in car production during the 1950s.

Bernd Pischetsrieder, BMW boss and nephew of Sir Alec Issigonis, who led the audacious dawn raid on Rover.

British and German employees, analysts and commentators first knew of the deal when televisions and radios were switched on on Monday morning, 1 February. They heard that Honda had told the Tokyo Stock Exchange that BMW were buying Rover from the parent company, British Aerospace (BAe).

Although the offer was made, negotiated and signed in twelve whirlwind days by a cabal of senior BMW and BAe directors - allegedly not even Rover's managing director, John Towers, knew of the deal until the last minute - it was the previous September's Frankfurt Motor Show which convinced the men from Munich that the once-ridiculed British motor industry had something to offer. While the punters were queuing up to experience BMW's multi-media event, others were standing five deep round the Land Rover display with its fashionable range of 4x4s, booking demonstration drives and confirming orders. It set Wolfgang Reitzle, BMW's head of research, thinking and on an appraisal programme of all Rover products; his verdict - as good as BMW. What is more, Rover's European sales continued to climb and by the end of the year they had become the only manufacturer to buck the trend in a declining market and increase their share by 8.9 per cent to 361,000 - only 9000 behind BMW themselves - and with a

model range that was improving markedly with each new car introduced.

Though bigger than Rover - BMW at that time built half a million cars a year and had 70,000 employees, compared with 400,000 and 30,000 respectively - BMW knew they had a problem: they had to expand into unknown product niches to ensure a long-term future without diluting the carefully nurtured BMW image. They also needed to increase productivity while decreasing costs. The problem was that Germany's motor-industry labour rates, at £22 per hour in 1993, were the highest in the Western world, almost twice the UK's £11.32.

BMW were also coming under pressure from another direction - arch-rivals Mercedes-Benz. At the same Frankfurt Show where Land Rovers, Discoveries and Range Rovers were wowing the Germans, Mercedes-Benz had unveiled the Vision A concept car and clearly signalled their intention of building a VW Golf-sized car by 1997. What is more, only two months later, Mercedes' head of passenger cars, Jurgen Hubbert, announced a £200 million factory in Alabama, to build a new challenger to Discovery/Range Rover, to replace the dismal G-Wagen. BMW might have had reservations about

Dr Wolfgang Reitzle, BMW's head of research, who became Rover's chairman after the takeover.

putting their moniker on anything other than a sporting/luxury saloon/coupé or a roadster, but Mercedes apparently had no such qualms.

While Mercedes hogged the limelight, BMW were quietly forging their own destiny. Reitzle had used the excuse of BMW supplying Land Rover with diesel engines for the new Range Rover to inspect Rover's assembly plants. He returned to Munich suitably impressed, not only by the build quality but also by Rover's lean manufacturing processes - learned, of course, from Honda.

BMW made their first tentative overtures to BAe in November 1993 and then went away while Honda were given the opportunity to respond. Nothing happened until 20 January 1994, when BMW made it formally known they wanted to open negotiations. Two days later Honda made a counterbid, offering to increase their share in Rover to 47.5 per cent, pumping £165 million into the company and valuing it at £600 million. Honda further suggested that a similar-sized stake should continue to be held by BAe, with Rover employees owning the remaining 5 per cent.

With their fourteen-year relationship, a 20 per cent stake and a joint model programme ahead of them - the Honda Concerto/Rover 200 and 400 replacement due in 1995 - the Japanese position looked unassailable. But this ignored BAe's desire to return to their original core businesses and their need for a large cash injection to fund new projects. BMW's £800 million provided the cash as well as freeing BAe of Rover's debt burden.

In the final analysis, neither Honda nor BAe wanted Rover. While a management buy-out seemed a vague possibility, the willingness of British investors to keep pumping in cash for new model development and maintain buoyancy during turbulent times could not be guaranteed and Rover would always have been susceptible to a multi-national predator. There would also have been qualms about Rover's most profitable division, Land Rover. If that was sold off separately it would leave the car division even more vulnerable to takeover.

It was a shame that the man who had to break the bad news to Honda's president, Nobuhiko Kawamoto, was the person within Rover who, above all others, believed the Honda road was the right one for the group - George Simpson. Perhaps that was one reason why Simpson left shortly afterwards, in spring 1994, to take over at Lucas; he was succeeded by John Towers.

While BAe must have been very pleased with themselves, it was obvious that the whole

process had left a sour taste in Honda's mouth. European and Japanese business ethics are as disparate as their languages and cultures, but it seemed inevitable that the relationship which saved Rover from going under would gradually be devolved over the next decade. Although Pischetsrieder flew to Japan in the hope of persuading Honda to retain its share, it was always a forlorn journey. The Japanese were likely to view the ruthless Germans and perfidious Albion with a jaundiced eye and prefer to plough their own furrow in Europe, concentrating production at Honda's Swindon plant.

Pischetsrieder made all the right noises, but one thing was certain - 'Buy British' wouldn't have quite the same ring to it when a customer next walked into a Rover showroom.

Pischetsrieder's £800 million swoop on Rover gave BMW instant access to a model range which dovetailed almost perfectly into their own, presenting the Bavarians with an opportunity to expand into unknown territory without jeopardising their carefully nurtured and jealously guarded image. Not only that, but Pischetsrieder gained instant access to some of the most evocative, unused names in the motoring dictionary.

A nephew of Mini inventor Sir Alec Issigonis, Pischetsrieder talked about rekindling marques such as Austin-Healey, Triumph and Riley as well as investing in a new, updated Mini and going ahead with PR3, which would clash head-on with BMW's own American-built roadster.

Meanwhile Honda, once scorned as the company which would sound the death knell of the British motor industry, found new friends. Politicians from both left and right aligned to praise the Japanese and pillory the way in which BAe had dumped them after fourteen years of faithful service. There was no doubt that Honda president Nobuhiko Kawamoto felt aggrieved at the short shrift meted out to his company and the about-face which Rover's former owners had performed: 'We did not want to make Rover Japanese. We wanted to increase Rover's Roverness. We wanted it to be more British . . .'

Fine words, but they ignored the rancour often felt and privately expressed by some senior Rover personnel over the way in which the Japanese had railroaded the 600 project and refused to listen to Rover criticisms about interior packaging. But that was all water under the bridge now.

The Japanese market was contracting for the first time since the last war and the deal couldn't have come at a worse time for Honda; their strategists would have to rethink the company's future plans. As well as securing Rover's four-

wheel-drive expertise, BMW gained breathing space and set back Honda's plans to challenge them on their European home ground by several years.

It took just ninety minutes, talking on Monday 21 February between Nobuhiko Kawamoto, President of Honda, and Bernd Pischetsrieder, Chairman of BMW, for the Japanese to decide they wanted out of Rover.

Unknown to Rover at the time were BMW's plans to launch its own roadster, the front-engined rear-wheel-drive Z3.

Honda's 20 per cent cross-holding in Rover and Rover's 20 per cent share in Honda UK reverted to the parent companies.

Fears that Rover would be left behind technically by BMW proved unfounded. At the time of the takeover they had 2000 design, development and engineering personnel capable of taking cars, engines, gearboxes etc. from concept to production; they also had the 90-acre advanced research facility at Gaydon with 26 miles of test track. What Rover lacked was the money to develop their own projects: they were spending a meagre £200 million a year on new model development, putting cars into production, updating existing models and upgrading and maintaining plant and equipment.

Very often their collaboration with Honda - or the use of Peugeot engines and VW gearboxes, for example - was forced on Rover by lack of money to develop their own units or, more sensibly, prudent housekeeping. 'Why go to all the expense of developing something when it can be bought off the shelf?' said one Rover director. However, Pischetsrieder wanted Rover to spend at least 7 per cent of its £4.3 billion annual sales, or slightly more than £300 million, on design, development and engineering.

'The BMW buy-out didn't have any impact at all, says Towers. 'It's important in terms of the way we've organised our respective programmes that we don't, except at the very highest levels, actually seek to get too much cross-over of opinion when it comes to the fundamental issues . . . and suddenly find that we've got an MG, Rover or Land-Rover that's being configured with BMW values.' Even more important, says Towers was that 'Pischetsrieder, Reitzle and Co. were very happy with the car [PR3]'.

If Towers' statement reads as if it's shrouded in corporate-speak, then it's typical of the measured replies he always gives, which tend to belie his enthusiasm for Project Phoenix. After all, he was largely responsible for encouraging Nick Stephenson in the early days and will, if pressed, admit to a particular thrill about the project: 'I have to be a bit careful because I regularly drive all the new cars, but human instinct takes over and you'd want to drive PR3s all the time and you've not got to do that. You've got to say to yourself, "Are you doing your job or being a kid enjoying yourself?" And you could say "Yes" to both.'

Nick Stephenson, on the other hand, can barely contain his enthusiasm for the BMW takeover and his relationship with the German engineers: 'I claim they arrived in the design studio on day one and have never left, because they are such car enthusiasts. They spend all their time talking about cars. I can recall the first sessions when we were reviewing the cars and the first thing that came out was that they had a small sports car coming out as well. It was going into similar territory as they had some very aggressive pricing on that vehicle as well. The initial reaction was, "Well, we've both got a sports car, we need to make a decision." Their reaction to the car was very positive, partially driven by relief that when they saw it, it looked very different to theirs.'

In the weeks immediately following the takeover there was considerable debate about which Rover programmes would continue and which might even be revived. PR3 came under the microscope, and with BMW developing its Z3 roadster there were some lively discussions about the merits of having two sports cars from sister companies - echoes of MG versus Austin-Healey or Triumph? As Stephenson relates, 'It

was very much in their minds that if the two cars were to live, and that decision hadn't been taken at the time, that one should be seen as a German sports car and one as a British sports car. So the debate about Britishness was very much on their list.'

According to Stephenson, BMW saw Britishness as more retro than Rover did, which was in line with the thoughts Gordon Sked and Gerry McGovern had over the car's interior and became quite a heated topic in the media when the car was eventually revealed.

'We're certain that Britishness isn't always about looking back in time and there is a very strong contemporary element. So there was a debate around that; many of the characteristics, the use of wood and leather, maybe a touch of eccentricity - those are things maybe we see as characteristic of Britishness and there was no disagreement about that.

We pretty soon got comfortable about the definitions we were talking through and over this period there was a lot of open debate and viewing. It occurred to me that we weren't helping ourselves by showing the cars in the least British colours, so we repainted them and that was a small breakthrough and they became completely relaxed about it. The paint brought back the British character.'

The paint in question, recalls Gordon Sked, was an experimental colour, 'Lipstick Red', which changes its hues according to the conditions. 'It went quite blue in some lights and then an orangey- pinky colour. Even for Sked it was a weird colour.'

Brian Griffin's recollection isn't quite as subtle: 'In the meantime we'd been playing around with unique colours for the VVC models and a colour that had looked great on the plaque was this "Lipstick", it was the kind of pearlescent red that went from blue to dark red when the light fell on it. So we sprayed up the fibreglass model in this colour and it looked bloody awful. Nobody liked it. Even the guys in the paint shop were saying, "You have to be kidding!" when they rolled it out. But that's the colour the car was when BMW first clapped eyes on it.'

Weird colour or not, Gordon Sked and his team had got used to it and such was the swiftness of BMW's takeover that there wasn't sufficient time to respray the car before the Germans wanted a product review.

Sked kept Reitzle and his colleagues waiting, leaving PR3 to the very end of his presentation. 'I'd taken the sheets off all the other cars and left PR3 till last. They were horrified and shocked, shocked on a number of levels when I took the dust-covers off. The first thing was the colour, of course, but I don't believe they realised the car was mid-engined. They had this impression, because they had come from their own roadster and they were used to looking at that sort of proportion and architecture, that the MG was going to be similar - front- engine/rear-wheel drive. They were absolutely shocked.'

Although 'Lipstick Red' looked like one of the more outlandish colours that German tuners favour, BMW were not amused, as Nick Fell recalls: 'They tend to be fairly traditional when it comes to things like sports cars, especially if it's a brand that's got a massive past, if you like. The word came back that they were somewhat shocked and immediately asked for a programme review.'

The review was only a few weeks away, on 4 March, so Fell and Sked decided to respray the car British Racing Green for that event. 'They began to warm to it. But the irony of the situation is that they didn't expect that "Lipstick Red" on a British product, whereas it might have been more acceptable on a German one.'

Although there were some speculative rumblings in the press that BMW would cancel PR3 because it clashed with the Z3, Nick Fell believes that neither Pischetsrieder nor Reitzle ever really contemplated that: 'Well, it would have been very difficult for them to do it, because it would have been seen as an incredibly hostile first move. But I think because the cars were actually quite different, that made it a much easier fit in terms of product line-up. Part of the reason for keeping it was that nobody had an affordable, mid-engined roadster. We thought that would keep the car distanced from theirs. Also, we felt it would help its longevity in terms of being an aspirational product - we didn't think that too many people would go down that route because it's not easy and PR3 would stand out from the crowd.'

Although Nick Stephenson largely agrees that 'Lipstick Red' might not have been in the best possible taste, it did illustrate a point: 'The colour issue was important. I think it shows what a contemporary car we've got, because if you paint it heritage colours, its history comes out, but if you paint it in some of the more exciting colours its modernity comes back.'

In the ensuing months BMW took an avid interest in PR3's development, although according to Stephenson they remained at arm's length and rarely interfered: 'They've taken a very active interest in it. I've had some very exciting drives chasing Pischetsrieder and getting Bernd to drive on the right route because he was getting carried away.'

There has been a more serious element to

BMW's senior management appreciated this British Racing Green MGF far more than the Lipstick Red one they saw first.

BMW's takeover; according to Stephenson, 'quite rightly we had a focused business debate on whether to keep the two cars. Looking at their potential, however, we swiftly came to the conclusion that there was room for both. In terms of the corporation, the two cars were different enough to do battle with the competition and do it in different ways. There would be some cus-tomers who would migrate either way, but in the main we'd be battling it out with the competition and not ourselves.'

The takeover also had repercussions beyond Rover, as Motor Panels' Hugh McKenzie recalls: 'In the contract negotiations one of our biggest concerns was what happens if something affects Rover because we've put a lot of money into the programme, and it was one of those issues people couldn't answer. When it first happened our reaction was "Told you so." We were a bit surprised, unsure of the implications. Then it got interesting because BMW had got their own sports car and I am sure the Project Phoenix team and Rover must have felt the same, because both cars were geared to not dissimilar production levels and timing, there was uncertainty.'

Like the Project Phoenix team, Motor Panels believed in the PR3 programme and as time went by, they started to feel more certain of the car's future: 'When BMW made statements they gave us a warm feeling as they believe in marque values and MG is the classic marque value. They analysed the programme and endorsed it.'

Listening to Nick Stephenson it is impossible to believe that Rover's life with BMW will be anything other than rosy: 'Their focus on attention to detail has been tremendously helpful and they do it in an enthusiastic fashion. They're car enthusiasts you can really respect, they really know what they're talking about. They are very, very good product people.'

It is this depth of knowledge, the appreciation of what makes a good car, allied to the respect which BMW have for Rover's understanding of what an MG is in the mid-1990s, and

what it might lead to, that helped preserve Project Phoenix. Nick Stephenson also believes strongly that the Z3's traditional front-engine/rear-wheel-drive configuration and PR3's far more radical mid-engined layout helped to distance the two and strengthen Rover's argument: 'That was helpful to the debate, as well as positioning, style and what we're trying to do with the car. If we'd had the same mechanical layout we'd be more tense about it. I think MG customers are a broader base with a very high female take. There will be more MG customers who will use their cars as a daily means of transport, practically daily use, so we'll have more first-car usage. They've got a more focused customer base, whereas we're trying to pick up everybody to whom MG means something. We'll also have a wider age profile.'

The fact that Rover isn't going into the American market with PR3, but that the BMW Z3 is being built there and will be sold there, was yet another factor which helped settle the argument that there was room for two sports cars from the same corporate stable.

As the countdown towards the car's début accelerated into its final twelve months, Rover's confidence in how acceptable PR3's radical engineering would be to the buying public was about to be put to the test.

The early market research conducted by Greg Allport and his colleaguesconfirmed there was a pent-up demand for a new MG, but it also revealed that having the Octagon badge was a double-edged sword. Yes, a new MG would sell and wearing the Octagon would make that task easier, but the new car didn't just have to equal its rivals, it had to better them. 'Those questioned regularly told us they were waiting for a new MG "to redefine the sports-car market". They wanted the car to be "forward-looking", "modern in design and technology". It had to be the best handling and have an affordable price tag,' says Allport.

The acid test of whether the Project Phoenix team met those targets came in early 1994 when a series of customer clinics were held in principal European markets such Italy, France, Germany and Spain as well as in the UK and Japan. At each clinic some eighteen potential customers were invited to review the car and its rivals and asked a series of carefully formulated questions; they would also be videoed so that their physical reactions to the cars could be studied. Analysing the answers would help the marketing department determine pricing strategy, advertising campaigns and dealer requirements, as well as confirming whether the car was generally well received. Those invited didn't know it was Rover who'd asked them and the car was kept badgeless to retain its anonymity.

Allport and his team had already determined that cars such as the Toyota MR2, Mazda MX5, Peugeot 306 Cabriolet and VW Golf GTi would be typical rivals to the new MG, and it was against these that PR3 was lined up at the clinics.

The immediate reaction of many who attended the UK clinic was that PR3 wasn't only a new MG, it was a 'very modern MG'. The marque recognition wasn't as strong in other countries, but it was still there. The Japanese added that if the car wore an MG badge, it would command a premium price above rival marques such as Mazda, Toyota and even BMW. The marketing team were also heartened by the reaction to the hard top: 'Being affordable, people said it would give them two cars in one. A coupé for the winter and a convertible for the summer.'

The universal reaction to the car was very

positive, says Mike Ferguson, who worked with Allport on the clinics: 'In the UK, where the MG marque has been kept more alive through the clubs and there are plenty of MGBs still being used, PR3 was immediately identified as an MG. Although that wasn't as strong in Europe, the car was seen as being British, which was very important.'

There were, however, sufficient warning messages coming from the clinics about the car's interior for Gerry McGovern secretly to observe a clinic in Germany. At this stage, the prototypes still had the brightwork in the interior on the gear knob, ashtray and trinket tray. 'The results from the Italian and French clinics said that while everyone liked the exterior design, they were confused about the interior,' recalls McGovern, 'because it was partly modern and partly retro.'

At that third clinic in Germany, McGovern suggested it should be explained to the customers that PR3 was a modern car which recognised its heritage and that was why the brightwork had been included. Armed with that explanation people began to understand and appreciate it, says McGovern, but that didn't save it from being deleted.

The second major issue the clinics raised was that of whether or not power steering should be standard. For Rover Japan there was no question about it - their customers would expect a car of this calibre, class and price to have power steering as standard. On the other hand, the Greek market, for instance, wouldn't want a mid-engined sports car to have power steering. 'It's a more chauvinist market,' says MG's brand manager, Lisa Faulkner, 'and male drivers wouldn't want power steering.'

Lisa Faulkner was responsible for defining a modern MG image for the advertising and promotional programme as well as the dealers.

This early data provided Allport and his colleagues with the foundations for briefing the advertising agency, Ammirati & Puris/Lintas, to develop a media campaign for the car. 'It was crucial,' recalls Allport, 'that the car shouldn't be positioned with nostalgic overtones, but as forward-looking. Not so much that the marque is returning, but that it's restarting.'

The target audience was ABC adults aged between twenty-five and forty-five who led a stylish life and were driving hot hatches, coupés and cabriolets. 'They probably saw MG as a classic marque, "They don't make cars like that any more" sort of attitude. We wanted the advertising to make them think, "What a stunner, I must take a closer look. It's an MG, but obviously a brand new car.'"

It was equally important, says Allport, to convey the five marque values which had acted as guiding beacons throughout the car's development: 'The first value is desire, it relates to sex appeal, to driving a new MG, "wanting to own" factor. The second value is exhilaration, which comes from the car's performance and superior handling, freedom and release for the owner. Thirdly the car is distinctive. Recognise its prestige and exclusive nature, it's a car for individuals who want to be viewed differently from the crowd. The fourth value was this Britishness encompassed in the car's authenticity and originality. If you take the sports-car market of the 1970s, we used to dominate it, we were the best and we haven't lost our edge. The fifth and final value,' explains Allport, 'recognises its affordability. The accessibility of the car, not only through its purchase price, but running costs as well, competitive insurance, the cost of ownership.'

From this point on the advertising philosophy began to gel into three or four key areas that would be used where appropriate across all the markets. For instance, in the UK in the winter months, the campaign might concentrate on cars

pictured with the hard-top to emphasise the car's dual nature and the additional security it affords. However, Faulkner explained, security isn't a problem in the Far East, so that would be ignored, but air-conditioning would be emphasised. A distinct advantage of having the MG Octagon badge is that the advertisements don't have to spell out that it's a British sports car, the badging does that automatically. 'We've always looked on the MG badge as icing on the cake,' explains Ferguson. 'Without the badge it's still an amazing sports car.'

Wherever possible, says Faulkner, they have tried to use the same catchlines for the advertisements such as 'It lives, do you?' or 'We could have said a lot more'. Local sensibilities have to be accounted for, however, so that in Singapore, Hong Kong and Japan, for instance, 'It lives, do you?' has been replaced by 'The new MG, it lives'.

A major problem that Lisa Faulkner, who took over managing the MG brand in spring 1994, had to confront was how to devise a dealer network for selling and servicing the car. Rover dealers had been out of the sports-car sector for so long that it was felt a new strategy was needed not only in the UK, but in Rover's overseas markets as well.

Rover was planning on building only 15,000

If you can't afford the real thing there's always the Corgi model. To ensure accuracy the original buck for this model was milled on the same five-axis machine using a down-scaled version of the same programme Rover used to produce the full-size car.

It's not just a car you sell, but an image – hence the range of MG branded goods.

cars a year at first, increasing production to 20,000 if a consistent demand was demonstrated. Spread that around more than 1500 dealers worldwide and it's very slim margins for everyone. Furthermore, the sports-car market is a specialised sector, very different from retailing family saloons. Ferguson says, 'We wanted to ensure that the dealers had a viable business from MG, but it was also

important from the customer's standpoint that the dealer had specialised salesmen and technicians, people who were focused on the marque and knew what they were talking about.

The customer clinics had identified the fact that potential owners wouldn't object to travelling further to an MG dealer, especially as the car might only need servicing once a year, and they didn't necessarily see Rover dealers as being MG dealers. With this in mind Lisa Faulkner set about analysing the Rover network to see which ones met the criteria she was setting: for instance, they had to have achieved a minimum customer satisfaction rating of at least 85 out of a 100 to qualify. She then asked the dealers to put forward business plans - how would they deal with trade-ins against the new MG, bearing in mind that many of them would be used sports cars? From those replies the final list of 120 UK dealers was determined. Faulkner admits that they are some gaps in the markets, but maintains that it is better for an MG owner to have to travel a bit further to get the level of service they expect than to compromise MG's reputation. In addition it makes the MG marque aspirational for those dealers who haven't got it.

Initially this approach wasn't well received by dealers - especially by those who believed they deserved to be allowed to sell the car - but Faulkner is unrepentant: 'If the criteria and measurements are right, then you can justify why one dealer has got the franchise and another hasn't.'

Lisa Faulkner's team were also responsible for developing the sales image for the revitalised brand, from the corporate signage and point-of-sale material used by the dealers through to the brochures and the accessories programme. As with the press advertisements the brochures ignore MG's heritage - a deliberate ploy, according to Faulkner: 'We wanted to establish MG as a modern sports car. It's very important that it appeals to a younger audience which hasn't grown up with MG. We had to position it as a modern sports car from MG, with a cult appeal to a younger audience.'

The need for some car owners to parade their marque loyalty in public has resulted in a hugely profitable merchandising market. No longer is this merchandising restricted to key fobs and jackets or to the younger, sporty end of the market. Nowadays all car companies are offering ranges of merchandise which reflect their own products and no one is too proud to take part, from Rolls-Royce, Bentley and Ferrari at the mega-expensive end of the spectrum to Mini-Coopers at the other extreme.

Rover were quick to realise the value of the MG marque and are exploiting it fully with the

'MG Collection' of clothing, watches, pens and the like, with much more on the way. 'There's been tremendous interest in MG since the launch and we've registered the marque in all the countries where the cars will be sold,' says Faulkner. Perhaps one of the most popular items in the range will be the 1-18th scale Corgi model of the car, made from a miniature buck carved by the same five-axis equipment that was used to machine the full-size buck for Motor Panels.

It had been decided that the new car would be unveiled at the 1995 Geneva Salon, held in March, but before that the car would have to be revealed to the dealer network or, at least, those who had qualified for the franchise.

An architect by training, Pat Ward is responsible for managing all the Rover Group's conferences and exhibitions, so it was down to him to organise a dealer launch. The chosen venue was the British Motor Industry Heritage Trust museum located next door to Rover's Gaydon technical centre.

As well as displaying cars which trace the history of the constituent companies which have made up Rover in the past, the BMIHT also houses all the company's archives, engineering drawings and many concept cars which never made the light of day. It would make an ideal historical setting for dealers, especially those from overseas who were a little hazy about MG's own heritage.

Ward's team worked through the nights leading up to the event to build a set in the middle of the museum's display area. Although the walls appeared to be solid as dealers from more than thirty countries trooped in for their briefings, as soon as the lights came up the curtains became transparent and those present found themselves surrounded by past MGs. After briefings by senior directors on the car's development and Rover's sales and marketing pitch, two new MGs - one red, one green - rose out of the floor on turntables.

'Because we'd managed to keep scoop pictures of the car out of the press, the dealers didn't know what to expect,' recalls Ferguson, 'but there was a tremendous buzz when the cars appeared. They were really enthusiastic, with an incredibly positive attitude to the cars.'

Those dealer meetings were held on 24 and 25 February 1995. Ten days later the new MG would be revealed to the world at the Geneva Salon. Behind the scenes, as the marketing and sales departments were evolving their strategy and Pat Ward was developing the various launches, Brian Griffin, Nick Fell and the rest of the Project Phoenix team were slaving away to ensure PR3 stayed on course.

SELLING A LEGEND

224

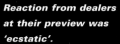

*Reaction from dealers
at their preview was
'ecstatic'.*

20

The decision to go with Motor Panels wasn't the only new ground broken by Project Phoenix - the facility in which the car is manufactured represents a breakthrough for Rover as well. Car Assembly Building 2 had lain dormant for eight years, and resurrecting it gave Rover the opportunity to extend their 'Rover Tomorrow' programme. Neil Jauncey, who had been responsible for body-in-white and final assembly at Land Rover, transferred to Longbridge in July 1994 with a brief not only to put PR3 into build but also to bring CAB2 on line.

'Rover Tomorrow is a new way of manufacturing with worker empowerment . . . we've got good people here who can do more than just put vehicles together, they can contribute to better ways of working, resolve problems and do a lot of it themselves, which is what we're trying to do, push that ownership lower into the organisation.

Not abdication by management at all, we're still very much there in a leadership, mentor, coaching role,' explains Jauncey. 'There's a lot more satisfaction if a work team has a problem that affects them - it might be as simple as the layout of their rest area or the lighting - if they can resolve it themselves or we can put people in to help them resolve it. It broadens the job and makes coming to work much more pleasant, so we want to engage their brains as well as their manufacturing skills.'

The majority of those working in CAB2 are new to Rover and were the successful applicants in a rigorous recruitment campaign which saw an 80 per cent rejection rate. Rover have seen the benefit of that, says Jauncey, in a rate of absenteeism only 20 per cent of what it is in the rest of the company. 'They do job rotation, train one another and help out when there's an absentee. Moreover, there's a pride in their job and work, they're likely to say, "I build MGs" rather than "I work at Longbridge".'

Although the majority of cars which come out of CAB2 are MGs, it also produces the Rover 200 Coupé and Cabriolet, and it was these models which ironed out any production-line hiccups. Jauncey's job was further complicated by a brand-new and ecologically friendly water-based paint shop being built at Longbridge at the same time. We got all the problems and launch start-up process out of the way before MG had to come on stream.

In Project Phoenixs early days the engineering programme was led by Brian Griffin; once it was given the green light Nick Fell took over as project director. Although Fell retained overall control Neil Jauncey's role became more crucial as the car neared production.

It is during this stage of a car's development that engineering theory is translated into manufacturing fact and to help make that transition as short and immediate as possible, Nick Fell and his team transferred to temporary offices adjacent to CAB2 at Longbridge. At the same time, Jauncey was making sure the relationship with Motor Panels was working efficiently and there would be no disruptions in the flow of bodies. 'I had at least two jobs when I arrived in '94. I was manufacturing manager bringing CAB2 on stream for the cabriolet and coupé and I also had launch responsibility for PR3. So, while I was the end internal customer in final assembly, I also had to ensure the process chain was ready to accept the product and that extended to Motor Panels.'

As you move through and get nearer to the point of volume the lead responsibility changes, the product design is complete and it's only the quality maturation type changes that are going on. The manufacturing people tend to take over the lead role, ready for the final phases into manufacturing.

Until this point in late 1994, all the engineering-phase cars, D1 and D2, had been hand built as prototypes, but in late October the final few went down the production line in CAB2 - another first for Project Phoenix.

'We had never done that before at Longbridge,' says Jauncey, obviously relieved that the operation had gone smoothly, especially as CAB2 wasn't fully commissioned. 'There was a lot of concern about manufacturing PR3 in a building which was not quite complete. We still had external contractors in, finishing conveyors and engine marriage, glazing cells and we tried to keep the wraps on the car. From a security point of view we were taking PR3 from within a very controlled, secure engineering area to one that could never be totally secured.'

In the beginning there were some thirty or forty people building the cabriolets and coupés, stopping and starting the track as it was fine-tuned to handle the different bodies and sub-assemblies; small things like making sure the centre of gravity was perfectly balanced on the body slings.

Gradually the numbers of production-line

*Once painted the body
shells are transferred
by overhead track to
CAB2.*

*Installing interior trim
is still one of those
functions best per-
formed by humans
and not robots.*

Engine and rear axle sub-assemblies waiting to be mated up with the body shell.

Final touches being put to the body shell as the wiring harness is installed.

employees grew, with each new batch being trained by their more experienced work mates and, again, it was a two-way learning process. Those on the assembly lines passed along ideas and suggestions that would make their job easier, and improve final quality, to Nick Fell's engineering team.

'We went into the Quality Prototype build phase with increasing numbers in the team who were going to build the car. So we were actually getting far more feedback from those who were going to build the car from very early on. Again, it's fine-tuning the build methods. How can we make sure the harness routing is correct, do we need more instructions or colour co-ordinated harnesses and locators? All very simple stuff, but it all adds to the robustness of the product as it moves into its volume phases,' says Jauncey.

'Each QP phase had about twenty cars in it, broken down into lots of four or five built at a time. We'd build those four or five, learn from them, correct any problems and then move on to the next batch and so on throughout the QP programme,' explains finance man Nick Boneham.

It was a nerve-wracking time for Jauncey: 'It was a continual balance and that's when the launch manager shows his mettle and has to say, "No, it's not right. We were promised this change, it's not arriving for another two days so we'll wait." That gives us other problems because volume dates have been set and marketing strategies put in place and the finance man wants to start getting some revenue back. That's when the brave have to stand up and say, "It's no use building numbers if you're not getting the quality maturation you wanted." You do need to be brave to say, "No" and wait another twenty-four hours until the supplier is coming off production tooling. That's the balance, at that point going from components off prototype tools straight into volume tools. A lot of trim items have to go that way, as there's no intermediate low-cost tooling . . . The danger is everybody believes everything will be right first time and a very high percentage are, but you've got to deal with the few that aren't.'

A lot of these problems are dealt with by the engineers responsible for that component even before they get to Neil Jauncey's area. Others, like the additional bracing to regain torsional stiffness, have a knock-on effect. Not only did that result in the sill bins being abandoned, but the carpet tooling had to change as the shape of the carpet had altered.

Road mileage in prototypes whose hoods being constantly folded and erected had resulted in the PVC fabric stretching and creasing around the B posts. Steve Garrett thought it looked untidy, so he decided to change the specification to a much more expensive fabric, as used by BMW and Audi on their convertibles. According to Garrett, 'Nick [Fell] wasn't best pleased when I first told him, but he was completely won over when he saw a car with the new hood fitted. It puts the car in a class above its rivals.'

Garrett and his team also used a novel way of measuring hood deflection on a moving car. They had been working very hard throughout the programme to ensure the car was quiet and windproof with the hood erected, and Pininfarina had insisted that it shouldn't deflect more than 15mm between bows. The problem was, how do you measure that on a moving car?

The answer came partly from Rover's own advanced optics group and aerodynamicist Trevor Haynes. He and Garrett devised a system of lasers that projected a web of light beams criss-crossing the hood surface so that as the canvas roof flexed any deflection could be measured and captured on computer. The system was tried in MIRA's and in Rover's own climatic wind tunnel at speeds up to 70mph; it allowed Garrett's team to tension the hood precisely and reduce bowing to an absolute minimum.

Increasing the torsional stiffness of the body forced John Cooper and Phil Turner to rethink their ride and handling strategy. They had already developed a longer limb joint between the suspension arm and Hydragas unit to give more articulation over small bumps so that it didn't lock solid, increased the anti-roll bars' diameters to 19mm front and 18mm rear to reduce the contrast between power-on and power-off cornering when they had to retune it all to allow for the chassis' improved torsional stiffness.

All the early development ride and handling had been done on the weaker chassis, which tended to act as an extension of the suspension medium, becoming one big spring and helping to smooth out the ride. However, this meant that the suspension itself was pretty stiff. With the stiffer body shell those forces were fed straight through to the driver and passenger, so Cooper and Turner had to recalibrate the damping to achieve optimum ride and handling.

The moment of truth for Project Phoenix was approaching. Rover were locked into revealing the car at the Geneva Salon, Pat Ward and his team had designed the stand to incorporate the cars and a launch routine had been written and rehearsed.

The roll of honour of past greats launched at Geneva includes some of the world's greatest motoring badges: Aston Martin, Bentley, Mercedes-Benz, Lamborghini, Ferrari. Even in this elevated company 1995's Geneva Salon will

*Body drop, where the
shell meets up with
the mechanical sub-
assemblies.*

*Oils, coolant and other
liquids are loaded into
the car's systems.*

The badge is the very last item to be put in place.

Finished MGFs waiting to be transported off.

be remembered as the venue where a stunning quartet of sports cars, two from Italy and two from the UK, were unveiled. Two of the cars were head-on rivals, pitching for the same customers, the other two rivalled each other only in their exclusivity and outrageous prices.

The latter were Bentley's magnificent Azure convertible, yours for a trifling £215,000, and Ferrari's latest supercar, the £329,000 F50. Also from Italy came Fiat's *barchetta*, a two-seater front-wheel-drive sports car that oozed Italian charm, especially in its heavily retro interior.

But if there has been a press revelation more eagerly awaited at Geneva in the past decade than Rover's was that morning, I can't remember it. Among the hordes of international motoring press there was a palpable air of excitement and expectation. After a press conference (350 were invited, double that number showed up) in a room adjoining the central exhibition area, during which 500 MG lapel badges and a similar number of press kits disappeared in less than eight minutes, John Towers led the media pack across the main hall to the Rover stand.

Other manufacturers must have wondered if their stands were out of bounds. All round the exhibition hall stands were deserted except for the staff. Everyone was crowding around the Rover display. Then, as 9.30 a.m. approached, the covers were hauled back to reveal a pair of sports cars - one bright red, the other, appropriately, British Racing Green. And to the strains of a melody specially written for 'Fairer Sax', the MGF was finally launched to a rapturous response.

From John Towers downwards there were looks of justifiable pride in the new car. There wasn't a member of the Rover management whose face wasn't split by a beaming smile. Quite simply the MGF stole the show.

'In terms of emotional experience the high point of Project Phoenix was the launch. The whole Geneva show stopped for that presentation . . . There were tears in people's eyes. It was extraordinary,' recalls John Towers.

Up until the launch, only an inner circle of Rover personnel knew the car was going to be called the MGF. Most of the media had speculated that it would be MGD, following on from the A, B and C models, but D had been used on an aborted prototype and E on the experimental mid-engined car that had stopped the Frankfurt Show back in the 1980s, so F it was.

For Nick Fell it was a case of, 'Blimey, I hope they like driving it as much. I suppose that in some ways my knowing that we still had some time to go before people got to drive it caused reservations. It was one great big tick in the box, but I was acutely aware that there was another big tick required before we had it all stitched up. Everyone underwrote the concept of the car and the style, which was quite a departure for an MG, so that was a huge relief, but there was also this sense that the driving experience had got to live up to something now.'

Both Gordon Sked and Gerry McGovern were justifiably proud of the reception accorded to the car's styling, especially from fellow designers. For Brian Griffin, 'The biggest pleasure was the fact that once the wraps were off we could then drive the car any place, any time, within reason. It's extremely frustrating to develop a car when you can only drive it under camouflage in the dead of night, when everybody else is in bed. You end up with a lot of people working an awful lot of hours purely because of the need to retain the security.'

As soon as the show cars were returned from Geneva, Griffin and his team of appraisers went up to the Yorkshire Moors to get a feel of the undisguised car on public roads. 'It stopped the traffic,' recalls Griffin. 'Going through rural towns you could see all the pedestrians stopping and turning round.'

The MGF had captured the public's attention so firmly that it made driving quite hazardous at times, says Griffin: 'Motorways were

quite a problem as you'd be cruising up the middle lane at 80mph and you'd get a car full of business people coming up in the fast lane and they'd whack on the anchors right next to you and then tail you. You needed to have your wits about you, because other road-users weren't paying attention to their driving.'

By now it was almost too late to make any changes to the car, unless they were absolutely necessary. The team were confident that they had met any problems and solved them, but mention headlamps to any of them and they groan, head in hand. Well, Brian Griffin does: 'Oh the headlights, yes, bloody hell. When we got the first off-tool headlamps we ended up with these torch beams bouncing vertically off the chrome bezels, which you only noticed in mist or fog or when driving down tree-lined lanes. You'd suddenly find you had these very concentrated pencil beams going straight up into the sky.'

The team had put a lot of development effort into the car's lighting system. There's not much point, says Griffin, in having a wonderful sports car that you can't drive at a sensible speed as soon as it gets dark.

The problem was cured by introducing a series of longitudinal corrugations on the bezels to diffuse the light: 'It was a bit of a nail-biter because it was quite a big tooling change with a long lead-time, late in the programme.'

Right through to midsummer the ride and handling team were constantly honing the car's characteristics. It was almost an obsession with them. Mid-engined cars aren't the most benign when it comes to on the limit handling, but the MGF team were determined that their car would live up to MG's 'Safety Fast' slogan. They even called in Le Mans, F1 and CART driver Mark Blundell for his opinion. His views coincided with what the team were already thinking and working towards, says Fell. He was impressed with the ride quality and the car's stability under cornering, but wanted crisper turn-in from the steering. 'He helped confirm to us that the direction we were going in was absolutely the right way to go. We were trying to get a balance between crispness and turn-in and sensitivity at high speed. So he helped us optimise the direction we were going. There's always a balance: do you make it absolutely superb on twisty roads or do you make it superb on motorways?'

Deciding to go with one tyre supplier, Goodyear, and just a single rear-tyre size, 205s, had made matters easier as well, says John Cooper. There had been one stage in the programme when the less-powerful 1.8 would have been fitted with slimmer 185 tyres all round with the option of 205s at the rear, but this was aban-

The calm after the storm. Rover's stand at the Geneva Salon the evening after the car had been given a rapturous reception by the world's motoring press.

doned when it was realised that the bigger tyres had considerably more grip under hard cornering. Additionally, they helped to signal the onset of understeer as the car reached its cornering limit, as Nick Fell explains: 'We found that our test drivers were exerting far more lateral acceleration with the MGF than they were doing on any other car. That made us realise that customers were likely to be driving quicker than they would do otherwise. So we wanted to set a standard that was extremely high, if you like at a speed where most people would never get themselves into an uncomfortable situation.

'We could make it more exciting by putting 185s on, but we felt it was our duty to protect the customer from themselves. It's a bit like our approach to safety and also the reason we've set the car up so that it's got slight understeer. If you're really pressing on you will get some warning bells that you're going too quickly because the front starts to understeer a bit before you lose adhesion at the rear.' The combination of being able to test undisguised cars and the new relationship with BMW meant the PR3 team could make use of BMW's test facilities on the outskirts of Tokyo. Japan's capital city has extremely demanding driving conditions, especially in the summer when road temperatures can soar to 40°C (104°F) with extremely high levels of humidity. Ally that with traffic moving at walking pace in endless traffic jams and the demands put on the engine-management system, the engine cooling and the air conditioning are some of the severest encountered anywhere. And since Japan would be a principal export market for the MGF, the car had to cope with those conditions. Thankfully for Peter Kavanagh and the rest of the team stationed in Tokyo that summer the systems did cope: 'We felt we'd probably developed the car to the worst case in the wind tunnel and then when we were out in the real world, we'd got this comfortable margin.'

As the QP phases merged into one another through the summer months, CAB2's build rate slowly started to increase, so that by 3 July the final Method Build - an old Honda term - commenced. Basically this is a repeat of QP4, which itself is a repetition of QP3. Each stage sees the car that little bit more refined and edging towards its final production levels of quality and specifications.

Fifty vehicles were built during M-build, but not in a single batch. The first body from Motor Panels in this sequence, known as the 'Kite Flyer', would be carefully measured, then sent through the paint process and down the production line at the projected build rate. Any problems would be flushed out at that stage - for instance, there was concern over speedometer flutter that needed to be cured - and then five or six more cars would be sent through at the line rate. As the cars were finished they were returned to the Project Phoenix team for detailed inspection; any faults or problems were cured and the results reported back to CAB2, where they'd be put into practice for the next batch.

This process continued throughout July until volume production started on the 24th. Seven days later VIN 000251 left CAB2. The first all-new MG in more than three decades had been finished and was handed over to Fred Coultas, managing director of BMIHT, for permanent display in the Gaydon museum.

It didn't take Rover Japan and Rover France long to start suggesting national one-make series. The Japanese competition is a series of track races in very lightly modified 1.8i's. Apart from safety items and a stylish hard top styled by former Lotus and McLaren F1 designer Peter Stevens, the car is remarkably standard. The suspension is stiffened and the rear top mountings beefed up and cross-braced, standard discs are retained and fitted with competition discs. The only engine modifications are the conversion of the camshafts to mechanical operation from hydraulics, increases in engine and oil-cooling capacities and a change to the VVC's final drive

ratio - nothing to increase the engine's power output.

Development work was headed by Rover Sport's technical manager, Roy Ford, working with Tony Pond and Wayne Mitchell. Much of the development work was done in the high temperatures of South Africa to replicate those that would be experienced in Japan. 'We wanted an inexpensive, reliable race car and that's what we've got,' says Ford. During more than 2400 race miles, the car behaved perfectly and even the standard brake discs withstood 2000 race miles before starting to show signs of fatigue.

And what did former rally ace Pond think of the car? 'Absolute fun. It's tremendous, you can chuck into corners and get the back out on opposite lock or drive it neat and tidy. It does what you want it to, not what it wants to do. For £4000 on top of the cost of a car, it's great value.'

If that £4000 seems expensive, the cars are built up by Janspeed Engineering of Salisbury and then sent back to Gaydon for final suspension adjustments before being shipped to Japan. Even before the first batch of twenty-five was freighted to Japan in mid-March, there was talk of a further twenty-five being ordered for 1997.

The French championship was more ambitious, being a combined series of tarmac rallies, races and hill climbs, although the car's specification won't differ that much from the Japanese racers except, perhaps, for differently tuned suspension. That the MGF had captured the attention of both the media and motoring enthusiasts the world over was undeniable. When UK prices were announced in mid-July - £15,995 for the 1.8i and £17,995 for the 1.8i VVC - Rover already had orders for a thousand cars and the order bank continued to grow. The interesting thing, says Lisa Faulkner, is that customers are loading their cars with extras; demand for the £1000 hard-top outstripped production and Rover and their suppliers were frantically looking at ways of meeting customer requirements. A bigger concern was interest in the more powerful 1.8i VVC model which, again, was outstripping expecta-

Fred Coultas, managing director of British Motor Heritage Ltd, receives the keys to the first MGF off the Longbridge productionline.

tions - some 40 per cent of customers specified the more powerful, and costly, engine package.

All this was before the car's press launch, the first opportunity the media would have to drive it. Foundations for the international launch, which was held at the splendidly medieval Coombe Abbey in the Midlands, had been headed by Mike Kennedy, who later handed the reins over to Bernard Carey. Centrepiece of the event was the elaborate 'Octagon Club', complete with British Racing Green upholstery, a library atmosphere and walls hung with paintings of past MGs as well as a number of cars on display. It was supposed to invoke a bit of good old British nostalgia for the carefree golden days of MG motoring. With bar billiards, darts and skittles available for the journalists when they tired of driving the MGF or talking about cars, it was a relaxed and informal atmosphere that helped instil the continuing theme of Britishness that is core to all MG, and Rover, products.

John Towers and all the senior Rover personnel can recall many a late-night session with some of the invited journalists, explaining why the MGF wasn't so retro, why it was mid-engined. 'There were some pretty hard-headed journalists who have to find something wrong with a car, no matter how good it is,' recalls Towers, 'but even they were won over. They were really absorbed with the excitement of what the car provided, to the extent that, maybe, there were one or two things they didn't like about the car but couldn't bring themselves to talk about it.'

Almost inevitably, talk turned to the future, something that Rover traditionally won't talk about, but John Towers is prepared to give an inkling of what might be: 'MG is safe, it will continue. It has to, you can't do this and let it go. There's got to be a successor to the F. I am not sure there's got to be additional MG products, the jury is still out on that one. There's the problem that when the jury comes back it will say another sports car is a bigger sports car and, arguably, that won't be an MG. MG has always been the affordable sports car. I always say that a bigger sportster would be Austin-Healey, some say Triumph.

'It won't be a question of there's no new MG programme, so look at the financial hit we take. That's irrelevant. There's a sense of integrity, you restart it and don't allow it to fade and die.

'A lot of people says there's too many sports cars in the world for a finite market and there is, but it's surprising the number of people who are saying, "Thank goodness for that. I wanted a sports car and I was cheesed off that the only sports car to have was a Japanese one. Now I can buy a proper sports car."'

21

IT'S BEEN A LONG TIME COMING.

There was the glorious-looking EXE which stunned the Frankfurt Motor Show back in the 1980s. A mid-engined supercar that could have conquered the world. But it didn't, and it remains to this day a styling concept. At least EXE made it part of the way and we've seen some of the many other MG drawings, concepts, studies and reports that were produced, discussed and discarded. How many others are lying forgotten at the bottom of dumped filing cabinets, we'll probably never know. All we do know for certain is that Britain's once-independent car-maker - variously called BLMC, BLMH, Austin-Rover and, finally, Rover during those times - abandoned its position as the pre-eminent manufacturer of affordable sports cars and handed it over lock, stock and barrel to the Japanese, and to Mazda in particular

Admittedly, in those dark days, the management had other concerns, like survival. The money to spend on niche products like sports cars simply wasn't there and, anyway, the cynics Nelsonian eye couldn't see a market, even if Mazda's success with the MX5, proved otherwise. As Rover's confidence grew, so did rumours that it would produce a sports car, that 'MG' - once relegated to be-decalled Metros, Maestros and Montegos - would once again take its rightful place on showroom floors as an independent marque in its own right.

We waited and waited and still nothing came. Then the MG RV8 appeared - a limited edition run of Rover V8-powered two-seaters based on the antiquated B bodyshell. The Japanese loved it - to the extent of buying 1200 of the 2000 built - and so did I. Apart from its cost it reminded me of what MG motoring was all about: it was quick - but not too quick - enough to have slidey-out tail fun without needing F1 reflexes to catch it. But for twenty-somethings it was just old-fashioned.

But, and this is the important part, it revived interest in the MG marque. It heralded the return of the Octagon.

For me it was a long six months between first seeing the MGF at Geneva and driving it. But every second was worth it.

Normally, you wait till the end to find out if the car's any good. But I won't do that; the good news, the wonderful news, is that MG is back with a car - give or take a few niggles that can easily be cured - equal to, and better in many cases than the MX5, *barchetta*, Elan, TVR, Alfa Spider et al. And, let's face it, it had to be that good to stand a chance in the marketplace.

Britain's dry, dusty drought of a summer had gone the week before I was due to drive the F for the first time, and had been replaced by the remnants of a hurricane that had sidled across the Atlantic from the Caribbean and was lashing the UK in howling winds and teeming rain. Just my luck. I had programmed myself for a couple of days of hood-up soggy sports-car motoring, despite the blue skies and sun that warmed the Midlands as I drove to collect the test car. I could hardly believe my luck when it turned out to be the British Racing Green example that was parked at Rover's Gaydon test facility and not the Volcano (metallic orangey) or Amaranth (purple!) examples that flanked it. The omens were looking good for the day.

Away from the lights and crowds of Geneva's crowded Salon you're immediately struck by how compact the MGF is, how tightly formed between its wheel-at-each-corner stance. There isn't a gram of wasted metal. Its tight packaging has been moulded around the minimal dimensions demanded to house an engine, two tall adults and some luggage.

Unlike some roadsters, the F looks good with the hood up or down. With the hood in place it takes on a far more wedgy appearance, the rise from the headlights to boot lip more discernible than when the hood is stowed away.

Despite the boldly shaped rear lights, it's the back view that is the most disappointing. The panel between the lights is bland, broken only by a single MG Octagon badge. The addition of a high-mounted stop light might alleviate that. But it's the view beneath the bumper that really lets the back down: twin vents give those following an excellent view of the silvered transverse silencer box, which also extends marginally below the rear lip. Lotus had exactly the same problem with their Elan and got round it by using black gauze between the vents to mask the silencer. Rover should do the same. They should also paint the silencer black or somehow shroud it.

The F's success, though, comes with any view that includes the front. The grille's shape, the use of black 'egg-crate' mesh and the manner in which the bonnet badge is mounted conjure images of bygone MGs - especially the B - without parodying them. Match that to the bold

The MGF is a handsome car from whichever angle it's viewed. Apart from such subtle hints as the raised badge mount on the bonnet, there are few acknowledgements of MG's past. The most obvious link is to the EX-E.

headlights and you have a car that is almost smiling at you when it comes down the road. During my time with the car it was variously described as 'dinky', 'cute' and even 'sweet' and I think it's because the MGF looks fun, inviting to drive.

There are also some nice styling touches like the racing filler cap and a couple of stainless steel strips on the rear deck lid, complete with Allen key fixings. Nor is the car festooned with MG badges which would have been the easy and crass thing to do. The F doesn't need to shout, 'MG' - it *is* an MG. There are but two - one front and one rear - updated versions of the original cream and rusty red Octagon badges that adorned my MGA of twenty years ago.

Hell, there's only one way to drive a convertible when the sun's up and that's with the hood down. After unzipping the rear plastic panel and laying it flat on what doubles as a small parcel shelf when the hood's in place, it's a simple task to unclip a pair of over-centre catches and fold the (Pininfarina-designed) hood back. The fiddly bit comes when you try and fix the tonneau: fumbling to thread the thin wire beading into its location is tiresome and requires patience; unless done exactly right the thing soon comes adrift. The hood itself is a single-layer affair which was given a stern test twenty-four hours later when that dying hurricane did a U-turn and swept back

across the UK with lashings of rain. Apart from a minor whistle, where it didn't seat fully against the passenger's window, it was weatherproof and didn't balloon too much at speed. And, just as in my A, there was the requisite drip of rain on to the seat as the doors were opened.

The only driving problem was caused by the broad B posts which make pulling out of acute-angled junctions difficult, as it is in most rag-tops

The interior is as intimate as the rest of the car is compact; driver and passenger sit almost rubbing shoulders, and there's plenty of leg room even for lanky six-footers. The car wraps itself round you, with the high door-line and rear decks combining with the low seating position to emphasise that you're sitting in the car and are one with it.

It's a good driving position, straight-legged with your right foot naturally falling to heel 'n' toeing position on the drilled throttle pedal. I could have done with the chunky-rimmed steering wheel being an inch higher, but even so it never once detracted from the driving pleasure.

In your line of vision there's a simple instrument display, in traditional MG rusty red figures on a cream background that echo the Octagon badge. The minor controls you'll recognise from Rover's parts bin and they're none the worse for that. Twist the key and Rover's new 1.8-litre,

118bhp engine springs into life with anticipation; blip the throttle and the needle swings easily round the tacho accompanied by an eager engine note. The fun factor is growing by the second.

I take the first few miles gently as I play myself into the car, feeling my way round the five-speed 'box and the novel (optional in the UK) electric power-assisted steering. All the controls are light, but not sloppy; the pedal efforts are well balanced, the stalks and switches operate with a satisfying 'click', the power steering takes away the effort but none of the feedback, while the engine responds immediately to the throttle.

Only one niggle persisted and that was third gear: hurried up- or down-changes - especially fifth to third - often resulted in a 'box full of neutrals as the linkage balked - character-building if you're rushing down into a tightening bend.

As the roads open up and miles slip by, confidence gains and speed builds up. The Hydragas suspension absorbs all the ripples and pot-holes, but simultaneously controls body movement so there's no pitch or wallow. Only on the roughest of surfaces does it get upset and feed through to the driver and passenger, the windscreen frame betraying the occasional shimmer.

A snaking series of bends unfurling themselves towards the horizon are attacked with gusto in fourth gear, 80-90mph on the speedo, and succumb to a series of fluid steering inputs. The electric power steering is uncanny in the way it remains evenly weighted throughout the lock: there's little or no kickback, yet all the pertinent information is there at your fingertips. Neither is there any body roll to upset your chosen course, or caution you to back off. The MGF does - to fall back on that over-quoted phrase - seem to corner on rails

Its overall attitude is neutral, shading to mild understeer at very high speeds that warns you of imminent oversteer, but so benign is its onset that you'd have to be a complete hoodlum seriously to kick the tail out. The F reminds you of Lotus's standard-setting front-wheel-drive Elan in the manner in which a small-engined, well-balanced car can eat up the miles with far less effort than a bigger car with more power.

I spent much of the drive in convoy with a colleague in a Honda NSX Targa F-matic (not the best of the breed, it has to be conceded), and this man, no mean driver, was often hard at work maintaining station with the F, only closing or opening large gaps when the Japanese supercar's superior horsepower came to the fore.

Rover's latest incarnation of the K series is superb. Maximum torque - a healthy 122lb ft at 3000rpm - and 118bhp at 5500rpm are well below the 8000rpm red line, but so flexible is the

*The interior is simple
and smartly finished.
The seat styling is
redolent of the early
MGBs, but more com-
fortable.*

*Cream and red instru-
mentation is smart
and effective.*

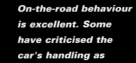

*On-the-road behaviour
is excellent. Some
have criticised the
car's handling as*

engine and so intoxicating its note that it would be a sad soul indeed who never used that limit just for the sheer hell of it

The MGF is an invigorating, intoxicating car to drive. In a year in which we've been seduced by Fiat's *barchetta* and Coupé - OK, a bigger car, but still a sportster - and succumbed to the rakish Alfa GTV and Spider, Rover had a daunting task on its hands with a new MG. Many were the cynics who said they didn't possess the depth of engineering talent to succeed. Well, they were wrong.

In the MGF we have a car that not only looks fun to drive but is fun to drive. It possesses huge reserves of talent and character in the way it rides, corners, handles, performs. There are, undoubtedly, quicker straight-line cars, but sports cars are for the twisty bits, scything and arcing through swooping bends in the open air, and at this the F excels.

At times 118bhp might feel insufficient, though for most it will suffice, but in the 143bhp Variable Valve Control version sports-car fans have a deceptively fast car that concentrates the mind. The distinguishing features of the VVC models are not any flashy, in-your-face sign writing, but five spoke rims instead of six, a leather steering wheel and half-leather seat trim. That's it, until you switch the engine on and you hear its

note - crisper, more urgent when you blip the throttle than the ordinary 1.8i. It doesn't have the snarling, visceral scream of Honda's VTEC or its sudden slam in the kidneys as the valve profiles switch in, but a powerful surge that's always on tap whatever the gear, whatever the revs.

As I explained in an earlier chapter, the VVC operates throughout the engine's rev band - increased to 7200rpm thanks to its freer breathing characteristics - and that means you can remain almost oblivious of the car's acceleration until you're hammering down into a bend several miles an hour faster than anticipated. The MGF's chassis deals with such circumstances admirably, but because of the extra power of the VVC, your speed through the corner and acceleration can start the rear tyres chirruping as they lose and gain grip, something you'd never hear in the 1.8i. The VVC has enough power in an oh-so-competent chassis to tingle the palms as you drive.

Some commentators have criticised the MGF for being too benign, too user-friendly, but that's to ignore the fact that the vast majority of potential owners aren't closet F1 drivers. What the majority want is to feel as if they're driving swiftly without necessarily having the skills to do so. Don't forget MG's slogan - 'Safety Fast'. But for those who need an adrenaline fix, the

VVC will provide it. Don't, however, expect slam-in-the-back acceleration, just glance at the speedo to see what you're cornering speeds are - they'll be higher than you think. This version of the MGF is a great cross-country car that would leave many bigger-engined rivals gasping in its wake. Maybe the steering could do with slightly less assistance, but its pointability and ability to change direction without over-reacting are exceptional. It is this in-built security that has made the basic 1.8i such a good basis for the Japanese one-make series. A bitingly cold and occasionally snow-swept Castle Combe isn't the best circuit to try the little racer, as it's too open with fast, sweeping bends punctuating the flat-out straights. Furthermore, the car is shod with partially grooved Dunlop racing tyres and the almost Arctic temperatures mean there's little warmth in them.

It's the first time the racing version of the MGF has been seen out of captivity; there are two on show, an open white version and a British Racing Green example with the Peter Stevens-designed hard top. I like the conventional roof, but the racing one has a rakish stance that's appealing. Unfortunately that one's for show, the driving car is open to the elements.

Once you've threaded yourself beneath the low-slung roll cage and into the race seat, the fas-cia and controls are pure MGF; the door trims are still in place, but the rest has been stripped bare, as has the boot. Fire up the engine and there's the familiar K-series beat, though the exhaust is muffled by your crash helmet. The gear change and pedals feel exactly the same as the standard car, though you've been told there are tougher Mintex M1166 pads gripping the discs. Even the EPAS system is unchanged.

After an exploratory lap getting the feel of the car and the circuit, you sense a harder ride but certainly not a harsh one. The brake pedal has more feel to it, also - a by-product of the servo's additional bracing perhaps?

With some heat in the tyres you accelerate down past the pits and uphill into Folly, reaching 7000rpm in fifth with the daunting Quarry to tackle. The dilemma is, do you brake before or after the brow at Avon Rise to set the car up? Unlike Tony Pond, who had chauffeured me round the track earlier in the day, I brake before Avon Rise, change into fourth and turn in late for Quarry, letting the car drift outwards to the left. I can feel the understeer building up, warning me that oversteer is approaching, but it never quite arrives. Then it's hard down the flat-out Farm Straight, if you're brave enough, to the appropriately named Hammerdown. I am not and lift slightly, but the F feels rock solid as I

The Japanese specification racing version of the MGF.

approach Tower. Another bitch of a bend, with all the ingredients for a major off: it's more than 90 degrees, you approach it over a brow, it's partly blind and the turn-in is against the camber. They've also resurfaced it. Even Mr Pond uses third here, so at least I am in good company as I snick the lever forward from fourth, braking as I do so.

The F's secret is keeping the power on, balancing it on that edge between under and oversteer as you fly into Westway, another bumpy slight right-hander before the gentle descent into Camp. There's a false apex here and, again, it's an irregular bend. As you clip the apex which aligns with the rear of the grid you let the car drift wide to the left before it's flat-out up Folly and into fifth.

It's an exhilarating drive, and also uncannily comfortable for a race car. Usually, even modified road cars ride race-tracks as if they were washboards, but the F just soaks it all up. The steering, as with the road cars, is maybe a shade too light, but it does make driving at racing speeds less strenuous and the brakes are mightily responsive and effective.

The secret of driving a relatively under-powered car like the MGF 1.8i on a fast, open, sweeping circuit like Castle Combe is to carry its speed through the bends. The F isn't a point-and-squirt car, there's insufficient power low down to catapult you down the straights if you've pottered though the corners. As such it's a satisfying race car that will reward the driver without biting back. The Japanese race series will be run on much tighter circuits, which will suit the MGF's nip-and-tuck characteristics ideally. But the overriding impression of Britain's best two-seater to date - be it a 1.8i, 1.8iVVC or racer - is not of an MG built by Rover, but of an MG conceived and built by MG.

The Octagon is back.